Impact

IMPACT

How Law Affects Behavior

LAWRENCE M. FRIEDMAN

Harvard University Press

Cambridge, Massachusetts
London, England

2016

Library of Congress Cataloging-in-Publication Data

Names: Friedman, Lawrence M. (Lawrence Meir), 1930– author.
Title: Impact : how law affects behavior / Lawrence M. Friedman.
Description: Cambridge, Massachusetts : Harvard University Press, 2016. |
Includes bibliographical references and index.
Identifiers: LCCN 2016011341 | ISBN 9780674971059 (cloth)
Subjects: LCSH: Effectiveness and validity of law. | Law—Social aspects. |
Law—Psychological aspects. | Obedience (Law) | Compliance. |
Sociological jurisprudence.
Classification: LCC K260 .F75 2016 | DDC 340/.115—dc23
LC record available at https://lccn.loc.gov/2016011341

For Leah, Jane, Amy, Sarah, David, Lucy, and Irene

CONTENTS

A VERY SHORT PROLOGUE

This small book, as the title suggests, is about impact: about how law affects behavior. In 1975, I published a book called *The Legal System: A Social Science Perspective*. Two chapters in that book dealt with the subject of impact.

That was forty years ago. In the past few years, I decided to revisit the topic. A lot of water had gone under the bridge; and more to the point, a lot had happened in the world of law-and-society scholarship. My aim was to bring the subject up-to-date and to bring myself up to date. The outcome, I hoped, would be a more contemporary, more comprehensive treatment of the subject.

The study of impact—rarely so labeled—had mushroomed during this period. On one small topic—does the death penalty deter?—oceans of ink had been spilled; the studies apparently run into the hundreds or even more. On the question of when, how, and why regulation of business works or doesn't work, another ocean of ink. There is also increasing interest in cross-cultural studies. Even in the English language, more and more studies concern countries other than the United States or compare two or more countries, often (but by no means always) including the United States.

The sheer volume of work is a problem, a barrier. And the work comes from all branches of social science—from economists, criminologists, psychologists, sociologists, political scientists, anthropologists, and historians. This rainbow of approaches only increases the need for some kind of summation, some conceptual framework. I thought I saw a real value in treating the subject synthetically. Value in trying to simplify. Value in setting out an outline, a structure, the bones and the skeleton, leaving out (as one would have to) the muscles, nerves, and glands. Value in trying to show some sort of order underneath the chaos, some sort of harmony in all the conflicting voices and noises. Value in trying to provide a series of hooks to hang all the scholarship on. Value in trying to classify and to suggest some meaningful categories. The result, in the pages that follow, is my modest attempt to do these various things.

Impact

1

INTRODUCTION

THE COHORT of law-and-society scholars has grown greatly in the last two generations and so, of course, has the work they have been doing. Looking at the way law and society relate to each other is an extremely important task for legal scholarship. No social scientist working today has any doubt that legal systems matter a great deal in society, or that legal systems are linked to their home societies. Today, there are a number of national and international associations devoted to the study of law and society. Scores of scholars work in the field. Specialized journals, in a number of languages, come out regularly.

It is hard—no, impossible—to sum up the work in one neat package. On the other hand, much of the work, maybe most of it, can be described as an attempt to answer one or both of two fundamental questions. The first is this: Where do the laws, decisions, rules, and regulations come from? They are, we assume, in some real sense, products of society, of social forces. But which social forces, and how, and why? Under the rubric of this first question, we can list all the studies of lobbying and interest groups, all the studies of the way in which social change makes its mark on the law, how the making of law has been affected by the industrial revolution, the Russian Revolution, the sexual revolution, the computer, air conditioning, the automobile, antibiotics, democracy, the human rights movement, and, perhaps, even sunspots and the movement of the tides.

Underlying these studies is the question of the autonomy of the legal system. To what degree does it march to its own drummer? To what degree do legal systems in general move and change independent of social forces, answering to their own inner logic, laws, and traditions? No reputable social scientist thinks that a legal system is or can be wholly autonomous. (What orthodox legal scholars think is another question.) Probably very few social scientists think legal systems are not autonomous at all. But they probably think it is much less autonomous than traditional legal scholars think, and probably many lay people as well. Clearly, social context matters. Social context, to some extent—to a great extent, in fact, or even an overwhelming extent—makes the law what it is, what it was, and what it will become.

The second big question is the question of impact.[1] Once you have a law, rule, doctrine, or legal institution, what happens then? What kind of impact or influence do any of these acts within the legal system have? By *impact*, I refer to behavior tied causally, in some way or other, to some particular law, rule, doctrine, or institution. (More later on as to what this means exactly.) I began with the impression that research on impact, on this second big question, is less voluminous than research on the first question (or research on legal personnel and institutions—on judges and lawyers, for example, or courts and legislatures). But this was only an impression. True, not too many studies explicitly label themselves "impact studies."[2] And there are only a few general discussions of impact, in one context or another.[3] Perhaps the richest (explicit) area of impact research deals with the United States Supreme Court and whether its decisions make much of a difference in the world.[4]

But in truth, there are actually a huge number of impact studies; they merely lack the label. In socio-legal research, nothing is more common than to look at the difference between formal law and the law in action. But any study that does this is, in a way, an impact study. Do easy divorce laws lead to family break-up? Do tort rules and medical malpractice cases cause changes in the behavior of doctors? Do the rules of corporate governance make companies more efficient or less? Do these rules make prices on the stock market go up or go down?[5] Impact studies would also include such things as the many, many studies devoted (probably in vain) to the deterrent effect of the death penalty. This, of course, is an impact question, and it has attracted scholars like bees to honey. And the countless studies of regulation of business—what techniques work, what techniques fail to work; these, too, are impact studies.

If every exploration of living law is, in a real sense, an impact study, then we are unlikely to isolate general rules to explain the whys and hows of impact, except at some very high and perhaps useless level of abstraction. Most studies are pretty specific; they explore one subject, at one point in time, and in one place, and with one particular group of people (psychology students, for example, the favorite guinea pigs of experimenters in the social sciences). They are careful not to go beyond an invisible boundary line. Good studies, of course, do prove something, and the something may be quite important. And analysis of groups of studies, too, might demonstrate something more general than the particular situation of the case studies: patterns of impact, and even some mid-range generalizations. Grand theory is quite unlikely to emerge. But to make definitions clearer, to expose assumptions, and to classify types of question, types of method, and types of answer can be a real contribution to the field.

This book will discuss, on a fairly general level, but with examples, the question of impact. I will pretty much ignore the other macro-question, about the sources and roots of law. Of course, the two are not unrelated. They can be separated analytically, but in real life, they are intertwined. After all, one of the key sources of law, one of the social forces that make law, is the reaction to past laws and legal states. And that, too, is a kind of impact. California passes a law to give consumers protection against lemons sold by car dealers. Car companies hate this law, and they put pressure on the legislature; the legislature modifies the law, responding to this pressure; the new law tells customers the disputes have to be resolved through the internal mechanisms of the carmakers.[6] This sort of feedback loop, this eternal dance of action, reaction, and more action, is obviously common in every modern legal system—in developed societies and in other societies, as well. Pushback against a law, or some consequence of the law, is an important part of the impact story.

Nonetheless, to take that fully into account would blur the distinction between the two meta-questions I mentioned, and would make the whole subject even more difficult and confusing. I think there is value in isolating impact studies and putting them under the magnifying glass. The aim, then, of this book, is to set out some sort of checklist that might (one hopes) bring a bit of order or clarity into a vast, oceanic, and somewhat chaotic body of studies, and to generate some middle range conclusions. Anything beyond that? Probably not.

Roughly, the plan of the work is as follows: first, a discussion of prerequisites to impact. Any new law, or old law for that matter, along with any rule, doctrine, or dogma, embodies a message, and it is addressed to some audience or audiences. A simple rule, making burglary a crime and prescribing some sort of punishment, is a message to the general public: do not burgle. Also, in this case, it is a message to police and other functionaries. It gives them authority to arrest and prosecute burglars. A statute that says a valid will has to be in writing, signed, with two witnesses who also sign is a message to the general public: this is how you execute a valid will. It is also, of course, a message to estate planners on what advice to give. And a message to probate courts, telling these courts which wills to recognize as valid.

Obviously, a message has an impact only when it reaches an audience. Any analysis of impact, then, has to begin by considering how legal acts get communicated. (By *legal acts*, I mean laws, rules, regulations, decisions, doctrines, and whatever else emanates from the legal system, all the way from a police officer giving a ticket or directing traffic to the adoption of a national constitution.) And one has to ask, to whom do these legal acts get communicated and what sorts of communication are more effective than others. One must also ask whether the audience understands the message, and if not, how and why the message is misunderstood.

Next, the book will deal with types of impact—direct or indirect. Obviously, there is no sharp divide between these two categories; the extremes are fairly clear, but there is a large gray area in between. If the law insists that people in the United States who earn money must file a tax return on or before April 15, the number of returns filed is one measure of direct impact, not to mention the billions of dollars that flow into the treasury. The income tax law, of course, has indirect influence on economic behavior. Since taxpayers can deduct money given to charity, the tax law stimulates charitable giving; people give more money than they otherwise would. Some of this money, say, goes to an organization looking for a cure for diabetes. This new money stimulates research on this disease, and attracts more doctors and more Ph.Ds. to the study of diabetes. And so on. The ripple effects of the laws can be endless.

We also have to consider the scale of impact. Some laws, for example, are meant to have an impact on everybody in society; others, however, have a more limited range. Laws licensing taxicabs have a direct impact on taxi drivers, an impact (somewhat less direct) on customers, and an indirect impact on traffic conditions. But the taxi rules for New York City have little or no impact on people who live in Los Angeles; and definitely not on people in Singapore.

A law is passed and communicated. What happens then? The third part of the book deals with this question. Do people do what they are supposed to do? And if so, why? Some people obey, some disobey, some do something in between. There is a difference between tax evasion (a crime) and tax avoidance (probably not a crime). A business can fully comply with some regulation, or partially comply, or figure out a way to comply without complying (so to speak), or just plain cheat. The larger the organization, the more complex, the more likely the reaction to the laws will be a tangled skein of behaviors.

Conventionally, scholarship divides the factors that influence impact into three general categories. The first is rewards and punishments. People avoid parking overtime because they might have to pay a fine. Punishments deter, or are supposed to deter. Incentives are supposed to have the opposite effect. The second factor is the immediate social context—peer pressure, in other words: what family, friends, and others think of your behavior, what your tribe, clan, religion, or cohort wants and expects. This, too, is surely an influence on impact. The third factor is the inner sense, conscience and related psychological motives: the sense of morality, of right or the opposite; of legitimacy and illegitimacy. Some cynics may sneer at the idea, but there is no doubt that this third factor can be a powerful influence on behavior, and the social science evidence confirms this commonsense notion.

Each of these "factors" is not a single factor at all, but a cluster of factors. We have to consider, too, how they relate to each other. What happens when they act together? What happens when they conflict? In a crunch, is peer pressure more powerful than conscience? Is it less powerful than the threat of prison? Do moral appeals have more impact than the opinions of neighbors and friends? A fair number of studies have tried to answer questions of this nature, with mixed results.

We will also look at how culture, tradition, and personality impact impact. There is no reason to think that iron laws of human nature or universal psychological mechanisms govern the impact of law. Time and place make a difference. Most of the studies I will mention come from the United States or from other developed countries. And they are, for the most part, quite recent. Young people and old people might behave differently. Men and women might also have different reactions to law; the same for children, members of different religions, or different ethnic groups within the same country. The question for every study is: How far does it reach? How far can it reach? How much can we learn from this study? Sometimes only modest amounts, but these are at least a beginning.

2

GETTING OUT THE MESSAGE

Every act done inside the legal system aimed at people or institutions outside the legal system gives off, in a way, a distinct message, and usually at least two messages. In addition to the message to the public, or some part of it, there is the inside message, the message to legal authorities, calling for or allowing some sort of action. In fact, this second message can be quite complicated. Making burglary a crime, for example, implies, obviously, a complicated message to police officers, prosecutors, judges, and perhaps also to juries, prison guards, wardens, and the like. Not to mention manufacturers of locks, bolts, and alarm systems, and it may be a factor, too, in peoples' decisions to keep at home a large, loud dog with big teeth instead of a kitten or a pet turtle.

Communication can be direct and explicit, or indirect. The government publishes the *Federal Register*; in it, the Food and Drug Administration (for example) will make public any rules and regulations it intends to lay down. A lobbyist for a major drug company will comb through the volume looking for material that concerns his client. Government agencies issue a blizzard of directives, guides, manuals, brochures, and pamphlets of all sorts. Speed limits are communicated in the most direct way possible: on big signs on the side of a highway. On the wall of a room inside a building, a sign says "No Smoking." On a different wall, in a restaurant, probably near the kitchen, a sheet tacked to the wall gives information (in small print) about labor and safety regulations, for the benefit of the restaurant's workers. An appeals court in Pennsylvania decides a case on child custody. It is printed in the state's official reports and also available online. A family law specialist may read the text. All these are examples of direct and explicit communication. The speed limit applies to all drivers, the "no smoking" sign to everybody in the room; drug regulations pertain to a single industry. A warrant or a subpoena are direct forms of communication, and they are quite specific: one place or one person. They also get delivered directly and literally to the subjects.

But most legal rules do not get transmitted or delivered this way. The penal code of a country or a state is a thick book of rules, perhaps a thousand pages long, or more. Nobody ever sits down and reads this book. Lawyers and judges are familiar with some of the provisions (never all or even most), and they might have precise knowledge of the text of a few clauses and sections. A lawyer who specializes in criminal law surely knows more about the penal code than a tax lawyer. The public knows next to nothing about the code; yet they have a general idea about some of the basic things inside the code. They know, on the whole, what murder is, and also what constitutes burglary, arson, and rape. They know that drunk driving is against the law. They probably do not know how much alcohol in the blood it takes to be legally drunk. The public also has a handle on the core meaning of freedom of speech, or the press, or religion, but little or nothing about the vast body of case law that spells out the details. The public knows what it means to own property, generally speaking, knows what marriage is, and divorce, and maybe knows how to make out a will. But almost never do they know the exact details.

Still, people do know something. The question is, where do they get their information and their ideas from? Sometimes from direct experience—they sued someone; or someone sued them; or they were a witness in a case, or served on a jury. But most people pick up what they know about law from other sources. They learn something in school; they learn something from parents and friends. Life is a process of learning the rules: rules about sports, rules about how to behave, rules about what is and what is not a crime.[1]

Popular culture, no doubt, is a source of information (or misinformation) about law. The airwaves are saturated with material on criminal justice, for example. Laws, crimes, police, judges, legislation are all featured on the evening news. Cops and robbers, lawyers, judges, and detectives are staples of television shows. *L.A. Law*, a program that centered on a law firm and its members, was an extremely popular television program in the United States at one time. Crime shows are popular in other countries as well. In Germany, for example, the sheer mass of television shows with a legal theme is astonishing.[2] A certain amount of basic information about law comes this way, but what these programs *teach* is probably seriously and systematically distorted. I say "systematically distorted" because the distortion is not random. It is tilted, for example, toward criminal justice and, especially, big trials and dramatic events. In the United States, even major Supreme Court cases do not get as much attention as lurid murder trials, and the coverage of Supreme Court decisions hardly presents the reader with models of accurate reporting.

The results are unsettling. Surveys suggest that Americans generally feel the criminal justice system coddles criminals and that it is much too lenient.[3] The media seem to reinforce this idea. Yet, in fact, American criminal justice is quite harsh compared, say, to European systems.[4] In theory, a presumption of innocence protects the accused, and the law provides the accused with all sorts of safeguards and procedural rights. People probably think this is a good idea—in principle. But in practice, they show great impatience with "technicalities." If I had to guess, I would be inclined to estimate that more people are unjustly or unfairly convicted or mistreated in some way by the system than the number of bad people who find a way to wriggle through the net. Of course, there is no way of measuring these things. One thing, though, is clear: any list of movies and television programs that exalt due process and defendants' rights would be extremely short. In *Dirty Harry*, a wildly successful movie from 1971, Callahan, the main character (played by Clint Eastwood), is a policeman on the trail of a vicious serial killer. The killer, Scorpio, is caught, but the system lets him go because of technical glitches, including a search without a proper warrant. In the end, Callahan kills Scorpio, but throws away his badge, presumably because his actions were illegal and would doubtless cost him his job. For Callahan, the hero, the story has two villains. One is Scorpio. The other is the code of rights for defendants, highly technical and full of tricks for criminals to use.

Star Chamber, a movie from 1983, is another film that smears mud on the niceties of due process. The main character is Hardin, a Los Angeles judge. He feels forced to release—on a technicality—two vicious, awful men who raped and murdered a boy. Another judge, who sees that this incident has made Hardin very unhappy, lets Hardin in on the secret of the "star chamber." This is a group of judges who meet quietly at night and more or less retry criminals who went free on "technicalities." If the judges at this night session find these villains guilty, they hire assassins to kill these men. Hardin is invited to join. There are many twists and turns in the plot, and the message is at best ambiguous. Still, the audience is asked, for the most part, to sympathize with a group of rogue judges. What they do is, of course, totally against the law. But the results are good: they rid Los Angeles of a crop of killers and thugs.

The media, also, by implication at least, spread the idea that crime, especially violent crime, is everywhere. In general, the media report what is news, and what is news is what is flamboyant, unusual, or catastrophic. As Elayne Rapping put it, the "disparity between what one 'knows' to be fact and what one sees portrayed on television programs" is "something almost schizophrenic."[5] She speaks about "global voyeurism," which makes tragedies into huge media events: "storms and earthquakes, babies trapped in wells and mourning relatives of victims of hideous deaths, weddings and funerals of the rich and famous."[6] The public is bombarded with this "information." In all of it, there are messages about law as well as about society; the unusual and the deviant get exaggerated. Surely this has some sort of impact on the public, but what sort of impact and how much?

This question—about the impact of the media, and the impact of the media on impact—is hard to answer. Do the distorted messages about crime and punishment on TV, in the movies, or spread by the Internet make a difference in the way people think about the law or the way they behave? It seems likely, but it is very hard to prove. Sex and violence are pervasive in the movies and on television. Does this produce more sex and violence in the audience? A German study went so far as to claim that violence in the media led to violence outside the media; that this influence accounted for a solid 10 percent of all juvenile crime. Later scholars were skeptical about this claim.[7]

In the United States, there has been considerable discussion of the so-called CSI effect. *CSI: Crime Scene Investigation* is the title of a popular television program. People who watch this program are fed a constant diet of forensic magic: hair follicles, DNA, fibers, and other modern miracles of technology. The question is, does this bamboozle jurors into unrealistic expectations? The fear is that juries will refuse to come in with a guilty verdict unless they see some scientific evidence. A study of more than a thousand people summoned for jury duty in Michigan cast considerable doubt on the "CSI effect." People who watched the programs tended to be more sophisticated than non-watchers; they did expect more from the evidence—but it was not just scientific evidence that they wanted.[8]

In the United States, "judge" shows in daytime television are extremely popular; and one of these shows, *Judge Judy* (featuring Judge Judith Sheindlin), was, at one point, the most popular daytime show of all. The judge shows are basically structured like small-claims courts; at least, they look that way. Real people appear, with real complaints, before judges who used to be real judges but are now making a fortune as television stars. The judges decide quickly, on a commonsense basis. They also question, harangue, and browbeat the litigants (mostly, of course, the losers). There is some speculation (and a small amount of research) suggesting that people who watch these shows develop different attitudes toward law and judging than non-viewers do.[9] Of course, shows like *Judge Judy* are as distant from the real world of civil litigation as the crime shows are from the world of criminal litigation. They are not even much of a guide to actual small-claims courts.

Tort law is another field of law where media coverage, in the United States at least, is twisted in systematic ways. The reader and viewer can easily get the impression that the system is running amok, that the dockets are crammed with crazy lawsuits, and that millions of dollars are awarded for phony or inflated claims. A prime example is the way the media covered the notorious case of hot coffee at McDonald's. In

1992, Stella Liebeck, who was seventy-nine years old, bought a cup of coffee in Albuquerque, New Mexico, at a drive-through window of McDonald's. Her grandson, Chris, was driving the car. The lid of the coffee cup came off and coffee spilled onto her lap. She ended up in the hospital. She had third-degree burns in the groin area and lesser burns elsewhere. She spent over a week in the hospital and had to have painful skin grafts. She was permanently disfigured "and was partially disabled for up to two years following the accident."[10] She complained to the company, asking them to do something about the temperature of their coffee and to cover her medical expenses. The company offered her $800, but stonewalled on the main issue. It was at that point that she went to a lawyer. When the case went to court, Stella Liebeck won her case. There was strong evidence that the coffee was, in fact, dangerously hot. The jury awarded substantial damages, including punitive damages. The judge, however, scaled down the punitive damages.

At this point, the media stepped in. Now the story they told was about a reckless old woman who won an "absurd judgment." The incident was a "stunning illustration" of what's wrong with the system. These quoted phrases are from a newspaper editorial. The newspaper also suggested that "greedy copycats" would "soon . . . be happily dumping coffee into their laps in a bid to make a similar killing." A talk-show host talked about a "suing epidemic," and later accounts railed at "bone-headed jurors giving away millions for cuts and scrapes at the demand of greedy gold-diggers and their ambulance-chasing lawyers."[11] In general, the media turned Stella Liebeck into the "poster lady for tort reform."[12] Aided and abetted by comedians, talk shows, and, probably, word of mouth, the media glommed on to the saga of Stella Liebeck, and similar stories, to make a moral point. Greedy, dishonest, or, at best, simply stupid plaintiffs were bringing wild, unjustified lawsuits, with the help of clever shyster lawyers. The plaintiffs won in court because jurors always punish the deep pocket. Damage awards, moreover, were absurdly high. Needless to say, this picture is a gross exaggeration of reality, if not downright false.

Tort law may be an extreme case, but distortions in the media are quite pervasive. Rarely does one get an honest, accurate picture of the way the system works. There is, for example, a dramatic discrepancy between newspaper accounts of cases about employment discrimination and the actual results in actual cases. In one study, "an astonishing 98 percent" of reports sampled in the media were reports that plaintiffs won their cases. But in reality, plaintiffs were successful in only 41 percent of the jury cases in federal district courts.[13] If you went by what the newspapers reported, you might think the median jury award was over a million dollars; the true median recovery was on the order of $150,000.[14]

Evidence of distortion in the media is easy to find, but findings on the actual impact on behavior is much harder to scrape together. Or findings on the influence of the Internet and social networks. True, in this day and age, ideas and attitudes fly about the world almost instantaneously. Even revolutions seem to get started on cell phones and social networks. Revolutions, of course, are complicated movements; they have many parents and progenitors. Most of us who live in well-off, comfortable countries take free elections, democracy, and the like for granted. In other parts of the world, governments are autocratic and there is a simmering pot of discontent, which can lead, in the end, to outright revolution. Demands for human rights, of course, do not rise up spontaneously out of some primal soup. The human rights culture is a strictly modern phenomenon. Preliterate tribes did not rebel against their chiefs, crying out for voting rights, travel rights, gender equality, and the right to change religions. But in the world of today, that culture is pervasive and powerful. It has generated a great deal of "hard law," including constitutions, bills of rights, human rights treaties, and decisions of high courts. The media and the Internet spread the message of human rights all over the globe. The messages fall on fertile soil, to be sure, in a way that would not have been true during the Roman Empire or for a Brazilian tribe deep in the Amazon jungle. The impact of the message depends on a receptive modern culture but also, in part, on how it was communicated—and to whom.

Legal Knowledge

As I said at the outset, communication is a prerequisite to impact. An unknown or uncommunicated law has (by definition) no impact in itself. But, of course, "communication" is not a simple concept. Sometimes, it is direct; sometimes it reaches the audience secondhand, often through the media. Many times it reaches the audience in distorted form. Even when the communication is direct, and even when it is face-to-face, we cannot be sure that the audience really hears it, or hears it accurately; or that the message is understood. Indeed, often it is not, as we will see.

Much depends, of course, on the message itself; the nature of the message as a variable (more on this later). An important body of research focuses, however, on the audience. How many people actually get the message? Or, a related question: What do people actually know about law, rules, decisions, and other aspects of the legal system? We might make a distinction between two kinds of legal knowledge. We are much more likely to know that shoplifting is a crime than to know how often shoplifters get caught and what kind of punishment is in store for them. This second kind of knowledge will be discussed in a later section on perceptions of risk.

A number of studies have tried to measure legal knowledge. They tend, on the whole, to find more ignorance than knowledge. But finding out, for example, how many Americans are aware that nine justices sit on the Supreme Court, or how many Frenchmen know the difference between the European Court of Justice and the European Court of Human Rights, is not necessarily germane to the issue of impact. More relevant are studies on whether people know and understand their rights and duties.

The studies of legal knowledge in various societies usually come out with more or less similar conclusions. They find that lay people are fairly ignorant about the law (no surprise), except for some very basic, very general chunks of it. In 2006, Germany enacted a sweeping and comprehensive law against workplace discrimination. Two years later, in a survey, only about a third of a sample of the population had heard of the law; another 15 percent might have heard of it but they weren't sure.[15] And this, of course, does not tell us whether people who heard of the law knew anything much about what the law actually said. A study in California, in the 1960s, tested what registered voters in six counties knew about statutory penalties for various crimes. There were eleven questions. Nobody answered all of them correctly. More than two-thirds knew the answers to three or fewer of the eleven.[16] People in Tucson, Arizona, studied in the 1970s were not much better. They were not, however, completely off base. They had a "general" rather than a "detailed" knowledge of statutory penalties.[17]

The results of these studies are not particularly surprising. People know, of course, that murder, rape, and arson are illegal; the same for burglary and armed robbery. And while, naturally, they do not carry in their heads information about the maximum, median, or modal punishments for these crimes, they do know that you can go to prison, and for years. Murder is against the law and everybody knows it. Only lawyers know the quirks and wrinkles, but the public gets the general idea. The same is true of arson, burglary, embezzlement, indeed, all the obvious, classic crimes.

Knowledge and ignorance of the law are not randomly distributed. Lay people know a few fundamentals. Beyond this, not much. What do people know about the punishment for, say, using marijuana? Very little, it turns out; and their ideas about the maximum penalty have only a slight connection to what the penalty actually is (or whether there is any penalty at all).[18] In fairness, one should point out that the actual punishment varies a good deal from state to state; there are federal statutes as well as local ones to contend with. The law has been in a good deal of flux; and enforcement effort varies greatly from place to place.

People's ideas about law are, on the whole, sporadic, distorted, and often just plain wrong. They have general ideas about property rights, divorce, and a few other fields of law. They know the basic rules of traffic law. On the other hand, vast stretches of the law are *terra incognita*, extremely technical and highly specialized. In the United States, the Internal Revenue Code runs to thousands of pages, and is written in a weird, crabbed jargon; even lawyers have trouble understanding it. People do get the basic point: income has to be reported, certain deductions are allowed, and so on. They know they have to file a tax return, and they even know when. They also know whom to ask for help. People in trades and professions usually have a general idea about the basic rules that apply to their job. Taxi drivers know how to get a license and how the taxi business is regulated. Owners of laundries will know the rules about laundries; building contractors will be familiar with building codes, and so on. People in various occupations get their information from word of mouth; or from other taxi drivers or psychiatrists or building contractors; or from newsletters, bulletins, brochures, and the like.

People and businesses, of course, have an incentive to know about laws that affect them directly. Taxicab drivers, after all, have to know about the licensing of taxis. They have to be knowledgeable about traffic laws. Some cab drivers, of course, will know more than others. And one wonders exactly how detailed and accurate this "knowledge" on the part of taxi drivers actually is. In 1957, the United States Supreme Court, in *Roth v. United States*,[19] upheld, as constitutional, state obscenity laws. This decision was certainly immediately and directly relevant to booksellers. Yet a survey of these sellers (somewhat later) found that 42 percent were "not familiar with the case," another 32 percent had heard of it but didn't know "many details"; 16 percent claimed to know the "major points"; and a mere 10 percent said they were "very familiar with the doctrines."[20]

With regard to general knowledge of law, class, education, and income make a difference. An older study, in Texas, found that educated people knew more than the uneducated, a finding which will surprise absolutely nobody.[21] A survey in a western American state in the 1970s found that the higher the educational level (and income), the higher the level of legal knowledge.[22] Vilhelm Aubert, in a classic study, tried to measure the impact of a Norwegian law giving rights to housemaids.[23] Very few housemaids had a clue about the law, even though it was directed specifically at them. But, of course, Norwegian housemaids, like housemaids the world over, were politically powerless and had low levels of education. A survey of old folks in Israel tried to test knowledge about laws that one might think were directly relevant to them. But the subjects knew very little about Social Security and about the national health system. They knew more about certain other areas of law, such as pension rights and taxes. The authors suspect this difference in legal knowledge was because Social Security and national health rights were "automatic"; people would benefit from them without needing to know much about the actual programs. In areas where rights were "not automatically granted," but were the "personal responsibility of the older person," subjects tended to know more.[24] This was simply a guess, but a plausible one.

Perhaps we can extend this finding. Where people are required to take some sort of positive step to comply with the law, they are more likely to know about this step (and to do something). I imagine, for example, that most people in the United States are aware that April 15 is the deadline for filing an income tax return. To be sure, people have all sorts of ways to learn this simple (and widely broadcast) fact. Not acting carries with it strong negative consequences. People who do not file can go to jail. If you are entitled to a juicy refund, too, you have a strong incentive to file on time. People also understand they need a license to get married, or to hunt for deer. Here, too, they are forced to take specific steps. They, more or less, know the steps and they also have a strong urge to get what the law is offering: marriage and dead deer.

In a recent study, researchers interviewed day laborers in Tucson, Arizona. Freshly enacted laws had strengthened the rights of these workers. There were rules to make sure, for example, that employers paid at least minimum wage. Most workers, like Aubert's housemaids, knew nothing about these laws, or even less than nothing (that is, they mixed them up or got them wrong). But the ones who did know something were more likely to try to improve their lot, more likely to take advantage of legal tools.[25] These workers also wanted changes in the laws and in the modes of enforcement. Whether this translates into better enforcement—that is, a greater impact—is an open question. Day laborers notoriously lack political power. One wonders, too, whether workers who wanted to see improvements felt this way because of their legal knowledge or whether a desire to make a difference led them to find out more about what formal rights they had.[26]

It is common, in short, for people not to know their rights, or to get things wrong, and even for businesses not to know about regulations that bear directly on them. In 1993, Congress enacted a Family and Medical Leave Act. Employers with at least fifty workers were required to offer twelve weeks of leave after the birth of a child (though without pay). The act applies both to fathers and mothers. A study done a few years later showed that as many as a quarter of workplaces covered by the law were not in compliance.[27] Why was this? For some employers, it was because of a kind of inertia, a failure to update older policies and arrangements. Some employers simply misunderstood. And men rarely took advantage of the act—partly because they were unaware of their rights and partly because both workers and bosses tended to think childcare was for women, not men.

But when people do know their rights, they are (other things being equal) much more likely to try to enforce them. Obviously, then, educational programs and outreach can be potentially powerful. Important social movements begin with awareness. Sally Merry's work on campaigns against gender violence is full of examples. Battered women, especially in traditional communities like Fiji, one of the societies she studied, tend to be politically apathetic. Elite women work with these victims, encouraging them to learn about their rights and to take action.[28] All over the world, constitutions, laws, and regulations make bold pronouncements about rights of women, minorities, workers, and many other groups. Enforcement often meets with massive resistance from the rich, the powerful, the entrenched. Impact depends on enforcement, and enforcement does not come automatically. It requires, often enough, vigorous social movements; these movements feed on, and make use of, education in the broadest sense, including propaganda, mobilization, and agitation.

Of course, the law itself is to blame, very often, for gaps in legal knowledge, as we will see. Laws can be vague and cloudy, or technical and complicated. As we will also see, there are intermediaries, or information brokers, that help to remedy this problem. But still, major pieces of legislation are almost always compromises between interest groups, and the result of the pushing and pulling can be a complicated mess. The Affordable Care Act, a monster of a statute, had to balance (shakily) interests of insurance companies, pharmaceutical companies, the general public, doctors, and hospitals; buried in the text are dozens of compromises and accommodations for the benefit of specific groups or businesses.

Businesses and businesspeople have strong incentives to know about regulations that affect them directly. Big corporations will almost certainly make an effort to get this information, and they do get it; smaller companies sometimes less so. Hazel Genn's study of health and safety regulation in England[29] found that large companies had specialized safety personnel and got information about safety regulation from a number of sources. Smaller companies could try to stay abreast, but it wasn't easy. She asked one small businessperson: "How do you keep up-to-date on changes in regulation?" His answer was, "Honestly, I don't." She asked how many sets of "different regulations are there covering your activities?" His answer: "God only knows."

Ignorance of the law is common, ubiquitous. But ignorance of the law, as the old maxim puts it, is not a legal excuse for breaking the law. If you did something deliberately, you take the consequences, even if you did not know you were doing something forbidden. The doctrine is firmly established, but not, it seems, absolute. In *Lambert v. California* (1957),[30] a Los Angeles ordinance provided that anyone with a felony record had to register with the chief of police within five days of coming to town. Ms. Lambert broke the law; she was fined $250 and put on probation for three years. She claimed she knew nothing about the ordinance, and offered to prove this. The trial court refused to allow her to interpose this defense, but the Supreme Court reversed.

The majority seemed to put some weight on the fact that Ms. Lambert was punished not for doing something, but for not doing something (not registering). Does this distinction make any sense? You can be fined for hunting without a license, or failing to file an income tax return, to mention two out of many culpable "omissions." In a federal system, like the United States, people travel freely from state to state. Each time they cross a state line, they enter a new legal world whose special rules might be different from the home state rules. They are unlikely to know the home rules, and even less likely to know the rules across the boundary line. A law nobody knows cannot have an impact as such, but it can, in general, create a new crime.

The Supreme Court surely felt that punishing Ms. Lambert was unjust. Harsh, in fact. A more humane system would have simply warned Ms. Lambert: the law requires you to register; you failed to comply; you had better do your duty as soon as possible. The old maxim about ignorance of the law suggests a person can be punished without communication of a rule or norm. Yet it is unrealistic to expect people to know the more arcane rules. Business lawyers try to make sure clients know what they are supposed to know. Government inspectors, at factories, stores, and places of business, will often give warnings and reminders. Police sometimes let a driver go if a driver claims she had no idea there was a "no U-turn" sign: let go, and told not to do it again. But still, a rule is a rule. The Lambert case is something of an anomaly. The Supreme Court itself backtracked some years later.[31]

Case Law

What do people know about court decisions? For the most part, little or nothing. The exceptions are the striking, headline decisions—cases like *Bush v. Gore* or *Brown v. Board of Education*.[32] The messages of these cases are widely broadcast. But even here, what people know is basically only the actual result. The opinions of the Supreme Court are long, elaborate, confusing, and hardly models of literary style. Only a few lawyers and some law professors and political scientists (and some helpless students) actually read these opinions (sometimes in cut and edited forms). Even specialists can have trouble deciding exactly what the court decided and why. Famous cases, then, give out at least two separate messages, and probably more. One message is the actual opinion, what the justices actually said. Another is the bare, naked result. Even when newspapers try to explain what decisions mean, in quasi-technical terms, this message goes in one ear and out the other. The lasting message is simply who won, and not much more. This was true of the abortion case, *Roe v. Wade*.[33] Members of the public certainly never read the opinions. They knew little or nothing about the legal reasoning, but they got the basic point: a woman had a right to decide, at least in the early months of pregnancy, whether to keep the baby or not.

Probably not one person in a thousand could explain the legal issues in *Bush v. Gore*. People simply understood that Bush won, Gore lost, and Bush would be president. People understand the central point of *Brown v. Board of Education*: racial segregation was illegal and wrong. Few people read the opinion itself. Some members of the legal academy decided the result was just fine, but the opinion was poorly done—as if a "better" opinion would have changed anybody's mind, as if the Ku Klux Klan would have given up the fight for white supremacy. The message of big cases passes into a kind of folk interpretation. The abortion right morphed into a woman's right to choose on issues of sex and reproduction. *Brown* was about segregation in schools, but it came to mean that segregation was illegal and wrong, that the South had trampled on the constitutional rights of the African American minority. The Supreme Court itself made the leap to a broader meaning; but so did the public.

Legal logic, the structure of arguments, the treatment of precedent: these loom large in the minds of lawyers, but not for the rest of us. All that counts is the result, and the central message of the decisions. And the legitimacy of what the court had done: whether it had a right to decide as it did. For the most part, in many societies, a general, diffuse sense of legitimacy protects the court system. But for any particular case, the actual result and what the public thinks of it can be crucial. And opinion can have a definite effect on the impact of those decisions.

Misinformation

Ignorance of the law is understandable, and probably acceptable, as a general proposition. There are shelves and shelves of laws, rules, and ordinances in every modern country; piles and piles of texts; many gigabytes of data. Nobody could possibly know it all, or even most of it, or even half, a third, a tenth. This much is obvious. Besides, most of it, maybe the vast majority, has little or no bearing on our lives. When it does, we are likely to know a bit more, as we have seen. A man who has been arrested several times for armed robbery and drug dealing has a better grasp of the way the system works than a law-abiding citizen.

In some situations, people think they know the law but, in fact, they are wrong. A classic study looked at the impact of a well-known California case, *Tarasoff v. Regents of the University of California*.[34] In the Tarasoff case, a student told a university psychiatrist that he harbored violent feelings; he felt an urge to kill his girlfriend. Later, he did, in fact, kill her. The psychiatrist had never passed on information about the threat, either to the girl, her family, or the authorities. The family brought a lawsuit against the University of California, the psychiatrist's employer. The California Supreme Court held that the family did have a right to sue; in situations of this kind, there was a duty to warn. The decision horrified psychiatrists, psychologists, and social workers. Patients, they insisted, would be reluctant to seek help and to talk freely unless they could rely on total confidentiality. They asked the California Supreme Court to reconsider its decision. The court rarely does this, but in this case they agreed; and the Tarasoff case was reargued. This time around, the court modified its first decision. They retracted the idea that a therapist had an absolute duty to warn. Rather, a therapist had a duty to use reasonable care to protect people threatened by patients. Reasonable care might include some kind of warning, but not necessarily.

The Tarasoff study surveyed a sample of 2,875 psychiatrists, psychologists, and social workers in Los Angeles and San Francisco, and in other large metropolitan areas (Boston, Chicago, Detroit, New York, Philadelphia, and Washington, DC). They asked, first, whether the mental health specialists knew about the case. An astonishingly high percentage of them did—96 percent of the psychiatrists in California, for example. There was considerable awareness in other states, too, at least among psychiatrists and psychologists. The survey then asked for the source of their information. A fair number learned from a colleague, but most learned from professional organizations and professional literature (this was true, for example, for 65 percent of the California psychiatrists and 62 percent of psychologists in other states). For many occupations, professions, and trade groups, newsletters and bulletins to the membership report news about legal developments that are relevant, and this, no doubt, happened here.

The study turned up other interesting information. The health professionals thought they understood what the Tarasoff case had decided, but they got it at least somewhat wrong. They thought they had a clear duty to warn. The second *Tarasoff* decision simply eluded them. And this is understandable. What does "reasonable care" mean? A sharp, clear message is easier to grasp and to follow than a fuzzy one. A duty to warn is something a psychiatrist can understand; reasonable care is not. The second Tarasoff case was almost bound to be misunderstood.

I have used the words *knowledge* and *information*, but this has to be taken with a grain of salt. Maybe *awareness* is a better word. The message that any audience gets is bound to be skewed. In the Tarasoff case, as we saw, the mental health professionals had a high degree of awareness—they had definitely heard of the case. They got the general idea. But the subtleties of the actual decision escaped them. Professionals outside California were also misled. They thought the decision applied to them, when, of course, it did not—at least not formally; California decisions have no binding effect in Massachusetts or Illinois. In fairness, their notion was not totally irrational or ignorant. A tort lawyer in Illinois would surely be aware of the California case and aware, too, that it did not apply to Illinois. But she would also know—or guess—that the case was important, that it made it at least somewhat more likely that Illinois would go down the same road.

And one can ask, how wrong in fact were the psychiatrists, in their understanding of the Tarasoff case? Probably not that wrong. "Reasonable care" could include a duty to warn, and probably most of the time it would. What else would "reasonable care" entail? In this particular case, the misunderstanding was understandable, and (arguably) was approximately right.

Sometimes an error in understanding is more egregious. A study in the United Kingdom tried to find out what people thought about the rights of unmarried couples living together. Many people, it turns out, believed in what might be called the myth of common law marriage. That is, they firmly believed that if a couple lived together long enough, they would somehow earn the same rights as married people.[35] There is no such rule. No length of time turns cohabitation into a "common law marriage."[36]

Is there a pattern to the kinds of misinformation people have? The common law marriage myth probably does not come from the media, the movies, or television, although the media often use the term "common law marriage" somewhat loosely. But on the whole, no institution, to my knowledge, is peddling this notion. Where then does it come from? A study of workers in three states—Missouri, New York, and California—by Pauline Kim may shed light on this question. Workers were asked whether it was "lawful" or "unlawful" for an employer to fire somebody simply "in order to hire another person to do the same job at a lower wage." In fact, in all three states, the employer has a perfect right to do this;

to get rid of an employee, for any reason, or no reason at all. Employment is, generally speaking, "at-will," which means that workers on the whole have no job tenure. Nevertheless, an overwhelming majority of respondents in all three states thought the action was "unlawful."[37] Workers were quite convinced of this even when their company had handed out (for example) a personnel manual that said in plain English that the company reserved the right "to discharge . . . for any reason."[38] About two-thirds still thought this kind of firing was against the law.

Kim thought the source of the problem was a "confusion of norms and law." In other words, workers think it is unethical, morally wrong, to fire a worker just to get someone willing to work for less money. And if this is wrong, it must be against the law. This might also explain the common law marriage myth. If people think that couples who live together a long time should have rights with respect to each other, it is easy for them to assume that this must be legally so. The legal system, after all, is supposed to be fair and just (at least in democratic societies). People assume, then, that the law on some particular subject is fair. Another study, of employees in state universities in four states, on certain aspects of criminal law (for example, whether you can use deadly force to protect your property), also found that people tended to assume (often wrongly) that the law corresponded to their "moral intuitions."[39]

Law is, after all, a reflection of social norms. If people think the law ought to give rights to people who live together year after year, they may be wrong—for now; but, in fact, the law has shown signs of moving in this direction. Cohabitation does imply rights, at least under some conditions. And there are signs, too, that the "at-will" doctrine in employment cases is under some legal pressure.[40] The norm change comes first, then the law tends to change to conform, and the new law will, in turn, have its impact.

In the famous palimony case, *Marvin v. Marvin*,[41] Michele Triola Marvin lived for many years with the movie star Lee Marvin. They broke up and she sued Marvin, claiming they had an agreement: if she moved in with him and devoted herself to his interests, they would pool their incomes. His income, of course, was very large; hers was basically zero. Lee Marvin's defense: the two were sex partners, living together without getting married, and this made their agreement, if it existed at all, totally illegal and unenforceable. The California Supreme Court, however, rejected this argument. Cohabitation was no longer taboo, no longer a gross violation of society's rules. Times had changed. This kind of agreement, then, was no longer per se illegal. Michele Marvin had a right to prove her claim. The trial court had thrown the case out of court. The California Supreme Court reversed, and sent the matter back down to be tried.

In the end, Michele Marvin won little or nothing. After a long trial, a lower court decided Michele had failed to prove the existence of the agreement she claimed under.[42] But the media (and comedians) had a field day with the case. One cartoon, for example, showed two little kids and a mother. One kid is saying, "Mom, this is Suzie McWhortny. She was my valentine last year and now she's suing me for palimony."[43] The case was big news in newspapers and magazines. Millions of people not usually in the habit of following California decisions knew more or less what the case (supposedly) decided. But, of course, they got it wrong. People tended to assume that the case meant more than it actually did— that it gave rights to unmarried couples living together simply because they were together, which was not true at all. Also, like *Tarasoff*, it was binding only in California. But, as in *Tarasoff*, the public was not entirely wrong. The case had an impact: it led to a flurry of lawsuits elsewhere. A number of law firms began placing ads, offering their services in palimony cases. Some of the cases that followed were widely publicized, including a lawsuit (by a man) against the popular entertainer Liberace.[44] The decision also led a number of states to legislate on the subject.

The examples discussed have come from more or less democratic societies. The dynamic may be different in autocratic societies—societies that, often enough, lack legitimacy. If people think their system is, in general, evil or corrupt or fatally biased (with good reason, often enough) they may be less likely to confuse social norms and legal norms, less likely to assume that the law reflects their notion of justice. The bias may, in fact, lie in the opposite direction: they assume that they cannot and will not get justice. But each society, and each situation, may be different, may produce different frames of mind, convey different sets of information and misinformation.[45]

Ironically, then, as these examples suggest, misinformation can have an impact—this was true in the Tarasoff case. What the psychiatrists and others thought about the case made a difference to the way they behaved; it colored their actual practice. Perhaps workers who feel unjustly treated are more likely to go to the law when they think the law is on their side (even if they are wrong). And going to the law, if it happens often enough, puts pressure on the system. At least, this is a working hypothesis. A rule that is never challenged will never change. In the famous case of *Gideon v. Wainwright*, in the 1960s,[46] the Supreme Court of the United States held that a person charged with a felony had a constitutional right to a lawyer; if the accused had no money, the state had to provide him with counsel. Clarence Gideon lived in Florida. He was accused of breaking into a poolroom. He insisted he was innocent and demanded a lawyer. He said he had a right to a free lawyer. He was (legally) wrong; Florida recognized no such right. At least not then. Gideon's case, taken up on appeal, changed that situation. Gideon had conflated a moral and a legal claim; and in the end, his legal claim was vindicated. Michele Marvin was not so fortunate, but her stubborn insistence on a right she thought she had did have an impact on the law. She, too, was swimming with the current (unconsciously, perhaps), riding a trend that soon turned into laws about domestic partnership, and, ultimately, gay marriage.

Clear Messages, Cloudy Messages

Analytically, we make a distinction between communication and impact, that is, between the message and the result of the message. In practice, the message, the way people hear the message, and the way they interpret and react to it are links in a single chain, parts of a single social process. Communication is the first link in that chain. And it is built into the very structure of the legal system. Laws, rules, ordinances, court decisions—all of these are published. In the United States, proposed rules and regulations—from the Food and Drug Administration, or the Securities and Exchange Commission, or any other agency—must be printed in the *Federal Register*. This book is hardly bedside reading. Each year it runs to thousands of pages. It reached some kind of (dubious) pinnacle in 1980: the *Register* in that year bulged with 87,000 pages. Its size dropped significantly after that (to some 47,000 pages), but has since rebounded to a length between 65,000 and 85,000 pages—a truly monstrous tome. In 2013, 3,659 "Final Rule Documents" were published in the *Register*.[47] There are state registers, as well. Volume 38 of the *Illinois Register*, for the year 2014, ran to 24,081 pages.

This is communication with a vengeance. Some of the material in these registers, especially the *Federal Register*, is of enormous importance—rules and proposed rules that potentially affect thousands, maybe millions, of people. These millions, of course, are blissfully un-aware of what goes into the *Federal Register*, except in the rare case where a rule, say, for whatever reason breaks through the curtain of ob-scurity and makes it into the newspapers, or even better, onto the eve-ning television news. Nobody reads the *Register* for fun. Almost all of us never read it at all. This does not mean that publishing in the *Federal Register* is a pointless ceremony. Lobbyists and lawyers for unions, in-dustry groups, and NGOs make it their business to find out which pages concern their clients and constituents. Drug company lawyers will cer-tainly look for material from the Food and Drug Administration that might affect their clients.

A communication can be general or specific. It can be broadcast, as it were, to the whole world or sent to specific people or groups. There is a world of difference between announcing something on the evening news and announcing the same something to one or more particular people by phone or email. A rule can be general, also, in the sense that it applies to everybody: thou shalt not kill. Or it can apply to one person, or a group of people: taxi drivers need a license. Putting the text of a proposed rule in the *Federal Register* is a general broadcast in the first sense; anybody can read it. Most of these proposed rules are not, how-ever, general in the second sense: if the FDA announces plans to outlaw certain food dyes that might be carcinogenic, the plans can have a big impact on companies that make and sell those dyes. John Q. and Mary Public might be affected, but only indirectly (and they are extremely unlikely to get the message at all).

The type of message is also important. Legal scholars draw a distinc-tion between rules and standards.[48] Under the Constitution, the president must be thirty-five years old or more. This is a "bright-line" rule. A voter has to be eighteen years old. This is another bright-line rule. Rules, on the whole, are easy to understand (though there are always some border-line cases). A standard is much fuzzier: negligence, in tort law, is defined as a failure to use reasonable care, or something along those lines. A contract is unenforceable if it is against "public policy," or if it is "uncon-scionable." These are standards. Standards are harder to apply—and, often enough, they open the door to the exercise of discretion, to subjective judgments. If parents squabble over child custody, a family law judge is supposed to decide on the basis of "best interests of the child," an extremely general standard. This standard gives the judge a great deal of discretion—and power. Appeals courts find it hard to re-verse a decision based on a standard.

It is easy to understand why professionals got the second Tarasoff case wrong, or at least slightly wrong. The first Tarasoff case announced a rule; the second case announced a standard. Standards are fuzzy mes-sages, and they can confuse the audience. Complicated messages are also a problem. The messages in long judicial opinions never reach any-body but lawyers, and even they often fail to get the point. The message of the second Tarasoff case was delivered to the relevant audience, but it was too blurry for lay people to understand or to use. What often hap-pens is that fuzzy messages get bent out of shape, distorted, or converted into cleaner, brighter rules. The reaction of psychiatrists and others to the second Tarasoff case was quite natural. What could a psychiatrist or social worker make of the duty to take "reasonable care"? A duty to warn is concrete, simple, easy to grasp and to act on. (Though not without problems: warn whom? And about what?) People tend simply not to hear, or not to get, complicated messages or vague, general messages.

Schoolteachers, social workers, and others in Canada have a duty to take action if they suspect a case of child abuse. Their suspicions must be reported. But a study in Canada found a high level of noncompli-ance.[49] The duty might be clear, but the triggering situation is not. It is hard to make a bright-line rule for suspicion of child abuse. Sometimes there are hints but no clear evidence. Teachers, then, face a dilemma. A child comes to school with bruises—but from what? How suspicious should teachers be? Under what circumstances? Teachers did know the law—the duty to report—as a general matter. They also approved of the law; but one element (what is abuse and how do we know it?) was highly problematic. And probably had to be. This is another situation where impact gets bent or diluted. The rule itself seems clear but the trigger is hard to measure or define.

In Washington State, a twenty-three-year-old woman sued her eye doctors; they had failed to test her eyes for glaucoma and she developed this serious eye condition.[50] The trial court had held against her. The defendant doctors had claimed, successfully in the court's judgment, that it was not the practice to test younger people for this disease. The Washington Supreme Court reversed. The glaucoma test should have been given; it was "simple, harmless, relatively inexpensive, and effective."[51] The case was well publicized; eye doctors knew about it (and disliked it). Presumably as a result of lobbying, the legislature in Washington State passed a law intended to undo or mitigate the glaucoma decision. Any malpractice plaintiff had to prove "by a preponderance of the evidence" that the defendant "failed to exercise that degree of skill, care, and learning possessed by other persons in the same profession"; and also prove that he, the plaintiff, had been damaged as a result.[52] Surveys of ophthalmologists, however, turned up no evidence that the statute made any difference. The statute never explicitly mentioned tests for glaucoma. It was vague, general, and ambiguous. No statute of this kind sends an effective message, and is unlikely, therefore, to have an impact.

James Spriggs tried to measure the impact of Supreme Court decisions on administrative agencies. If a decision of the court concerned the work of the agency, did the agency change its behavior? He found, unsurprisingly, that vague, unclear decisions had less impact than more "explicit" decisions. Opinions that were "totally lacking" in "specificity" had virtually no effect, but when the court was very explicit, agencies almost always made "major policy change" (more than 95 percent of the time).[53]

The message of the various studies is clear: vague standards and directives either get ignored or, as often happens, get converted by the audience, either deliberately or unconsciously, into something more concrete, something easier to use. Take, for example, that everyday rule, the

speed limit. A speed limit of sixty-five miles per hour is easy to understand. Consider, however, the speed limit in Rhode Island. Under
Rhode Island law, the basic rule is this: "No person shall drive a vehicle
at a speed greater than is reasonable and prudent under the conditions
and having regard to the actual and potential hazards then existing"
(RI Stats, sec. 31-14-1). Then come the actual "speed limits," as most
people would understand them: fifty miles per hour, during the daytime, if "outside a business or residential district," less in those districts,
or during evening hours. Speeds above the statutory limits are prima
facie evidence that the driver was not driving at a "reasonable or prudent" speed. Probably very few people in Rhode Island know the actual
"rule." It is obviously too big and clumsy to post on big signs on the side
of the roads. As a message, then, it is ineffective. And even if people were
aware of the rule, it is pretty much unusable, because "reasonable" can
mean so many things. And what are "actual and potential hazards" that
a person is supposed to have "regard to"? The tendency is, therefore, to
convert the rule into something solid and concrete—an actual "speed
limit." This is what one finds on the highways in Rhode Island, and this
is what the driving public understands.

This process of converting the vague into the concrete is quite
common in the real world of law. In a classic work, *Settled Out of Court*,[54]
Laurence Ross studied the work of insurance claims adjusters. Tort
law—or, to be more precise, the law relating to auto accidents, the bread
and butter of the insurance trade—is difficult, complicated, and full of
standards rather than rules: the concept, for example, of the "reasonable" driver who is "reasonably" careful. The adjusters, who were not
law-trained, converted the slippery, subtle norms of tort law into rules
of thumb. There was no other way to deal efficiently with the huge
burden of claims produced by auto accidents. We have already seen a
similar process in the way mental health professionals read the meaning
of the Tarasoff case. The Spriggs study of administrative agencies suggests
another way to react to fuzzy rules: the audience does nothing, shrugs
its collective shoulders, and goes on doing what it did before.

A great many people have written about how businesses respond to
the complex regulations that they face, regulations that often contain
standards as well as rules. One response was just mentioned: vagueness

is turned into something concrete and usable. At other times, businesses create some sort of internal procedure, sometimes including an internal agency charged with coping with whatever the law requires. The Equal Employment Opportunity Commission is responsible for implementing the rules of the Civil Rights Act of 1964; this law forbids discrimination on the basis of race, sex, religion, and national origin. Big businesses get the message. But exactly what is the message? The law "simply mandates nondiscrimination," but it says nothing about how a business is supposed to handle the situation, when employees complain about discrimination. Nor does the statute offer a clear definition of discrimination. Some businesses, in response, set up "grievance procedures"; they created a framework, a structure, to cope with the statute's vague command. At the same time, they transformed a personal right—the right to be free of discrimination—into a corporate problem to be solved through internal measures.[55]

Simple, clear rules about property—who owns what; who is entitled to what—are, arguably, much more effective than fuzzy rules, generally speaking. This is because they communicate better. Economists would say that these rules are efficient because they reduce information costs. Of course, even simple rules can be misunderstood. This might happen when the channel of communication is full of noise, or is misleading. As mentioned, people and businesses often translate cloudy, squishy standards into bright-line rules, or create concrete mechanisms to cope with the standard. But the opposite process also takes place: that is, people translate or modify what seem to be clear rules into something quite different—something that may be cloudier and fuzzier than the rule itself. Take the speed limit in Rhode Island. The actual rule is a fuzzy standard. First, this gets translated into something concrete, a definite speed limit. But then speed limits, in turn, get modified, by common understanding and custom, into something much less definite. The actual, lived norm is that the speed limit is only an approximation. It is okay to go a bit faster. Everybody does, at times. But how much faster is okay? Not clear or distinct. A driver in a zone with a thirty-mile-per-hour limit would resent getting a ticket for going thirty-three. Sixty miles per hour: surely this is a violation. But what about forty? Thirty-seven?

Ambiguity interferes with communication. There are various kinds of ambiguity. A message can be cloudy or confused in itself. Or the ambiguity may stem from the way the message was given. Did whoever gave the message seem sure of herself? The message might seem clear, but did the speaker fumble and mumble and hesitate? The Supreme Court makes a decision. Does a unanimous court carry a different and more powerful message than a narrow, five-to-four decision? As Stephen Wasby put it, the "vultures who would pick over the bones of the Court" could conceivably use "split decisions, particularly those which are five to four" as an excuse for delaying compliance in the hope that the decision would get reversed in some future case. Does this actually happen? Wasby admits there is no evidence; the idea is simply a "hypothesis."[56]

The Supreme Court may agree, though, with Wasby. *Brown v. Board of Education* was unanimous; Chief Justice Earl Warren insisted on this. He wanted the court to speak with one voice. Did this matter? It certainly did not prevent bitter resistance. But it did tell people that the court was serious, that the justices were all on board, and that the decision was unlikely to be undone. In the following years, key cases and decisions on civil rights issues were unanimous. The court wanted its message to be absolutely clear and unambiguous: unanimity helped (in the court's view, at least). *Cooper v. Aaron* (1958)[57] was a school segregation case out of Little Rock, Arkansas. The governor of Arkansas tried to frustrate integration at Central High School in Little Rock. A district court issued an order delaying desegregation for two and a half years. The Supreme Court reversed this order, nine to zero. All nine justices signed the opinion. They meant to convey a message: we mean business.

The clearer the message, the more likely it is to have significant impact. But this is a tendency, not a law of nature. Two scholars compared industrial waste management in Japan and the United States.[58] In the United States, the Resource Conservation and Recovery Act (1976) was a complex fabric of rules, extremely hard to decipher and enormously detailed. By way of contrast, the Japanese used "administrative guidance." They avoided formal rules and used a mode of regulation that was "far more cooperative and nonadversarial."[59] The Japanese method has been, it seems, more effective. (I will return to this point when discussing modes of implementation.) For now, the point is that, as a message, precision and detail are all very well but there comes a point where the message can be lost in the detail, or the detail seems quite overwhelming. Perhaps the better way to put the general rule is that a clear and simple message is better than a cloudy and complex one. Or, perhaps, you could say that a statute that runs for some hundreds of pages can hardly be called "clear" no matter how explicit individual paragraphs might be.

Vagueness in a law, directive, or regulation can be simply the result of poor draftsmanship, but sometimes it is on purpose, as a way of dulling the impact of the law, of fudging hard issues, delaying actual results, or for other motives. Some laws are congenitally vague; they were born that way, perhaps because there was no other way to satisfy conflicting forces and clashing voices. The Sherman Antitrust Law of 1890 used terms like "restraint of trade" that had no clear-cut meaning. The point of the law, perhaps, was to persuade people that something real had been done about the giant and nefarious "trusts." The law was short; it set up no apparatus, created no agency to put meat on the bones of the statute. The effect, whether on purpose or not, was to put off any real action or decisions and to hand them over to whatever courts or civil servants might be given the job of implementation.

Vagueness, however, can also be empowering (consciously or not). Nothing could be vaguer, less meaningful in itself, than phrases like "due process of law" or "equal protection of the laws," which appear in the Fourteenth Amendment to the Constitution of the United States. Yet the Supreme Court has seized on these two phrases and used them to build a gigantic structure of doctrine, a palace of constitutional law. All the antidiscrimination decisions, for example, are tied to these two elastic phrases.

■ ■ ■

There is a lot more one can say about communication, but we have touched on at least some major themes. One key point is that communication is a vital prerequisite to impact. A necessary condition. Necessary, but not sufficient. The legal system gives an order. The order is received, but then, who obeys and disobeys, and why? The rest of this book deals with this issue.

Double Agents

Modern legal systems are, in general, hopelessly complex. The statutes of a typical American state, or the federal government, or the government of any country, run to hundreds or thousands of pages. To this huge mass, you have to add local ordinances, court decisions, and tons of rules and regulations of administrative agencies. And this is merely the formal part of the legal system. Customs, rules of thumb, and administrative practices add ingredients to this huge, legal soup in every modern country. How are people and businesses supposed to cope with all this complexity? The Internal Revenue Code of the United States, which sets out rules about taxation in the United States, is thousands of pages long and, as we said, it is written in an impenetrable jargon resembling ordinary English only remotely. Yet we are all supposed to pay our taxes, and on time. Most of us do. For many people, making out a tax return is no great task. But for wealthier people, and for businesses of any size, it can be quite daunting. How do they manage?

The short answer is, they use what we might call information brokers—middlemen, intermediaries—whose job it is to cope with this complexity. These brokers receive messages from the government, figure out what these messages mean, and store them in their brains or in files (today, more likely online files). They will bring these out of storage (so to speak) as and when consumers need to know about these messages. In the Tarasoff case, this job of spreading the word was done by professional literature and occupational newsletters. Bulletins, brochures, and information sheets pour out of government and private companies in enormous volume, analyzing, digesting, interpreting, and explaining. Social networks are another source (as are, of course, the media). In Taiwan, after a court awarded big damages in a malpractice case, newspapers and television programs trumpeted the news: "Hospital on the hook for $1,000,000. . . ." In addition, physician blogs and legal articles spread word about the case and reported the "shock, disbelief [and] anger" of doctors about the decision.[60]

Lawyers are also crucial information brokers. Consider, for example, the role of a divorce lawyer. By training and experience, she knows the rules, and also how the system works. When a client comes to see her, she converts legal messages (the "law of divorce") into understandable, usable form, which she then passes on to the client (accurately, one hopes). No doubt the lawyer can, and often does, distort the message somewhat, for whatever reason. In any case, the role of the information broker is indispensable. In the main, the law of divorce could hardly work without divorce lawyers and the advice they give their clients.

Divorce law, on the whole, is relatively simple. The intermediary has a much more elaborate role when the messages are incurably complex. The *Code of Federal Regulations* is a true monster. So is the *Federal Register*, mentioned earlier, which contains all proposed rules, executive orders, and all final rules and regulations promulgated by every federal agency. As I said, nobody uses the *Register* for recreational reading. But, as I also pointed out, lawyers who represent, say, the steel industry will keep an eye on the *Register* and try to catch anything that might concern their clients. Under the Administrative Procedure Act, every federal agency that proposes rules and regulations has to give the public a chance to comment. The public often does exactly that. Not, of course, the general public, but interested parties. Business groups, unions, trade associations, and NGOs may jump in (often through lawyers). In some cases, the agency will hold hearings in a number of cities; individuals and institutions may weigh in and give their views. Written comments may be solicited. For example, when, in 1999, the Securities and Exchange Commission (SEC) published a (proposed) Selective Disclosure Rule with provisions about insider trading, the SEC received several thousand comment letters.[61]

The Internal Revenue Code is another monstrous statute. For businesses of any size, or for individuals with money and complex investments, intermediaries are an absolute necessity. Tax advice is a big business. There are companies to help middle-class people cope with their tax returns. One chain, H&R Block, has 11,000 retail tax offices in the United States and 1,700 abroad. The bigger fish have their own tax lawyers and accountants. Commercial services provide tax lawyers and accountants with up-to-date information about rules, rulings, and regulations. Tax lawyers and accountants pass these along to their clients (along with advice on how to pay as little in taxes as possible without actually breaking the rules).

Tax lawyers and accountants are, in a way, double agents. Their main job is to help their clients. But they also tell clients how to comply, what strategies work and don't work, what an honest tax return might look like, and what kinds of evasive behavior are likely to lead to trouble. In a way, then, they are also serving the government. The tax system could hardly work without the help of the tax specialists, chewing the text, digesting it, turning it into small, bite-size bits, and feeding these bits to the clients. It may not be too far-fetched to compare them to microorganisms inside the stomach of cows. Cows eat grass, but cannot digest it on their own. Microorganisms inside break down the grass, making food for themselves and for the cows.

The role of lawyers as double agents is easy to overlook. Lawyers, as is well known, get paid for helping clients. They design and implement "innovative legal devices"; they help clients "in minimizing transaction costs, circumventing regulatory constraints, and pursuing various strategic objectives."[62] Helping people pursue "strategic objectives" is socially valuable. But just as valuable to society, perhaps, is the double agent role. It makes possible the success (such as it is) of that modern leviathan, the welfare-regulatory state. Huge numbers of laws and rules and regulations would have no impact at all if the public were forced to confront them naked, so to speak. The complexity would baffle and confuse people and businesses. They would be unable to cope on their own. They need the double agents.

Lawyers in many societies play the role of intermediary, or double agent. In some societies, other actors take this role: notaries, scriveners, or simply experts in this or that field of law. The basic phenomenon is the same: the messages of modern legal systems are too complicated to reach their audience unmediated. Or the audience is too naïve or unschooled to handle even a relatively simple message. Since impact without communication is impossible, there is a social niche for intermediaries, which is filled, one way or another, in every society—sometimes inadequately or badly, to be sure.

More on the Message: Auxiliary Carriers

Education, in the broadest sense, is one of the ways in which legal messages get transmitted to their audience. Education plays this role quite literally: what we learn in school about law, government, and the legal system. Popular culture, too, has an educational function. There are also organized campaigns to "educate" people about some aspects of the law. In late 2013, when the Affordable Care Act (Obamacare) was launched—a complex new program—the federal government made a great effort to tell people their rights and duties, tell them (for example) how to sign up for the program. At first, there was confusion and disorganization, but eventually things were straightened out, more or less.[63] Governments print, of course, thousands and thousands of directives, brochures, handbooks, and information sheets, much of this for the edification of the public. Governments also can force "disclosure," making companies give information to the public. Credit companies have to tell customers about interest rates. Notably, a company that goes public has to strip itself naked, so to speak, before potential investors. Registered sex offenders have to reveal where they live. "Mandated disclosure" is "a mainstay of the regulatory toolkit." The quote is from Dan Ho's study of "restaurant sanitation grading," whose "central idea is to summarize sanitation inspections with a letter grade ('A,' 'B,' or 'C')" and display them prominently in the front of the restaurant.[64] But whether all this disclosure makes a difference is, of course, an empirical question. Pennsylvania, for example, "spent millions of dollars to gather relatively sophisticated evidence on outcomes from cardiac interventions"; this was available to the general public. But very few patients were aware of this information, or used it.[65]

Private companies and institutions do their own sorts of educating. For example, the law prohibits sexual harassment. No doubt many people have at least a vague idea what this means. But the details can be subtle and complex. There is evidence that women define harassment more broadly than men do, which is no big surprise.[66] Many organizations—my university, for example—require training sessions or online courses or mock trials or proceedings, to spread the word, to explain sexual harassment and how to avoid it, and to set out university policy on the subject. Are these sessions effective? One study found some evidence of backlash: some men and women found the whole idea ridiculously overdone or even somewhat threatening. There were people who felt "they are walking on thumbtacks." One woman student thought that some women (obviously not her), "if they get flowers from someone they don't like then it's harassment, but if it's from someone they do like then all of a sudden it's sweet."[67] Prior attitudes toward gender were an influence on the way people received the message. But whether attitudes before, during, or after translated into behavior is another question that the study did not and could not answer.

Sexual harassment is a delicate and fraught subject. More neutral educational and information campaigns on more neutral subjects might be more effective. Companies, for example, often post on bulletin boards basic information about labor laws and the rights of workers. Employees can read about their rights and duties; some of them probably do try to absorb this information. Both government and private employers indulge in a good deal of outreach; whether this makes much of a difference depends, of course, on the circumstances and the subject.

The line between education and punishment can get blurred. In California, if you get caught for speeding or making an illegal U-turn, or commit some other relatively minor traffic offense, you have to go to traffic school. This is, in theory, educational. In practice, it is a kind of punishment—spending eight boring hours hearing about driving rules. Nowadays, it can be done online, which is less objectionable for many people. (There is even an online "comedy" traffic school, which promises to be fast, cheap, and funny, and does not require any reading.)[68] In Canada, a law passed in 1985 permitted the prosecution of "Johns" (male customers of prostitutes). In Toronto, in 1996, men charged with this offense could choose to go to the "Toronto John School Diversion Program," in which (in exchange for dropping the charges) the men were taught various things: how bad it is to have a criminal record, how dangerous it is to consort with prostitutes (they learn about "drug addicted prostitutes who have stabbed their clients with AIDS infected needles"), and how their behavior harms society. They see graphic slide shows about sexually transmitted diseases and they are instructed about safe sex practices. And all this is before the lunch break.[69] This was, of course, education with a vengeance, but also a form of (mild) punishment. It was also, apparently, effective in getting the message across.

Can We Believe It?

Most people, most of the time, assume that a message means what it says. But this is not always true. Many people, in many countries, would be wise to be cynical about messages coming from the government. In a dictatorship, constitutions (in a way) carry two messages. One is explicit: you have all sorts of rights. One is implicit: better not try to enforce these rights. Only a fool or a hero would have taken the constitution of the Soviet Union seriously, or the constitution of modern China, for that matter. The same for international treaties. Countries like the Sudan or Cuba sign human rights conventions without even blushing, but they have no intention of complying.

On paper, workers in China have strong rights. But the workers (according to one study) have little faith in the official labor code. The labor laws also give workers the right to file complaints about code violations. But workers do not, in fact, file complaints; they do not trust the courts. They see the courts as linked to local government, which is linked, in turn, to the interests of employers.[70] Those who do turn to the courts end up disillusioned.[71]

Another situation is probably also common: harsh laws that are weak and spineless in practice, or that seem to promise a lot and produce very little. All governments ignore some laws and enforce some rules that have no formal existence. The gap between the real and the ideal is probably greatest in a dictatorship, but it exists in every society. Legal systems have grown to enormous size—big beyond the reasonable capacity of government to implement, even assuming the state actually wants to implement the rules. Moreover, actors in all systems have at least some degree of discretion. The police officer who stops a speeder can decide not to give a ticket, if the driver tells a good story, say, a sympathetic story about a pregnant wife rushing to the hospital. No such excuse appears on the books, but the officer might just give a warning or do nothing at all. Those in charge of environmental laws, safety laws, and health laws also tend to have discretion. Enforcement of these rules is the subject of a vast ocean of studies. I will return to this issue in later chapters.

Enforcers

As mentioned, a legal rule can be seen as a message directed to at least two kinds of audiences. The law against burglary tells the general public that burglary is illegal (which they surely know already). The law is also, of course, a message to police and other enforcers. Enforcers, like citizens generally, may or may not get all the messages they are supposed to get; they may ignore, misunderstand, or misinterpret messages, just like the general public.

The role of the enforcers is crucial in any study of impact. Thomas Gawron and Ralph Rogowski distinguish between the "effectiveness" of a rule and the "implementation" of the rule. Research on "effectiveness" looks at the reaction of the public, and research on "implementation" focuses on the enforcers.[72] A legal rule is futile if the public message gets lost, but it can be equally futile if the message to the enforcers gets lost or if the enforcers resist it. The police certainly get the message about burglary, and understand their role in enforcement. But authorities can decide (for example) not to enforce rules against smoking pot, or that arresting prostitutes is pointless (a decision, historically, that was often greased with money).

The police are, in many ways, the chief enforcement agents of (criminal) law. How and why they behave varies enormously from country to country, from period to period, and from area of law to area of law. The police may be pillars of propriety, honest and hardworking enforcers and friends of the neighborhood, or they may be biased and corrupt or bigoted and unfair. In some countries, the police have been known to run death squads. The police in Japan have a reputation much different from the reputation of the police in some parts of Mexico, or in Honduras or Guatemala. Police scandals have erupted from time to time in the United States: scandals about incompetence, corruption, race discrimination, brutality. There is a massive amount of research on police behavior in various countries; research on who gets arrested and why; on selective enforcement; and on many other topics.

The criminal justice system is a big, loose, gangly system. In the United States in particular, no central authority is in charge—either at the federal level or on the level of the states. The impact of the criminal code depends on police, prosecutors, judges, and (sometimes) jurors. I have compared the system to a leaky garden hose. If you turn up the pressure at one end, water may never reach the other end, but simply squirt uselessly out of the holes. There are countless historical examples of laws dissipated at the level of enforcement. National prohibition in the 1920s is often considered the classical American instance, but every branch of the law and every era and every society could provide more instances. The message itself may be at least partly responsible; more often, probably, the will to carry out the message is missing or imperfect.

Historically, rape was almost surely an underreported crime. Police frequently seemed unsympathetic to victims. They often felt that a woman had "asked for it" or was "just trying to get back at her boyfriend" if she claimed she had been raped. Police made statements like, "She can't be raped, she's a whore."[73] In Harry Kalven Jr. and Hans Zeisel's classic study of the American jury, from the 1960s, juries were often unwilling to convict a rapist if the woman victim had gone to bars or had a rich sexual history, or (in the jury's opinion) acted in such a way as to invite sexual aggression.[74] This probably reflected general (male) opinion. In Germany, reforms in the laws against sexual misconduct had disappointing results, according to a study published in 2014. The public still believed common (but false) myths: for example, that women who accuse men of sexual misconduct are frequently lying.[75] The impact of the formal law of rape was stunted and imperfect; this was another leaky hose.

Each situation may be different; nonetheless, some general remarks can be made. Enforcement is always an issue, but particularly so when law tries to control or forbid popular behavior or outlaw a commodity that many people are eager to consume. The paradigm case is sex outside of marriage. Prostitution is, supposedly, the oldest profession, but this profession has rarely been recognized as legitimate. Brothels in the United States (outside of Nevada) were always illegal, but they were widely tolerated. In some cities, there were even guidebooks telling people where they could find the houses. One New York guide, published in 1839, had the pious title of *Prostitution Exposed*, and its writer used the wonderful pseudonym of A. Butt Ender.[76] In many cities, brothel owners simply paid the police to look the other way. In the early twentieth century, a strong movement arose to stamp out prostitution. It is safe to say that it failed. Prohibition, too, was a failure, and so, basically, is the war on drugs. And the battle against illegal immigration.

The police, of course, are not the only enforcers, and research on the police is only one type of research on the enforcement effort. There is a huge literature also on jury behavior, prison administration, and judicial decision-making; in short, on every aspect of the enforcement system. Courts are enforcers, too. And they, too, can be corrupt or lazy and inefficient. They may be committed to due process or not, independent of the regime or not, personally honest or not, dedicated to carrying out state policy or not. Every administrative agency is an enforcer, and every prison guard, warden, or official. Every major legal system employs thousands of inspectors, spot-checkers, arbitrators, an army of civil servants whose job it is to enforce the laws. What messages they get and how they understand these messages is a vital aspect of any study of law in action. So, too, of their identity. Who are they, how are they trained, how much do they know, how much do they care? The effect of civil servants on business regulation is a major theme of many studies; it will be dealt with later on.

The public, too, has an enforcement role. Criminal law would be badly off without citizen complaints. Civil rights laws would be dead letters unless people were willing to act. Public pressure on law enforcement makes a big difference (not always a good one). Pressure to be tougher on crime, or more lenient on pot smoking. Pressure to arrest and deport more foreigners or to grant more visas to foreigners with skills. Pressure to stop harassing minorities or pressure to make cities safe. Sometimes enforcement depends on whistle-blowing. This, too, is a theme to be discussed later on in these pages.

■ ■ ■

In this chapter, I spoke about messages to the public, or some part of the public; messages about rules, norms, regulations, and the like. The air,

so to speak, is full of these messages. But they are not the only important messages in the legal system. I mentioned messages to enforcers.
There are also messages about enforcement. That is, messages to people
about how much enforcement there is, of what sort, and against whom.
These are of extreme significance. If people somehow get a message that
laws against speeding are not enforced, this might lead to more speeding
on the highways. If they get a message about more police action, they
might speed less.

Later chapters will take up deterrence, shame, stigma, peer group
pressures, and other factors that affect the impact of law. Deterrence,
of course, refers to a system of rewards and punishments. But the impact comes not from rewards and punishments in themselves, but from
perceptions of rewards and punishments: what is communicated to
the public or some part of it. Shame, too (another possible deterrent),
depends on messages from a peer group. A person who does something
wrong, but invisibly and completely in private, is less likely to bear the
yoke of shame. These themes will be expanded on in the following
chapters.

3

AN ANATOMY OF COMPLIANCE

IMPACT HAS BEEN DEFINED as behavior that is causally related to some law, decision, or other action of government, or action by a civil servant, policeman, or any other enforcer. We can distinguish between direct and indirect impact, that is, between immediate impact and ripple effects. There is also what we might call legal impact. By *legal impact*, I mean how, say, a decision by Court A reverberates in Court B, or the effect of an appellate court decision on trial courts or other parts of the judicial system. Legal impact is of great importance to legal scholars. But on the whole, I will not take legal impact into consideration; for that I would need another quite sizable book.

The definition of impact given here is value-neutral. It is about changes that take place after, and because of, some activity within the legal system. In some instances, it is also about changes before the legal action but in anticipation of that activity.[1] To ask what impact a law has had is not the same as asking whether the law "fulfilled its purpose." That depends on what the law was supposed to do, which is not always easy to tell, objectively speaking. At worst, asking about the purpose of a law is posing an unanswerable question. Nobody can read the minds of a legislature. Of course, the purpose of a law is not always mysterious by any means. It is sometimes quite obvious.

The question—was the purpose of a law fulfilled?—is often an extremely important question. To be sure, impact and purpose are usually related, but they are analytically distinct, if nothing else. Obviously, if a law has, say, bad side effects, it can hardly be reaching its (presumed) goal, just as a drug meant to cure insomnia is a failure if it causes strokes and heart attacks.

This book, as I said, is about impact, and ignores, for the most part, effectiveness; that is, the match (or mismatch) between the impact of, say, a rule (the behavioral changes it leads to) and the (presumed) purpose of the law. Effectiveness deserves a book of its own. Probably many books. Any treatment of this subject would have to address some tough questions: how can we know purpose, and how can we measure whether the law actually fulfills that purpose? But the subject of this book is impact, not purpose. In any event, you cannot deal with effectiveness without first dealing with impact. I also suspect that effectiveness is extremely situation-specific, that it is even harder to discuss in general terms than impact.

The (presumed) purpose of a law is, of course, also quite different from the means chosen to achieve that purpose. If we want to know if a new law "works," we are really asking two separate questions. First, did it have an impact? And second, did that impact further the (presumed) goal of the law? Answering this second question is not just a matter of looking for side effects; it also asks whether the means chosen turn out to be wrong, because they do not move us toward our purpose or goal. For example, Germany, worried about a very low birthrate and a shrinking population, enacted a law that went into effect in 2007 which offered more generous payments to mothers and fathers who took maternity or paternity leaves.[2] The idea was to get people to have more babies (and also to induce fathers to play a bigger role in the life of these babies). The law had an obvious and measurable impact. You could count how many people applied for the money compared to the numbers who applied under an earlier scheme. A surprising number of fathers took the bait. Whether, however, the law led to a higher birthrate is another story. At first, the birthrate went up a bit (apparently), but later not at all. Too many other factors go into family decisions to have children or not have children. In short, arguably, the law, though it had an impact, failed to do what it was intended to do. This is surely a common phenomenon.

Compliance

Many studies of impact make use of the term *compliance*. Compliance is a response to some legal act, causally related to that act, which includes behavior purposely done to accord with that act and (more or less) congruent with the dictates of the legal act. Compliance, in other words, is some sort of obedience. Diana Kapiczewski and Matthew M. Taylor identify four distinct groups of studies that address compliance. Two of these are important to us: first, compliance by citizens—the usual meaning; second, compliance by "executives, legislatures, or bureaucracies."[3] There is, of course, also noncompliance, and various grades in between. Both compliance and noncompliance are complex concepts. The more complex the legal act (imagine a statute that runs to a hundred printed pages), the more likely it is that compliance is not an all-or-nothing thing. Neither, for that matter, is noncompliance.

Compliance and its relatives are obviously instances of impact, but the term *impact* has a much broader meaning than compliance. A word like *compliance* fits best when you talk about a criminal law. You comply by obeying the law against jaywalking, or by not committing burglary or shoplifting. You can also comply with a regulation: filing your tax return or, if you are a public corporation, disclosing financial information to stockholders. But decriminalization and deregulation also have an impact, which the word *compliance* hardly fits. Adultery was once defined as a crime. The law was repealed. Did this have an impact? In other words, did more people decide to commit adultery? South Australia loosens the laws about the use of marijuana. Do more people start to smoke pot?[4]

Impact also includes, for example, all sorts of indirect effects. The government passes a law asking all foreign nationals to register on or before a specific date, say August 1. Suppose the law excuses foreigners who are married to American citizens. An undocumented foreigner lives with an American citizen. They are not married. Now they decide to get married to avoid the need to register. This definitely would be an impact—it is behavior causally related to the law—but it would be straining language to call it compliance. Another foreigner simply decides to go back home. This, too, is impact, but here too the word *compliance* (or *noncompliance*) does not fit.

Obviously, *direct* and *indirect* are vague words. Extremes (as is often the case) are easy to see; in between, though, things get blurred. The most direct result of the famous Miranda case (which gave rise to the well-known "Miranda warning") was its effect on Ernesto Miranda. He had been convicted of a crime, the Supreme Court reversed, and he went free. The state of Arizona lost. In other cases, as a result of a decision, money changes hands; a mother or a father gets custody of a child; a prisoner goes free or stays in prison. Mental health workers found out about *Tarasoff* and changed their behavior. A state raises the fee for a hunting license; a sportsman applies and pays the fee. All these are direct and obvious impacts.

But all of them also have indirect impacts. If *Miranda* affected police behavior, this might be called direct impact, but whether or not it had an impact, and what the impact might be, has been disputed, and the case, consequently, has had political ramifications. It has affected the debate on police behavior, and on crime policy in general. These, too, are part of the indirect impact of the case.

An armed robber wearing a ski mask bursts into a store. The mask is there, obviously, to hide his face and his identity. The law against armed robbery is causally related to the fact that he puts on a ski mask. If there were thousands of armed robbers, sales of ski masks might go up. And this might have consequences for the textile industry and the gross income of sports stores. This is, to be sure, a far-fetched example. There are other, less bizarre results. Scared citizens buy more handguns. They avoid going out at night, and sales of concert tickets fall. You can spin out a scenario for almost any law, rule, or ordinance. The cumulative impact, direct and indirect, of the tons of legal material in modern societies is clearly great. An enormous range of behaviors can be identified as remote and indirect reactions to laws and decisions of courts.

Indirect impact refers to what we might call the ripple effect of some legal act. The state raises the license for hunting deer; fewer people pay; fewer deer get shot. Deer multiply in an area, and they invade more gardens and eat more plants. A woman becomes depressed, partly because deer ate her flowers and ruined her beloved garden. She goes to a doctor and he prescribes medication. The medication has a rare side effect and she dies. And so on. We can trace the chain of causation—more or less. But clearly, the more indirect the impact, the harder it is to measure, and the harder to line it up causally with the original stimulus. And the less it is predictable. After a while, the ripples are lost in the vast expanse of water.

The impact of the Tarasoff case on the way mental health workers acted has already been mentioned. Did the case also have an impact on patients? Some studies have suggested that it did. Psychiatrists have some sort of duty to warn, and a duty to tell patients about their duty. Some patients, then, after hearing this news, might be less likely to reveal violent thoughts, or seek psychiatric help at all. One economist even came to the startling conclusion that *Tarasoff* had the "unintended" (and surely indirect) effect of increasing the homicide rate by 5 percent.[5] This seems really unlikely. But a change in the pool of patients is certainly possible.

Brown v. Board of Education outlawed segregation in public schools. Later cases turned on specific situations: a city swimming pool, a municipal park. But people read these decisions—correctly, I think—much more generally: *de jure* segregation, anywhere and everywhere, was a violation of constitutional rights. There were important ripple effects: on attitudes, norms, mentality. The civil rights cases may have led to more roles in movies and TV for African Americans. It may have encouraged feminists, Native American activists, Grey Panthers, advocates for prisoners' rights. And each ripple had its chain of ripple effects.

The whole civil rights movement was within a circle of consequences; *Brown* did not create these consequences, but it surely reinforced them. One crucial result was a change in the national atmosphere of race relations. White supremacy, even in the South, ultimately lost legitimacy. A loss of legitimacy also occurred in the war on smoking. There was plenty of actual law here: high taxes, restrictions on advertising, bans on smoking in theaters and airplanes, and so on. These were joined with a relentless campaign to convince the public that smoking was dangerous, to smokers, and to the rest of us as well. The result was the "denormalization" of smoking, the "transformation of social norms surrounding smoking."[6]

In cases like the war on smoking, or the civil rights cases, it is hard to know how much is impact (direct and indirect) and how much is something else—processes in society, social changes, from whatever causes, that happen at the same time, or before, and which may influence the legal changes as much as or more than the influence of the legal changes on social change. And it is always difficult, and sometimes impossible, to disentangle cause and effect.

Ripple effects can add to the impact of a law. They can also be negative, like the side effects of a drug. Weighing good and bad effects is a formidable job of measurement. Does raising the minimum wage cost jobs? Or does it cut down on employee turnover in the fast-food industry? Or does it make no difference at all? A few cities still have rent control; those families lucky enough to live in rent-controlled apartments are surely better off. But what about the negative side effects? Economists are convinced that these outweigh any possible benefits: landlords refuse to make repairs; the housing market freezes; the stock of housing deteriorates.[7]

The law says you must wear a seat belt. Seat belts make driving safer. Or do they? Some economists (the kind who hate almost any government regulation) have argued, at least in the past, that the side effects drown out the benefits. Drivers lulled into a false sense of security will drive more recklessly. The seat belt lowers the cost of speeding and careless driving, "in terms of injury risk." A "decision to drive faster or more intensely" is a "decision to 'spend' some of the increased protection on 'purchase' of a reduction in travel time." After all, we "walk more cautiously when barefoot than when shod." Seat belts, in other words, do not save lives; they cost lives.[8] However, it was the cautious drivers, not the reckless ones, who buckled up. That they then went wild on the highway seems to fly in the face of common sense. In any event, as John Donohue pointed out, there are, after all, speed limits—in other words, other constraints on speed—not to mention traffic cops. And, most important, even if there were some tendency to drive a bit more incautiously, it would be dwarfed by the safety benefits of the belt.[9]

In the United States, the law requires sex offenders to register and let the community know who they are and where they live. This is the essence of "Megan's Law," named after a child victim in New Jersey. Megan's family in New Jersey had no idea that one of their neighbors was a violent sex offender. Outrage over the crime led to passage of the law in 1997; today, every state has its own version.[10] The point was not to heap additional punishment on sex offenders. These men, after all, had served their terms and were now back in the world. The point was to keep them from doing more damage. Whether these laws actually have this effect is hard to tell, and perhaps unlikely.[11] But what is clear is the impact on the sex offenders. These men (they are almost all men) find it hard to get jobs and to find a place to live. There is a ripple effect on their families: threats and harassment; landlords who refuse to rent to the men and their families; children who are ridiculed, teased, and pestered by other children; 77 percent of the children with feelings of depression. Arguably, these side effects outweigh any good these laws might do.[12]

Joseph Gusfield distinguished between symbolic and instrumental functions of "legal and governmental acts." Symbolic functions "do not depend on enforcement for their effect."[13] Presumably, a "symbolic" law makes an impact on society, even if nobody enforces it. Gusfield talks about rules that "remain as important affirmations of an acceptable code even though they are regularly breached." These rules serve as "ideals."[14] Erhard Blankenburg defines a law as symbolic when the lawmaker expresses a norm but does nothing to provide any means for turning its provisions into reality.[15] Presumably the public, unlike the government, will not ignore these laws. But I suspect that if a law is not enforced and people know it, the law loses whatever symbolic value it might have had. A purely symbolic law sooner or later stops working as anything, symbol or nonsymbol. A law, however, can be symbolic in a more literal sense. It can create symbols that have a meaning for people. Laws about the American flag are laws about a symbol of the country. The flag-burner burns the flag precisely to show contempt for what is symbolized by the flag.[16]

But in the usual case, it is hard to see why an unenforced law would have any impact at all, let alone a "symbolic impact." The history of unenforced or badly enforced laws suggests as much. Prohibition, for example. One can argue about the impact of Prohibition, but to the extent it was not enforced, it is hard to see any symbolic value to it. Indeed, the violators treated the law with utter contempt.

The Fifteenth Amendment to the United States Constitution guarantees the right to vote, regardless of race. During the Jim Crow era, African Americans did not, in fact, vote; the white South made sure of this, using a variety of methods, including violence and harassment. An African American in, say, 1910, in Mississippi, knew that trying to vote could cost him his job, or even his life. It would be hard to argue that the Fifteenth Amendment, nonetheless, had symbolic value in Mississippi in 1910. Unenforced laws usually have no value at all. Or perhaps negative value: an increase in cynicism, or, in some cases, hopelessness and despair.

Are there no exceptions? Situations when laws that make promises or express ideals have an impact even without any effort at enforcement? The law can catalyze action, can help in mobilization, can lead to demands for some official response—for real enforcement. Arguably, the school segregation case had this effect. Enforcement was, to say the least, pitifully slow and ineffective. The white South resisted massively. The real impact, arguably, was on the black community, on the civil rights movement itself. There are surely many similar instances: examples of legal mobilization, rules, and laws that stir up a community or an interest group. Mobilization takes needs and desires that were only half conscious, or inchoate, and turns them into concrete wishes and demands, as in Michael W. McCann's study of the movement for pay equity.[17] Impact, after all, depends on the behavior of an audience, and actual enforcement is only part of the story of how that audience reacts.

One can even argue that many, or even most, laws have a symbolic element. This is the case if the state fails to provide enough money and staff to reach the ideal level of enforcement. Symbolic laws and "real" laws, then, are not sharply divided; there is no single on–off switch. At one end of the scale, though, one can find the purely symbolic laws, laws that are, in fact, ignored or toothless; at the other end, those that are fully and vigorously enforced. Most laws are somewhere in between.

The interesting question is this: Why do we have these symbolic laws at all? Sometimes, bitter opposition to a law that might actually work is very strong; the demand for passage of *something* is equally strong; the legislature enacts a toothless law to pacify that part of the public that wants real action (but cannot get it). Jens Newig mentions the German ozone law of 1995, which he considers a classic example. Environmental groups demanded action against "summer fog," but an effective law was politically impossible. The law came about after a great to-do over holes in the ozone layer, but the provisions of the law were so riddled with exceptions that it never accomplished anything. Its real function was to calm the public, and it functioned as an alibi. The result was a toothless—or, if you will, purely symbolic—law.[18] Many state civil rights laws before the 1960s fell into this category.

Why would interest groups want a purely symbolic law to be passed? The short answer is: they don't. But a toothless law is sometimes all they can get; it is something they have to settle for. The drafters of the Fifteenth Amendment were not looking for a symbol; they never intended merely to express an ideal. They wanted to give blacks the vote. But the white South refused (and the North lost interest in the issue). Why were laws against prostitution routinely ignored? Moralists were not looking for a symbol; they wanted results. But customer demand, and corruption, frustrated them. For about a century after 1870, most American divorces were collusive, even though formal law refused to allow a couple to agree to get a divorce; they had to have "grounds." Moralists wanted tough divorce laws; they had to settle for what they got. It is possible to be cynical about this sort of law, to think of it as something designed to hoodwink the public, to convince people that something has been done when in fact nothing was done. Or it can be looked at as a first step—a way to start out on the journey. Either is possible. Symbolic victories are rarely victories, but they are also not always total defeats.

■ ■ ■

When we think about impact, we have to ask: impact on whom? Consider, for example, a simple rule in a penal code, making burglary a crime. There are two messages here, as I said. One is a message to the general public. The other is a message to legal authorities. Compliance or noncompliance is an issue for both audiences, and there can be impact on both, or on one but not the other, or on neither.

The burglary statute is fairly simple and straightforward. Modern law is a Gordian knot of complicated messages. The messages filter down through levels and layers of the bureaucracy. The federal food and drug laws set out general standards, and create an agency (the FDA) to carry out the mandate of the statutes. The FDA formulates rules and regulations. Companies in the food and drug business get these messages. The FDA will enforce its rules, through staff members helped by other enforcement agencies; businesses and the public will comply or fail to comply, or, at times, will bring complaints. Every major regulatory effort in every modern nation has a complicated structure. In the United States, the Affordable Care Act (often called Obamacare) is over 2,000 pages long (has anybody actually read it?). It set up a program of bewildering complexity; its messages go out to administrative agencies, state governments, the general public, the states, hospitals, doctors, nurses, pharmaceutical companies, insurance companies, and, no doubt, to many other audiences. There are issues of compliance and impact with regard to every single one of these audiences.

Action and Reaction

For many purposes, it makes sense to isolate the two macro-questions mentioned early in this book: the forces that make law, on the one hand, and the impact of law, on the other. Both macro-questions are important. We can ask: What was going on in society that led Great Britain to create a National Health Service? And, once in place, what impact did it have on British society? What was the background of the Civil Rights Law of 1964 in the United States, and what happened next? The two questions are analytically separate, but in the real world, they are not isolated from each other. Action breeds reaction. The topic in this book is reaction, not action, but reaction often includes interaction, a feedback loop, if you like the phrase. People do not simply obey, disobey, or evade; they act and react. In extreme cases, they might rise up in revolt. More often, they complain, write letters, demand changes. There is no lobby of burglars and potential burglars calling for changes in the law against burglary, but with regard to the Affordable Care Act, or the abortion decision, or so many other laws, pushback and interaction are important facts of legal life. One kind of impact that a law might have, in other words, is that it incites or stimulates some people to make efforts to change the law.

Backlash

One kind of pushback, or side effect, or backlash is worth more than a passing mention. A law or judicial decision that provokes "political reactions" may end up "undercutting" the "effectiveness" of the law or judicial decision.[19] Exhibit A in the so-called backlash theory is the school desegregation decision, *Brown v. Board of Education*. Michael Klarman has argued that this decision interrupted slow but steady progress in the South. It touched off ferocious resistance, it "propelled southern politics far to the right," it "exalted" race over all other issues, stimulated extreme versions of white supremacy, and weakened the position of moderate whites. Men were elected to office in the South who were "prepared to use virtually any means of resisting racial change, including blatant defiance of federal authority and brutal suppression of civil rights demonstrations."[20] Klarman later made a similar argument about the early decisions in states that took favorable action on gay marriage. These decisions, he felt, provoked strong backlash; they aroused conservatives to whom the idea of gay marriage was poison.[21]

Backlash is certainly real. Nobody expects people and institutions to shrug their shoulders and accept rules they absolutely detest, particularly if the rules go against deeply held principles. They might simply disobey (more on this later). But if they feel strongly enough, they could very well take action. Revolutions are giant instances of backlash. The American Revolution, the French Revolution, the Russian Revolution: all of these can be analyzed in terms of backlash against authorities or regimes.

Whether the backlash theory has gotten things right about the school segregation case is another question. Certainly, segregationists fought tooth and nail against desegregation. But that is not the issue. The issue is whether the backlash effect—the negative impact—swamps whatever positive impact followed this case, or the abortion case, or the cases that legalized gay marriage. It is impossible to make a definitive assessment.

My own intuition is that positive results outweighed the backlash, but this is not easy to prove. Klarman himself, despite his backlash argument, thinks the *Brown* decision was worth it in the end. Yes, it provoked a furious backlash, but it was also "indirectly responsible for the landmark civil rights legislation of the mid-1960s." Violent backlash "provoked an outcry from national television audiences," and this led Congress and the president "to intervene with landmark civil rights legislation."[22] There was, in short, a backlash against the backlash and, in the end, the results were positive.

In some ways, backlash was the direct impact of *Brown* and related decisions. The civil rights laws were part of the indirect impact, the ripple effect. And the backlash itself contributed to the strength of the civil rights movement and to the success, in the end, of the struggle for a strong civil rights law. The strongest way of putting the backlash theory, however, would have it that *Brown* and its progeny made things worse, at least initially. These decisions interrupted a course of slow but steady evolution. But is this true? Would segregation have died out gradually, and in a healthier way? Was resistance to the rights of African Americans stronger after the segregation decisions than before? Did the court's intervention slow down a natural process? I find this hard to believe. Yes, violence and turmoil followed *Brown*. But that, to me, does not suggest a stunted evolution; rather, it shows ferocious resistance to change. If anything, the bitterness of the "backlash" is evidence against the theory that race relations were evolving in a positive direction—at least in any reasonable length of time. Slavery had been abolished ninety years before, and the South was still segregated. Blacks were not allowed to vote, and the justice system was racist to the core. There were, to be sure, some changes. Race relations were improving in some ways and in some places, but the process was slow, halting—and ferociously resisted. Whether it would have "evolved" very much in another forty years, fifty years, or a century, without the court (and without the civil rights movement) is an open question.

On gay rights, especially gay marriage, here too the backlash was certainly real. The gay rights movement suffered a string of electoral defeats. Some elections turned on the issue; candidates opposed to gay marriage won races when voters, horrified by the prospect of gay marriage, flocked to the polls to strike a blow against the forces of Satan. On the other hand, when court decisions were favorable, this encouraged gay rights advocates and helped to mobilize them. They too became more active.[23] The decisions gave them hope, showed them a path forward. It made them feel that time was on their side. Which proved to be correct, in the not-so-long run. Gay marriage began to win victories at the polls in some states. The Supreme Court declared the Defense of Marriage Act unconstitutional,[24] and opinion surveys showed a remarkable change in attitudes toward gay marriage. Most young people simply accept gay rights ("What's the big deal?"), and the older folks are gradually dying off. Gay rights succeeded beyond the wildest dreams of people only a short time before. The Supreme Court delivered the final blow to the opposition in 2015; it declared laws against same-sex marriage unconstitutional.[25]

Brown may or may not have had a direct impact on school segregation in the Deep South (it probably made more of a difference in border states), yet *Brown* certainly influenced the civil rights movement, galvanized it, gave it important legitimacy. Nobody in the 1950s would have imagined an African American in the White House. The backlash argument has also been made against *Roe v. Wade,* the famous abortion case. The fuss over *Brown* has died down; gay marriage won signal victories; but the fight against legalized abortion seems to have abated hardly at all. *Roe v. Wade* is still with us—bloody but unbowed, so to speak, or at least bloody. It has come within a hair of getting overruled. It seems safe at the time of this writing (2016), but is still embroiled in bitter controversy. Here, the backlash argument has at least surface plausibility. But, again, it is hard to know what would have happened without this decision. No doubt there was an evolution toward a more permissive attitude, but is it really plausible to think that *Roe v. Wade* made the prospects worse? Surely not—at least in many parts of the country. On the other hand, the decision made the issue deeply political and, perhaps, affected the conservative movement. It made the goal of getting judges and justices appointed who were against *Roe v. Wade* extremely important.

If we reject the backlash theory, we should not make the opposite error—that is, giving too much credit, assigning too much impact, to decisions of the Supreme Court and other tribunals. There is no way to measure their impact accurately, especially their indirect impact, and certainly no way to measure indirect impact over time. To me, at least, it seems intuitively likely that cases on racial minorities, sexual minorities, and women's rights have had a positive impact, and certainly so in the long run. But society changes in so many ways that it is hard to tease out the causal contribution of particular legal acts in many situations. The progress of gay rights owes a lot to the sexual revolution and to ideas of individual choice. Court decisions may not be doing much more than limping along in the wake and backwash of social change. One kind of impact of judicial decisions, though, seems fairly clear: making laggards get with the program. In 2003, in *Lawrence v. Texas*, the Supreme Court struck down all existing sodomy laws.[26] In fact, most states had long since gotten rid of these laws; only a minority of the states, mostly in the Bible belt, were holdouts. This is, in fact, a common pattern. Supreme Court decisions may seem bold and forward-looking, when actually all that they are doing is forcing a minority of states to get in line. This was true, for example, of the famous case of *Gideon v. Wainwright*[27] in the 1960s. A right to a state-paid lawyer was already the rule in most states. Florida, Gideon's state, was a laggard.

Political backlash, according to Klarman, is "especially likely when a court decision not only contravenes public opinion but has supporters who are less intensely committed than are its opponents."[28] But was this true, in fact, for *Brown*, for *Roe v. Wade*, and for the gay marriage cases? Intensity is hard to measure. The civil rights cause certainly aroused intense commitment on the part of African Americans and their allies, and there was, or arose, a strong gay rights movement. Ultimately, backlash was swamped by acceptance, and by dramatic changes in public opinion.

In fact, there are two quite distinct backlash theories. One, which is Klarman's, carefully distinguishes between direct and indirect impact, and between immediate and longer-term results. For Klarman, one suspects, the cases he discusses, despite backlash, had happy endings. A quite different backlash theory would be one that insisted that *Brown*, or *Roe*, or the gay marriage cases retarded the march toward social change, that they made race relations, or the rights of gays and women, worse off than if they had been decided the other way. This second proposition seems more dubious than the first. The first has some grounding in law and society theory. Courts (and legislatures, of course) are never that distant from mass opinion. Like a platoon leader, they march along with the troops, or at best a few steps in front.

■ ■ ■

Direct impact depends on communication. As we noted, people who are unaware of a new law can hardly change their behavior because of it. Indirect impact, on the other hand, may not depend on communication. It might be a reaction to something done or not done by those who did get the message. *Tarasoff*, for example, had a direct impact on psychiatrists and social workers, who made more reports and warnings. But, as mentioned, some patients, perhaps, told about a duty to warn, might decide to clam up or stop seeing their doctor. This indirect impact would not depend at all on whether these patients had ever heard of the Tarasoff case.

In a well-known and controversial study, John Donohue and Steven D. Levitt pointed out a relationship between *Roe v. Wade*—decided in 1973—and a dip in the crime rate that took place in the years after 1991.[29] Crime, one must remember, is basically a young man's game. Legal abortion may have cut the supply of male babies, but the authors suggested a more intriguing possibility. Women who have abortions "are those most at risk to give birth to children who would engage in criminal activity." These women are "[t]eenagers, unmarried women, and the economically disadvantaged." Their children are "at higher risk for committing crime in adolescence." Unwanted babies born to such mothers are more prone to pathology and dysfunction as the years go by, compared to wanted babies. Liberal abortion rules meant fewer unwanted babies. Less pathology means less crime. This is an argument about an indirect impact—very indirect, as a matter of fact (and highly contested).

Jessica Wolpaw Reyes has suggested another legal change that, quite indirectly, might be tied to lower crime rates. Under the Clean Air Act, beginning in the late 1970s, rules required lead to be phased out of gasoline. Lead, it turns out, is "a dangerous toxin," especially for young children "at a sensitive stage of their neurobehavioral development." Lead exposure in children apparently can lead to an increase in "impulsive and aggressive behavior." Lead exposure, then, might be a "missing link" in the explanation of antisocial behavior, and phasing out lead might be one factor in a declining crime rate.[30] Of course, neither in Reyes's suggestion nor in that of Donohue and Levitt was communication a factor. Donohue and Levitt's ghostly, unborn criminals were not aware of anything, least of all *Roe v. Wade*, nor could clean-living males who grew up free of lead poisoning have any notion of the fate they had avoided.

Legal Impact

By legal impact, we mean the impact of a legal act—a rule, a law, a decision—within the legal system. High court cases, for example, have a direct impact on litigants; somebody wins and somebody loses. The general public is usually unaware and unaffected. But decisions, particularly the ones lawyers consider important, and which get reported and published, can have an impact within the legal system itself. Lower courts do what higher courts command. High courts in one state learn about decisions in other states, and sometimes this influences them. In many countries, cases from other countries or from international courts reverberate on the home front. New statutes affect what courts do, and also what the bureaucracy does, from the federal government down to zoning boards and school boards in the cities.

A huge number of legal studies (too many, in my opinion) are concerned with strictly internal impact (and ignore external impact). In this book, we will not follow this pattern. The internal chain of linked doctrines is not our issue. We should at least mention, however, one kind of legal impact. Important cases—*Tarasoff* is a good example—get noticed within the profession; they breed more lawsuits and they may also breed legislative change. *Tarasoff* was a California case, but there were lawsuits in other states as well. Other courts took notice; California passed a law to clarify the legal duty of psychotherapists toward third parties.[31] Diffusion of decisions from state to state is common. There is also legislative diffusion. Statutes start in one place and "diffuse" into others. "Megan's law" is a good example.

Legal impact (or supposed legal impact) is what law students study in law school: the ripple effect of decisions on other decisions, the way doctrine A gets modified or leads to doctrine B, and so on. This is especially the case in common law countries—countries, including the United States, whose legal system goes back ultimately to England. The common law system was, historically, a mosaic of doctrines, built up, tile by tile, by judges in the course of deciding individual cases and writing opinions. Civil law countries (in Europe, Latin America, and Asia) are, in theory, different; in these countries, the legislature and only the legislature makes law. In practice, the contrast between the two systems is probably not that great.[32] In both cases, however, purely legal impact, as defined here, is distinct from social impact or behavioral impact. But the boundaries between the two forms of impact are not as distinct as one might think. The effect of a law or regulation on the bureaucracy is, strictly speaking, legal impact, but it can also be looked at as a species of social impact. And, of course, legal impact often reverberates in the bigger world. Moreover, legal impact is not immune from its social context. Legal impact is almost never random or accidental, almost never mere fashion or habit. It is socially determined, and even though it seems confined to the legal system, as if it was in some sort of bubble, there is a tendency for impact to leak out.

Modes of Compliance and Noncompliance

We have used the terms *compliance* and *noncompliance* as if they were polar opposites. It would be better to say that they are, in a way, opposite ends of a scale. In between, there are many ways to react to a given law or doctrine; some of them are not easy to label.

Tax law (the Internal Revenue Code) requires people and businesses in the United States to file returns and pay income tax on their earnings. Tax law is a tangled mess of interlocking, sometimes mysterious rules. Some sections of the law seem clear. Some are anything but. Most people file their returns on time and (hopefully) make an honest attempt to comply with the law. The filing itself is unproblematic. You either do or don't file. If you do, you're in compliance. If not, you're breaking the law. But whether what's in your tax return is compliant is not so easy to say. Was it proper or not to deduct home expenses, on the theory that you used your study as a kind of office? Maybe. Wealthy taxpayers and companies hire tax lawyers or tax specialists to help them— to comply, yes, but also to figure out how to pay as little in tax dollars as possible. The trick is to get as close to illegality as you can without falling over the cliff. There are, thus, many shades of compliance. You can comply barely or fully; you can pretend to comply; you can comply in some twisted way that frustrates the very purpose of compliance. Or you can enthusiastically comply, or even give regulators more than they asked for. There is a sharp legal distinction between tax evasion and tax avoidance. The difference between them can be the difference between going to prison and not going to prison. But it is not always easy to tell in advance which is which.

Rules that are subtle or ambiguous, even rules much less complex than the Internal Revenue Code, make it hard for people—and enforcers—to tell if someone is complying. Drunk driving is against the law. But what does *drunk* mean? One way to decide is to measure alcohol in the blood. A person who is falling-down drunk should know he is drunk (if he is conscious). But a person who had a drink or two at a party might not know. Nobody carries around equipment to measure the level of alcohol in their blood.

Noncompliance (like compliance) can be, at times, simple and clear-cut. The burglar knows breaking and entering is against the law. But noncompliance is as complex as compliance; the rules may look black-and-white, but this can be an illusion. At times, they are shades of gray. A giant corporation pays for advice on tax shelters; it thinks it is complying; the Internal Revenue Service disagrees. Businesses are called on to react to regulations. Whole books are devoted to the problem of compliance: what it consists of, how we can measure it, how we can know it when we see it.[33] The same question can be asked about noncompliance.

An example or two might be helpful. Canada has a dense network of rules and regulations to regulate and control lobster fishing.[34] Lobster is delicious and in high demand. The problem is how to prevent overfishing. Poaching is common; enforcement difficult. Some fishermen catch more than the permitted number of lobsters, or catch lobsters out of season, or catch lobsters that, because of their size, are not supposed to be caught. Some catch lobsters without a license. Poachers come in three varieties. Communal poachers are small-scale poachers who use "techniques of stealth," make little money, and poach "for personal or family consumption." Outlaw poachers—illegal fishing companies—poach for profit. They are more organized than communal poachers, but their business is more precarious. They operate on a fairly big scale, which makes it hard to elude the authorities. A third type, business poachers, are regular, full-time, licensed commercial fishers who, in addition to their legal activities, also do some illegal fishing, violating quota rules, among other things.

All three types of poachers violate the rules, but the social organization is different for each type. Enforcement has to be adapted to the different types. Consider, for example, compliance with income tax laws. Here, too, there are small-scale, amateur violators. There are also businesses that cheat on an industrial scale and there are individuals and businesses who comply in general, but fudge a bit here and there—deducting a bit more than they should, for example. This is like catching an occasional lobster out of season, or wrong-size lobsters. Consider environmental laws. Think of the difference between, say, a hiker who plucks an endangered flower and the massive violators in the Amazon basin, destroying thousands of acres of jungle each year, or the poachers in Africa who kill elephants for their tusks and rhinos for their horns.

Noncompliance with regulatory regimes varies by agency and subject matter. The lobster-fishing industry has its amateurs and professionals, but the total numbers are relatively small. The tax laws apply to millions. The bite of the Food and Drug Administration is felt mostly by pharmaceutical companies (and makers of foods and cosmetics). There is a compliance and noncompliance schema, no doubt, for each industry and every law. The success of regulation depends on a whole cluster of factors. Cost of compliance, of course, is one factor. How much is demanded is another; whether we ask auto companies to make some minor change in design or ask them to do something difficult and expensive (like producing cars that are more fuel-efficient). But, surely, one factor is the style of regulation—tough, rule-bound, and harsh, or conciliatory and cooperative. We will return to this issue.

Measurement

Impact measurement has its own set of problems. On the whole, it is harder to measure indirect impact, compared to direct, and sometimes quite impossible. Impacts that consist of single, concrete bits of behavior are the easiest to demonstrate. Statistics can tell us exactly how many people filed income tax returns on time. All the techniques of social science can be deployed to ferret out impact: survey research, analysis of big data sets, close ethnographic observation, intensive interviews of key subjects, even lab experiments. Researchers have asked people their opinions on a bewildering array of questions, and have used vignettes and scenarios to try to tease out attitudes (from which presumably you can infer potential or actual behavior). The *Tarasoff* study asked a sample of mental health professionals whether they had changed their clinical behavior in the light of the case. Researchers can use random samples of some population, or captive populations (psychology students, notably) or, in some cases, snowball samples. Social scientists who conducted an "ethnographic analysis of burglary" did intensive interviews with thirty "active burglars" in an urban area in Texas, and asked them also to "reconstruct and simulate their past burglaries as nearly as possible."[35] There is obviously no way to get a random sample of burglars; hence, the study had to use the "snowball sampling procedure." The researchers started with three "informants" provided by "local criminal justice agencies." These, then, were asked to "recruit their co-offenders," and the co-offenders, if they cooperated, were asked to provide more names.[36]

A change occurs in behavior, and it seems, on the surface, to be connected in some way to a new law, rule, or doctrine. But how can we be sure about the connection? Correlation, as everyone knows, is not the same as cause. The Supreme Court, under Chief Justice Earl Warren, in the 1950s and 1960s, dramatically expanded the rights of men and women accused of crime: the right to free counsel in *Gideon v. Wainwright* and, in the Miranda case, rules about police interrogation.[37] The violent crime rate also rose dramatically during roughly the same period. William Stuntz argued that these two facts were connected.[38] Was he right? A connection would be extremely hard to prove. One would have to show how Supreme Court doctrines percolated down to the level of the station house and courtroom. Moreover, this was a period of rapid social change, turmoil in civil rights, a time when television became nearly universal. One could go on naming dozens of events and situations that were happening, some of which might or might not have had more to do with the crime rate than the decisions of the Warren Court— or not. The connection between a decrease in the crime rate and legalized abortion, which I mentioned earlier, is similarly intriguing—but it would be hasty to call the figures "proof."

If a legal intervention is simple, sharp, and time-limited, measurement can be easy, of course. We mentioned income-tax filings. In the United States, the date is April 15. It is easy to know how many people filed their tax returns by that date. This is a clear, transparent measure of direct impact. And if we know how many taxpayers could have filed returns, we have a good measure of noncompliance. The rule (about filing) is fairly clear, the meaning is obvious, and there is an easy way to measure whether it works. Moreover, we have a clean baseline for measuring impact. Before the tax law, filing behavior was zero. To take another example: in Taiwan, fathers were preferred over mothers in custody disputes in this traditionally patriarchal society. Then the highest court of Taiwan said no to this practice; the constitution prescribed equality between the genders. The legislature changed the law in response. Father preference was out; the new norm was best interests of the child (a common standard in legal systems). Did this new law have an impact? Yes in Taipei, the capital city; no in rural areas, according to a careful study of custody decisions before and after the new law. Why the difference between the two locations? No doubt because old norms of patriarchy were stronger and survived better in rural areas.[39] Because the change in the law was sharp and could be dated precisely, and because it had a direct bearing on custody cases, impact could be measured with some precision. Note that, here, *impact* refers to court decisions. Whether family situations changed, whether patterns of child rearing and caregiving changed, is another question entirely.

When a legal change is abrupt and takes place at some precise point in time, a before-and-after study can safely claim a causal connection. One classic study of this type, by Donald Campbell and H. Laurence Ross, looked at various jurisdictions that began to crack down on speeders.[40] In these studies, the "before" and "after" were quite clear. There was an abrupt and sudden starting point. Another study, by Julie Horney and Cassia Spohn, looked at reforms in the law of rape, as these played out in six different cities. Beginning in the 1970s, partly under the influence of the women's movement, state after state revised and modernized their laws against rape. The goal was to make these laws more realistic and less hostile to victims of rape. Horney and Spohn used time-series analysis. Under the new policies, would more women report rapes to the police? Would more rapists get convicted? Would rapists get more severe punishments? The results were disappointing. Except in one city (Detroit), the "reforms had little effect on reports of rape or the processing of rape cases."[41]

Why should this be the case? One reason was inherent in these so-called "reforms." They were weak; they placed, in fact, "few constraints on the tremendous discretion exercised by decision makers in the criminal justice system." This is the general problem of the leaky hose. Nobody is in charge. Legislatures can pass laws, but they do not carry out these laws. Police and prosecutors do, but they have their own set of values and priorities. The same for judges, juries, prison officials, and everybody else. There are veto powers, stalling powers, stalemate powers all up and down the line.

Horney and Spohn did think that rape reforms accomplished *something*. Officials in the six cities felt that victims were treated with more sensitivity. The reforms, in their view, sent an "important symbolic message." In the long run, this symbolic message was more important than the "instrumental change that was anticipated but generally not accomplished." The reformers wanted to "shift the focus in a rape case from the reputation and behavior of the victim to the unlawful acts of the offender." To the extent this occurred, what follows might be a "long-term attitude change."

I am generally skeptical about symbolic messages and impacts, as I have mentioned. And Horney and Spohn may have put the cart before the horse. Gender relations in the late twentieth century were already in flux. Males no longer dominated the criminal justice system as much as they had in the past. Women's voices were louder and were heard more often. If "reforms" were merely ratifying and formalizing changes that were taking place outside the law, their impact would be muted.

New laws and new decisions often merely seem to make a difference. Impact is always an empirical question. The change in custody laws in Taiwan made a difference—in court; but probably not much difference in the world of family relations. The *Tarasoff* decision did make a difference in mental health practice. The Washington State case about glaucoma (discussed earlier) had less of an impact. A young woman won her case against eye doctors who had failed to test for glaucoma.[42] Did eye doctors change their behavior? Somewhat, according to a study, but not a great deal.[43] It also turned out that many eye doctors did, in fact, test younger patients for glaucoma. The defense had argued that the decision would wreak havoc with the practice of eye doctors. Research showed this was not true. Courts have no way, ordinarily, of testing or measuring impact, and they resort, as a rule, to guesswork, intuition, and hunches.

Some before-and-after studies find that nothing much has changed. One reason might be a failure of communication. Or the law may fizzle out at the level of enforcement. There might be selective noncompliance; or, indeed, a heroic level of disobedience. Or, sometimes, there is nothing much to change: the change was already in progress. This was apparently what happened with regard to glaucoma treatment in Washington State.

Police sometimes mount a crackdown on drug markets. The idea is: flood the area with police and drive out the pushers. A city can get impressive results in this way. But there is always a risk of displacement; the pushers simply go somewhere else.[44] In 1994, after a terrorist attack on a Jewish community center in Buenos Aires, Argentina, the authorities jacked up police presence on blocks with Jewish institutions. Some evidence in a careful study showed that the "24-hour police protection policy displaced crime to other blocks" outside the protected zone.[45] The "red-light abatement movement" early in the twentieth century destroyed red-light districts in cities like New Orleans and San Francisco, and closed down the brothels. Sex for sale simply adjusted or went elsewhere.[46]

No principle of methodology is more important than the warning not to confuse correlation with cause. Places where people wear shoes are richer than barefoot communities. It would not be a good development strategy to buy shoes for barefoot people. Still, to confuse correlation and cause is as tempting as a rich dessert. A group of scholars tried to measure the impact of laws to prevent child marriages. After the laws were passed, fewer adolescent girls got pregnant.[47] The scholars concluded that laws setting eighteen as the minimum age of marriage were "associated with dramatic reductions in adolescent fertility." But the key word here is "associated." Their findings, they thought, undercut arguments that the law was basically "irrelevant."[48] Perhaps. Yet they also found evidence that "most countries experienced reductions in adolescent fertility in the recent period, even if they did not adopt any laws"; this, it seems to me, undercuts their conclusion. Many factors in the modern world depress the birthrate: women's rights, changes in family structure, better and cheaper contraception, urbanization, and so on. Laws against child marriage are probably not a major factor. And the causal chain might go the other way. Changes in gender relations, in social attitudes, might explain why the laws could be passed in the first place.

Time-series analysis is a powerful tool when we can use it, because it makes a plausible case for impact. Comparative analysis is another valuable tool. State X passes a law and we think we see a change in behavior. But suppose State Y has passed the same law and nothing happened. That tells us something. Suppose ten states pass this kind of law and another ten do not; we can look to see if there are systematic differences between the two groups. But life is complicated. X and Y can be different for all sorts of reasons, and state group A can be different from state group B for reasons that may or may not have anything to do with the law that was passed.

In the United States, rates of violent crime, which zoomed up after the Second World War, have been going down, somewhat mysteriously, in the twenty-first century. Why is this? New York City is, in Frank Zimring's phrase, the city "that became safe." In New York City, people point to the "broken windows" campaign. The theory was this: crack down hard on petty crime, and crime in general will decline. But crime declined in many other places, which tried other methods. Most explanations, alas, collapse like pricked balloons.[49] Impact is a slippery, wriggly beast.

Even rigorous before-and-after studies, though they can suggest causality, are not ironclad proof that some policy works. The timing of impact is relevant. A decision or law does not always "take" right away; it is not like a bullet through the heart. On the other hand, the longer impact takes (or seems to take), the more likely that other factors in society are mediating impact. What effect, for example, did the Brown case have on actual integration in southern public schools? Not much, according to Gerald Rosenberg, in *The Hollow Hope*. Rosenberg points out that southern states resisted integration, and with a great deal of success. For years, progress was dismal, minimal.[50] It was the Civil Rights Act of 1964 that actually made a difference. Rosenberg's case is strongest if you look at Supreme Court case law in isolation. The case had immediate impact in states outside the Deep South (like Kansas or Delaware), much less in the states of the old Confederacy. But it gave support to the civil rights movement; it gave leaders and members a powerful constitutional argument, as well as powerful moral claims. The court's role as a catalyst is hard to measure, but was almost certainly a reality.

Big, elaborate laws, which affect, or are supposed to affect, large numbers of people, usually have some impact, but the more complex the laws, the larger the number of people or institutions affected, and the more the laws ask people or institutions to do things that are hard, or expensive, or things they do not want to do, the more dubious the impact; and measuring impact precisely is likely to be more of a problem. The Americans with Disabilities Act (1990) was supposed to produce more jobs and opportunities for blind people, deaf people, people in wheelchairs, and so on. Did it work? A study published in 2014 reached some pessimistic conclusions. Workers with disabilities were employed at a rate 40 percent less than workers without disabilities. And they earned 33 percent less than the others.[51]

Does this mean the law was a failure? The researchers were cautious in their conclusions. Yes, people with disabilities did badly in the study, but maybe without the law they would have done even worse. To know that, we would need baseline information. Also, the study did not differentiate between different kinds of disability or face the issue of defining "disability." These factors might be relevant. Still, the real problem—and a persistent one—is (according to the authors) the attitudes of employers toward people with disabilities. Those who drafted the law hoped these attitudes would change, but attitudes can be stubborn and hard to move. Yet, if nothing else, the law made some people, and some employers, aware of the issue. It also handed a legal tool to people with disabilities. The Equal Employment Opportunity Commission got more than 25,000 ADA complaints in the 2014 fiscal year.[52] People in wheelchairs started cropping up as characters in television dramas. Businesses were asked to make accommodations. We began to see more ramps. Some buses can accommodate wheelchairs; some elevators have signs in braille. Some of these changes were mandated; others were not. Some were, in other words, indirect results of ADA. These changes remind people about Americans with disabilities, and perhaps awareness leads to attitude change. And attitude change, perhaps, in turn, leads to changes in behavior. Some of these changes are changes we would ordinarily (but perhaps mistakenly) classify as direct.

What about the effect on people with disabilities themselves? David Engel and Frank Munger conducted interviews and looked at the "life stories" of people who were "disabled" within the meaning of the law.[53] Not many of their subjects had actually filed claims under the law. But the law did have an impact on them; it altered their sense of identity—their self-definition. As Engel and Munger point out, throughout most of our history, "disabled" meant unable to work. No longer.[54] ADA is premised on the idea that most "disabled" people can work, should work; employers are supposed to accommodate them if it is at all reasonable. Whether they know it or not, the "disabled" came to have a new sense of themselves. ADA is not the sole source of this redefinition, but it has surely played a role. On the other hand, ADA itself flows out of a climate of redefinition. It flows out of the human rights culture, out of the culture that produced the civil rights movement, the women's movement, movements of aliens, indigenous people, gay people, and old people.

The educational function of laws, statutes, decisions—the effect on attitude change, knowledge change—is obviously hard to measure and easy to overlook. A law by itself—the words, the text—does nothing. That is, assuming people are even aware of these texts. But many laws do have an educative effect, at least on some people. This was probably true of ADA, and almost certainly true of *Brown v. Board of Education*. A recent study of hate speech laws in Australia claimed the laws made at least a bit of a difference; of course, hate speech was not stamped out, and not many people actually made use of the laws. Still, the researchers felt that the laws had an "educative effect"; and they reduced certain overt expressions of racial and religious hatred.[55]

Social movements are important vehicles of legal impact. Social movements are among the creators of law in the first place, and they stand ready to make use of these laws once they are on the books. The civil rights movement in the United States is a prime example. Civil rights laws—and other laws that are aimed at social change—put weapons in the hands of social movements. There was a civil rights movement before the Brown case, but the case gave the movement a powerful new channel for expressing its goals and taking action. The case also gave white America something to think about. The publicity mattered. In the background, massive cultural, economic, and political change was pulling the strings. Feminist movements and gay rights movements also profited from the ferment over race relations. But feminist movements and gay rights movements also flourished in developed countries without significant racial minorities. The human rights culture is global, and independent, to a large degree, from laws, treaties, and texts.

A recent study looked at the legal campaign in Senegal against female genital mutilation. Many African countries, including Senegal, have tried to outlaw this practice. The impact of the laws was much like the impact of *Brown*. The laws gave "added strength" to campaigns against genital mutilation. Some practitioners stopped cutting young women. The law was a weapon in the arsenal of the anti's.[56] Educational campaigns and public health crusades did their part. The battle, of course, is far from over. In Senegal, as in many less developed countries, Westernized, or at least educated, elites attack old customary ways that offend their sense of modernity and their sense of human rights: child marriages, segregation of women, honor killings, polygamy, witchcraft. But there are powerful forces on the other side: the deep but silent power of age-old practice, religious beliefs, firmly embedded customs. Each society, and each situation, has its own story to tell, its own trajectory of change.

In 1950, a survey asked people in West Germany whether they were for or against the death penalty. Fifty-five percent were for it, 30 percent against it (15 percent were undecided). By 1995, the numbers were reversed: 53 percent against, only 30 percent in favor. Between these two dates, Germany had eliminated the death penalty. Of course, the survey cannot tell us why public opinion changed. Change in the law itself may have played no role at all in this.[57] Another survey question pointed out that divorce was now a no-fault system and asked people if they approved. In 1977, only 35 percent approved; in 1995, even fewer (32 percent) approved. Divorce law was reformed in 1976; the fault principle was eliminated. Yet people did not seem to change their minds.[58] Why the difference between divorce law and the death penalty? There was no way to predict in advance which opinion was more strongly held, or more deeply rooted in the culture. In the United States, the desegregation case was decided in 1954; *Roe v. Wade*, the famous abortion case, in 1973. Nobody dares criticize the segregation cases now, but the opposition to the abortion case seems as virulent as ever.

It would be hard to argue that racism was less deeply rooted in (white) culture than opposition to abortion. Still, today, nobody openly defends segregation, not even right-wing political figures in Southern states. These same figures proudly proclaim opposition to *Roe v. Wade*. Desegregation ultimately affected a whole range of institutions, from baseball to the Army to the Metropolitan Opera. The role of African Americans in society, in universities, in government, changed radically after the 1950s. African Americans are on TV in dramas and commercials; there are black anchors, blacks announcing the weather, and, of course, a black president was elected in 2008. White college kids see members of racial minorities in dorms and classrooms. But abortion remains in the shadows. It affects the lives of a huge number of women (and their families); nobody, however, brags about it. Unlike skin color, it remains invisible. The women who take advantage of *Roe v. Wade* pass us by every day in the streets, but unlike racial minorities, they have no outer marks or signs to tell us who they are and what they did.

What does seem clear, in many instances, is that impact is mediated and influenced by some sort of learning process—a complicated process—that takes place within society. Americans learned to disapprove of segregation. They learned to expect ramps for people in wheelchairs. Attitudes do change over time. The income tax law in the United States dates from the early twentieth century. Wealthy people bitterly opposed it. Today, people may not like it but almost everybody accepts it as a fact of life—as a political and fiscal necessity. Only a few cranks and extremists still hold out. There is, of course, grumbling about rates, and everybody wants "reform," but repeal is basically unthinkable. Americans reject the idea of a national identity card (standard in many countries). But if we had one, it would become normal, a habit, in a generation or so, like drivers' licenses and social security numbers, which act more or less like identity cards and which people accept without question. At one time, people would have been outraged by security searches at airports. No longer. Young people cannot remember the prehistoric days when there was no such thing. The census has been a big issue in Germany, politically quite controversial. In the United States, the census dates to 1790, and is a recognized fact of national life. Habit is a powerful influence on behavior.

Here we will mention what we might call the law of small numbers. Trying to get a few manufacturers to put air bags in cars would be easier and more effective than convincing or forcing millions of people to buckle up with seat belts. True. And many people simply refused or were too lazy to comply with the rules, or thought that real men don't wear seat belts, or that good drivers didn't need them. And yet, after many years of coaxing and cajoling and propagandizing (along with a certain amount of enforcement), seat belts have become standard practice for most people in many countries. It has become a habit, an almost unconscious move. Campaigns against drunk driving or against cigarette smoking have also slowly made headway. Some laws, like good wine and good cheese, take time to mature.

4

A TYPOLOGY OF RESPONSES

THE SUBJECT OF THIS BOOK is impact, the responses that follow
some sort of legal act: a statute, a decision, a ruling, a regulation, a new
doctrine. The responses come in all shapes and sizes and forms. Sometimes we can talk confidently about compliance and noncompliance (or,
if you will, obeying and disobeying). But very often what follows the
legal act cannot be put into these pigeonholes so easily. A police officer
stops a driver and proposes giving her a ticket. Maybe she made an illegal U-turn. The driver can sigh and accept the ticket or she could make
excuses; she could try to persuade the officer not to give her a ticket ("I
was rushing to the hospital"). In some cities, at some points in time, she
might offer a modest bribe. She will either get the ticket or not get it,
but in this, as in many other situations, a person subject to the law can
try to wriggle out of the consequences. There is no such thing as half a
ticket, but sometimes a person or business can bargain; that is, try to
mitigate or compromise. This is common, even normal, when businesses deal with regulators. Or, a business may accept its medicine but
also complain, lobby, write to a member of Congress, or contribute to an
NGO that is working on matters relevant to the industry—the business,
in other words, can make efforts to change the rule, even as it complies.
This, as I mentioned, is part of the impact complex, a form of feedback.

Another kind of response is one we might call adjustment. A subject changes behavior because of a legal act but "compliance" or "noncompliance" are not terms that fit the behavior very well. Sometimes we can call the behavior evasion, but this, too, is a term that does not always fit.

Take, for example, American income tax law. Most people file their tax returns as they should, but they also try to take advantage of loopholes. Taxpayers adjust their behavior to pay as little tax as legally possible. Billions of dollars are spent on lawyers, accountants, and other experts who give advice on how to reach the nirvana of low taxes. So long as taxpayers do not cross the red line into illegality (a line that is often hard to see), they are fairly safe. What these crafty taxpayers have done is not full compliance; they haven't broken the law, but the whole point of their efforts has been to comply as little as possible. The behavior, of course, has consequences. For tax reasons, a person might shift, say, from stocks to bonds, or ship money to the Cayman Islands, or sculpt some sort of tax shelter; or, perhaps, give more money than planned to charity to get a bigger charitable deduction. She has, in short, adjusted her behavior in reaction to law. Adjustment, of course, is a ubiquitous feature of legal behavior; adjustment is a vital part of impact.

People who knowingly break the law also adjust their behavior to minimize getting caught. This is why a holdup man might wear a ski mask. This is why burglars stay away from houses if they feel people are at home, or pass by a tempting house when they see a neighbor staring at them, or avoid houses with big, shaggy dogs. This is why bank robbers like to have a getaway car nearby. Men who steal cars adjust their behavior to avoid the police. They try to create an illusion of normalcy. They drive as if they owned the car. They dress the part (if you steal a Mercedes, you had better not look like a thug), and, above all, they drive carefully and strictly obey all traffic rules—anything to avoid catching the eye of a police officer.[1] Hence, ironically, the most careful drivers on the road might be drivers who are driving stolen cars. Another group of careful drivers are "johns" who are cruising around looking for streetwalkers; they advise each other (online!) to "look like an ordinary guy driving around, not a horny dude. . . . Be sure to wear your seat belt." Also, if there is "anything about your car that might justify them pulling you over, avoid mongering [looking for sex] until you get it fixed."[2]

Probably any criminal, any gang, any criminal community, will develop defenses, tricks to fool the enforcers; otherwise, they could hardly survive. (As it is, most burglars, shoplifters, auto thieves, and other members of the larcenous tribe will be caught at some point in their criminal careers.) Each common crime constitutes a system, and to understand the system, you have to understand not only what law the criminals are breaking and why they are breaking it, but also how they manage the whole process of law-breaking, including forms of evasion and strategies to avoid getting caught. The strategies can be as simple as wearing a ski mask. Some streetwalkers and johns use Craig's List and similar sites to get together; this is safer than going on the street where the police are patrolling (and sometimes using "stings"), but it might raise the price of sex.[3] People who sell drugs might decide only to deal with people they are sure of—middle-class customers, for example, who have more to lose from exposure than the dealer does. These customers are unlikely to be "narcs" or informers.[4] One study of crack dealers, based on interviews, lists techniques for sniffing out narcs. True crackheads, for example, are dirty, sickly, and desperate, with runny noses and, at times, "blisters and black, soot-like stains and crud on hands and fingers" as well as "burns, blisters, and sores on lips." The police can hardly imitate these physical signs. Some dealers, unlike the ones who only sell to middle-class people, will not sell to anybody clean and well dressed.[5]

Compliance and noncompliance are terms that, on the whole, fit criminal law the best; they also fit regulatory laws fairly well. A company can comply with safety regulations, it can violate them, or it can adjust to them in one way or another. With regard to other parts of the law, it makes sense to talk instead about use and nonuse. The law of torts is a good example. If you are in a motorcycle accident and you think the other driver was at fault, you can sue for damages. The law of torts gives you the (doctrinal) tools to do so. You can sue or not sue, as you please. Similarly, you can use or not use (or misuse) the laws of contracts, property, wills, and trusts. Couples that do not get along can get a divorce. Or not, as they see fit. They can make these decisions for all sorts of reasons. Claims are a bother. Litigation even more so. Cost and time barriers are pervasive problems for the legal system. They help explain the so-called claims pyramid, which we will shortly discuss.

Adjustment is everywhere in the law of torts as well as in criminal law. Doctors hate malpractice suits. Some of them, supposedly, shift to what has been called defensive medicine. There is some evidence that they order more tests than they otherwise would.[6] They are careful to spell out side effects and post-surgery problems to patients. Patients also adjust. News about risks and side effects influences their decision to have or not have an operation, or to choose one kind over another. A high tax on estates leads an English movie star to move to another country; an American billionaire sets up a charitable foundation. An unhappy couple can decide to divorce or (in some places) try to get an annulment; or decide to live apart and ignore the law of divorce. Similarly, young couples can skip marriage laws and simply live together, a more and more popular alternative. You can make out a will or not; you can complain about a broken contract or put up with it; you can complain about your landlord or move out or shrug your shoulders and put up with cockroaches and a defective heating system.

Action or inaction might depend on what people know, what messages they get from the legal system (and from society), and, of course, on barriers of cost. Everybody knows there is such a thing as divorce but most do not know how custody issues will be handled or the rules for dividing up property. Most people know what a will is. They probably know it might be useful. Yet many people who should have a will simply don't bother. And, of course, adjustment is everywhere in civil law. A whole industry of estate planning is based on the needs and desires of people with money. Estate planners help these people minimize legal burdens, avoid bothersome procedures in probate court, and, incidentally, make sure their wishes are carried out after they die. Relations between businesspeople, or between businesspeople and regulators, or between businesspeople and customers, are best explained not in terms of formal law or even in terms of use and nonuse, but in terms of adjustments, compromises, and standard or customary ways of acting.

No legal intervention takes place in a vacuum. It lands in a crowded, preexisting social space, and what that space is like tempers and determines the reaction. In the next chapters, we will explore the motives for compliance, noncompliance, use and nonuse, evasion, and other responses to legal acts. Norms, culture, and the state of society are always determinative, always the background against which impact plays out. And the response is sensitive to time and place. The law in Taiwan about child custody generated one reaction in Taipei, quite another in rural areas. The U.S. Supreme Court, during the days when Earl Warren was Chief Justice, held that prayers and Bible-reading had no place in public schools; the court upheld a strict view of separation of church and state.[7] The decision, not surprisingly, were wildly unpopular, especially in the South (the Bible belt). Kenneth M. Dolbeare and Phillip E. Hammond looked to see how schools were reacting to the Supreme Court decision. The results were mixed. Before the decision, morning prayers were recited in 14 percent of elementary schools in the West; in the South, in 87 percent of the schools. The decision made a difference: the percentage of schools with prayers fell to 5 percent in the West and to 64 percent in the South.[8] The decision, in short, had an impact. Nonetheless, almost two out of three schools in the South stuck to their practice despite what the Supreme Court told them not to do.

In the South, the decision went against strong and deep religious traditions. Schools, people felt, should teach moral values, and that included religious values. Perhaps some districts never got the message, or never understood it. Besides, there was no enforcement mechanism. The decision called for fundamental change, but it was "cast adrift with very little institutional support available to induce compliance."[9] Unless somebody complained (an unpopular act) or brought a lawsuit (even worse), there was nothing to force a school district to change. Indeed, the real question might be: Why did any southern school district change?

A similar dynamic occurred after Supreme Court decisions on "hate speech" codes in colleges and universities, which presumably violated free speech rights. Some schools ignored these decisions; some schools complied. Close study and analysis of individual colleges exposed all sorts of local reasons and considerations that explained the reaction of particular institutions.[10] These reactions ranged from compliance, through "passive noncompliance, through evasion, up to outright confrontation."[11] But perhaps the word *confrontation* is a bit stronger than it should be. Since there was no obvious mechanism for enforcing the decisions, there was, in a way, nobody to confront. Here, too, unless somebody complained or brought a lawsuit, the schools were, practically speaking, free to act on their own. Free, that is, as far as outside pressure was concerned; not at all free from internal dynamics, student protests on this side or the other side, administrative issues, and faculty politics.

Many studies have examined the impact of Prohibition—the so-called "noble experiment."[12] Temperance campaigns had bubbled up to the surface from time to time in the United States; after a century of agitation, the "dry" movement had become enormously powerful, politically speaking. "Drys" actually succeeded in amending the U.S. Constitution: the Prohibition Amendment (number eighteen) prohibited the "manufacture, sale, or transportation of intoxicating liquors" in the United States. Prohibition went into effect in January 1920. But this "noble experiment" was gone by the early 1930s. It was, in many ways, a failure. It certainly did not stamp out drinking. For many Americans, wine, beer, and even whiskey were part of their culture. Enforcement would have been a massive undertaking; it was probably always impossible. A vast apparatus of evasion and disobedience grew up in the cities.

Probably there was, in fact, less drinking after Prohibition became law, compared to before, especially in rural areas. But millions of people found ways to keep on drinking. Some made their own liquor; most of them bought it illegally. Tons of liquor poured in from Canada and from overseas. Thousands of speakeasies sprang up in the cities, places where people could get their fix of alcohol. The drys had miscalculated. There were, to be sure, attempts to enforce the law. Thousands of people were, in fact, arrested and tried. Some paid fines; some went to jail. There were periodic crackdowns, periodic spasms of enforcement. Prohibition cases clogged the courts and filled the jails. But these defendants were simply unlucky members of a vast army of violators. The sheer illegality—the speakeasies, the culture of disobedience—might have made drinking the kind of forbidden fruit that has tempted people since Adam and Eve.

If this is true, then the attempt to enforce Prohibition rigorously was doomed to backfire. When demand for a behavior or a commodity is strong and inelastic, it is hard (and expensive) to jack up enforcement enough to make a difference. The metaphor of the old garden hose seems appropriate. Prohibition was a very leaky hose, badly rotted, and full of holes.

And certainly not the only example of this phenomenon. Prudish censors in Boston cracked down on books they considered "obscene" (including some venerable classics). Naturally enough, sales skyrocketed in other parts of the country. The censors were dealing with a very leaky hose. Perhaps they plugged a hole in Boston, but the water squirted out everywhere else.[13] In 1970, John Kaplan published a book with the intriguing title *Marijuana: The New Prohibition*. The National Organization for the Reform of Marijuana Laws (NORML) issued a report in 1997 with the title "Still Crazy after All These Years: Marijuana Prohibition 1937–1997." According to the report, more than seventy million Americans had smoked marijuana at some point, and some ten million were "regular" smokers. It was the "recreational drug of choice for millions of mainstream, middle class Americans."[14] The laws against marijuana are hardly dead letters; thousands of people are arrested and put in jail—many of them members of racial minorities. But the basic comparison holds: millions disobey the laws. At this date (2016), harsh federal laws remain in effect, but medical use of marijuana is legal in many states, and Colorado, Washington, Oregon, and Alaska have essentially decriminalized use of the drug.

I could mention many other leaky hoses. During the Vietnam War, thousands of young men tried to avoid military service through one means or another. The war itself had become extremely unpopular; draft evasion, thus, lost much of its stigma. Arrests were made and trials were held, but as the war wore on, even when defendants were convicted, they received shorter and shorter sentences.[15] In the face of public disapproval, attempts to crack down were almost bound to fail.

Dual Systems

The law on the books and the law in action are never identical. But sometimes the two differ so radically that we could almost describe them as two distinct systems. Laws are passed by legislatures; rules and regulations are promulgated by bureaucrats; high court judges create doctrines. What all of these have in common is that law is made by people who are, more or less, elite. Law, in other words, comes essentially from the top strata of society. The more stratified the society, the more this is the case. Ideology in democratic states has an egalitarian ring to it. But a certain elite bias is, inevitably, present, and in some societies, the bias is extreme.

This means that, as far as at least some people are concerned, in any society, a lot of the law goes against the grain. Of course, this is true for all laws, no matter how popular, although even burglars might want to keep the general law against burglars. But at times, elite law flies in the face of strong, entrenched customs and values. The campaign to end female genital mutilation in Africa; the campaign to end honor killings in Arab countries (and Brazil); national Prohibition in the United States in the 1920s . . . these are egregious examples. There are innumerable others, from many periods and societies, and to a lesser or greater degree. We can ask of any legal act: In whose interest is it? This question goes far beyond the scope of this book. But a study of impact has to recognize the unavoidable gap between what some, or most, people want and what they get from the law. This gap makes legitimacy and trust, which we discuss later, extremely important to any legal system.

In 1996, Thailand enacted a law to abolish or at least control prostitution.[16] The law, which replaced an older law (1960), outlawed child prostitution and reduced the penalty for (adult) prostitution. It also imposed sanctions on both prostitutes and customers, and it included a plan to give prostitutes vocational training, to wean them from the sex trade. Did the law have an impact? Not much, apparently, at least as measured by the number of arrests before and after. The prostitution law was a very leaky hose.

Thailand's experience is not unusual. Attempts to stamp out prostitution are usually failures. In Thailand, there was also a failure of communication: most people knew nothing about the law. Moreover, prostitution is big business in Thailand, and money can corrupt. Enforcement was spotty. But the main problem might have been the disconnect between the legislators and a large part of the public. The campaign against prostitution was led by elites and religious leaders. The customers had their own views. Drug addicts, drinkers during Prohibition, the consumers of products made from rhinoceros horns or ivory . . . these are other examples where a strong demand for illegal commodities makes enforcement difficult if not problematic. An elite moral code imposed on a recalcitrant public might, in some cases, result in widespread violation; in other cases, a chasm between official and living law. The formal law is displaced, or radically subverted. The result is what we might call a dual system.

The history of divorce law in the United States provides a classic example.[17] Before the 1970s, divorce required a court proceeding. The parties had to conform to certain legal rules. An innocent spouse had to act as plaintiff, claiming that the defendant, the other spouse, had committed an offense against the marriage. The local statute would list the offenses that opened the door to divorce. Adultery, desertion, and cruelty were the most common grounds for divorce. The formal law absolutely refused to allow divorce by mutual agreement. That both parties wanted out of the marriage was legally irrelevant. And collusive divorce was illegal: that is, telling lies in court to try to satisfy the formal requirements.

But for about a century (roughly the 1870s to the 1970s), consensual and collusive divorce was the rule, not the exception. The plaintiff (usually the wife) filed for divorce, alleging, say, cruelty, and the husband simply failed to defend himself. The demand for divorce, for complex reasons, was rising steadily, but the law was frozen in place. Religious leaders, in particular, considered divorce a social evil. Moral elites were strong enough to thwart any attempts at reform. The aim was to keep divorce rare and hard to get, except in egregious cases.

New York was an extreme and interesting case. In New York, basically, divorce was available only on the grounds of adultery. A practice developed that I have called "soft-core adultery." The husband would check into a hotel room and get mostly undressed. A woman would come in, and she, too, would take off most of her clothes. A photographer would mysteriously appear and take pictures of the couple. Then the woman would be paid, get dressed, and go. The photos would show up in court as "evidence" of adultery. Everybody, including the judges, knew what was going on. But the system persisted for decades.[18] England's laws, which also restricted the grounds for divorce, spawned a very similar racket.[19] In New York, too, actions to annul a marriage—rare in most states—were as common as dirt. This was also the case in Chile; until quite recently, divorce was simply not allowed in Chile; but there was an incredible outburst of annulments based on extremely dubious grounds.[20]

The "dual system" in divorce is now history, but dual systems thrive in other areas—for example, prostitution in Thailand and in many countries, immigration law, and the law relating to asylum. During the Soviet era, dual systems flourished in socialist countries, where the gap in, say, Poland or East Germany between official law and what the public wanted and did was particularly egregious. A moral or ideological or political elite makes the law. It ignores a high public demand: for divorce in the nineteenth century; for sexual services in Thailand and other countries; for cheap immigrant labor; or for "free market" sales under socialism. Loopholes and detours, modes of evasion and avoidance, spring up; the legal borderland, so to speak, is so porous that prohibited behavior slips easily through. The conflict between high law and low law blunts, distorts, or nullifies the impact of the formal law.

The leaky hose situation, like dual systems, represents a kind of equilibrium. Prohibition was a failure, but it was enacted; powerful forces pushed it to the top of the agenda. It takes enormous political muscle to force through an amendment to the American constitution. The drys had enough for that half of the equation, but not for the other half, the enforcement half. In other cases—divorce law, the Vietnam draft, marijuana—cases of dual systems and leaky hoses, we have a kind of stalemate. Two mighty social forces lock horns. Neither is strong enough to completely defeat the other. One force may control the formal law— this was true of divorce (before no-fault), or prostitution, or the use of marijuana. The formal law also represents what is, or seems to be, the moral high ground. The other side wins at the level of actual practice. Church leaders and other moral elites, for decades, blocked moves to loosen divorce law. Meanwhile, the divorce rate kept rising. The elites got their laws. The public got its divorces. In the case of Prohibition, the drys got their laws and the wets got their speakeasies. Such arrangements, of course, do not last forever. Prohibition died a painful death. No-fault divorce killed the old system of divorce. Sooner or later, the balance of power is likely to shift, and one side or the other, perhaps, will come out on top.

The old divorce law was a dual system, a stalemate between two strong forces. The moralists, who hated divorce, held the high ground. They wanted to make divorce rare and difficult. The consumers— unhappy married people—wanted a cheap and easy out and a chance to start over. Under modern no-fault statutes, from the 1970s on, the consumers win. Divorce as such is both easy and cheap. Traditionalists are still unhappy; they feel that easy divorce is a curse. This rests, per- haps, on an assumption about the impact of divorce law. Tough divorce laws, they think, will save marriages, will force people to work things out. But this is empirically dubious. Divorce laws do not disintegrate families. Happy couples do not care whether divorce is cheap or expen- sive, easy or hard. In a society without divorce, there will still be miser- able and dysfunctional marriages, and marriages will break up, but in informal ways. Changes in family structure, in gender relations, in the culture, have impacted marriage and divorce far more than the formal laws.[21]

The Claims Pyramid

Modern life is a buzzing whirlwind of activity, and every day, no doubt, things happen to people that, in theory at least, might give them the right to complain, express a grievance, or even file a lawsuit. A woman buys an appliance and it doesn't work. A man is fired from his job for no particular reason. A landlord is slow to fix a leak in the roof. A person slips on an icy street and gets hurt. In all these cases, we can ask, is somebody to blame? Take the icy sidewalk. Is the city responsible? Should they have done something? Much of the time, in the situations mentioned, nothing much happens. The woman returns the appliance (or doesn't). The man who was fired files for unemployment. The tenant moves out and finds a better place to live. The person who slipped on the sidewalk stays home for a day and takes aspirin.

How often do people have an experience that might at least in theory give them a legal claim? How often do they take some action? A few scholars have tried to find out. Hazel Genn, in England, in the 1990s, surveyed a sample of the population. She found that about 40 percent of the population had "experienced one or more justiciable problems during the previous five years." She also studied what they did about it. Some did nothing, some asked for advice, some even went to court.[22] Much depended, of course, on the situation. Take our pedestrian who slips on the ice and is injured. Out of, say, a hundred people in this situation, how many will follow up and make some sort of claim?

A well-known Wisconsin study examined the "emergence and transformation of disputes." The first step in the process is perceptual: Does the person think in legal terms at all? Some do. The Wisconsin team called this step "naming." The next step is to transform this notion into an actual sense of grievance—this they call "blaming," that is, the feeling that somebody or some institution might be responsible, that it is somebody's fault. "Transformation" occurs when a person with a grievance "voices it to the person or entity believed to be responsible and asks for some remedy." This they call "claiming." Even after naming, blaming, and claiming, only a few claims turn into an actual dispute or go to law.

The Wisconsin study drew a figure in the shape of a pyramid to show what happens when people encounter what is potentially a legal experience. The base of the pyramid is, of course, the broadest. As we move up the pyramid, from naming to blaming to claiming, more and more subjects drop out; out of a large crowd of potential litigants, only a small number will actually go to a lawyer or some other agency and file a claim. Even fewer will end up in a court of law. Every sort of legal incident produces a claims pyramid, though the exact shape will be slightly different.[23] Hazel Genn's survey shows the same kind of pyramid. For example, 76 percent of the people who had a problem with faulty goods and services talked or wrote to the "other side" about the problem; 30 percent looked for advice on the issue; 18 percent threatened the other side with action; 3 percent actually went to court.[24]

Similarly for medical malpractice. Every day millions of people go to doctors for advice and millions undergo procedures, ranging from a simple tap on the knee to major surgery. Naturally, things can go wrong, and if they go wrong enough, a patient can make a complaint or, ultimately, bring a lawsuit for medical malpractice. Most patients, in fact, never name, blame, or claim; they decide to do nothing (they "lump it"). Some will do something, but nothing that looks like a claim. They may, for example, change doctors. The malpractice pyramid has a broad base; but it rises to a quite sharp and narrow point.[25] Very few will go so far as to file a lawsuit.[26] Of course, the more serious the injury, the more likely that a lawsuit will result. Nobody will go to court, or even consult a lawyer, over a hangnail. A botched operation ending up in paralysis or death is far more likely to spawn a claim.

The enforcement side can also be analyzed in terms of an enforcement pyramid. Robyn Fairman and Charlotte Yapp, studying food safety regulation in the United Kingdom, describe such a pyramid. At the base are 544,840 inspections carried out by the authorities. These lead to a much smaller number of "written warnings" (165,696). At the very top of the pyramid are "692 prosecutions" and "491 convictions" for violation.[27]

Bringing a lawsuit is expensive, in time and in money. In the United States, the contingent fee mitigates this factor somewhat, at least in tort cases (and a few other types of case). The lawyer gets paid only if the client wins the case. A person with a strong claim but without much money is not shut out of the system. The lawyer, of course, will take a healthy chunk of whatever money is recovered, a third or more. But two-thirds is a lot more than nothing. The contingent fee system also gives the lawyer an incentive to filter out dubious or flimsy claims. If she takes on a claim that is hopeless, she will waste time and effort, and get nothing in return. She will only take on cases she thinks she can win, or where she can get a good settlement.

Lawyers, in other words, have an important role near the top of the claims pyramid and, in general, in the life cycle of disputes. They transform the raw stories that clients tell into legal claims—or, contrariwise, talk the clients out of going any further. Stewart Macaulay found that lawyers often "cool out" clients who come to the lawyers with certain kinds of dubious complaints.[28] On the other hand, lawyers can act as litigation brokers; they can stitch together dozens of small claims into a single class action. If individual claims are below a certain threshold, nobody will take them to court or even make any sort of claim for compensation. Lawyers who patiently knit together class action suits are doing a job that might be valuable, not only for the clients, but also for society. In the process, of course, they can make a lot of money. And stir up trouble. The class action suit is, therefore, rather controversial.[29]

Lawyers are not the only agents who influence the shape of the pyramid. The police also play a role. Suppose a woman calls the police; her drunken husband or lover is acting violently. When the police arrive, they might arrest the husband or, instead, try to "cool out" the couple, or adopt some other tactic. Potential claimants, in other words, are not the only actors who determine how the pyramid gets climbed; intermediaries and enforcers play a role as well: civil servants who work for the Food and Drug Administration, or the Equal Employment Opportunity Commission, or the Securities and Exchange Commission, and all the other federal, state, and local agencies, and, of course, the corresponding officials and enforcers in other countries. These middle people strongly influence impact; like a prism, they bend impact in significant ways. The law of domestic violence is not just the statutes on the books, nor is it only the reaction of victims. The living law is also the response of police, friends and relatives, advocates for women's rights, and so on. And every other branch of law—torts, securities regulation, food safety—has its own cast of characters, its own cluster of factors that bend and mold impact, and in every jurisdiction and society.

Cost, of course, is a tremendous barrier to claims. Cost in money, cost in time, cost in aggravation. Culture and tradition are also significant as barriers or influential in the opposite direction. There have been studies across cultures trying to show similarities and differences in legal behavior, including propensity to bring claims: for example, England or Australia, as opposed to the United States.[30] Morality and religion powerfully influence claims and uses of law. Devout Catholics shun the divorce courts, no matter how miserable the marriage. Victims of accidents in Chiang Mai, a large city in Thailand, studied by David and Jaruwan Engel, tended not to pursue their rights, not to make claims, not to seek compensation—for reasons of religion and culture. Prayat, an "agricultural extension worker," was riding his motorcycle when a car struck him. The other driver "visited Prayat in the hospital and accepted total responsibility," but Prayat "refused to accept any payment from him or even file the papers that would provide payment by the other driver's insurance company." This is because Prayat "attributed his serious injuries to his own karma."[31] The Engels found other examples of this attitude among accident victims. Buddhism was one factor; another was a strong belief in ghosts, in haunted trees and other locations. Some people blamed ghosts for their troubles rather than the immediate (human) cause. Mark Massoud, writing about the Sudan, reports that people in the Sudan tend to accept their fate stoically and passively; what happens is "part of God's plan." They do not "mobilize" against actions of government; government is "not seen as ultimately responsible." What happens, simply happens; it is all basically the will of God.[32]

People in the United States, or Finland, are unlikely to invoke karma, or ghosts, or even the will of God as reasons not to assert their rights. But the underlying process—"attribution"—is significant everywhere. People who "blame themselves for an experience" are unlikely to sue somebody else.[33] One man who slips on the ice will feel the city should have rectified the problem; another will consider himself a clumsy fool who brought it on himself. Women who are victims of domestic violence may blame themselves for their predicament or feel too helpless and fearful to call the police. Or they may be fatalistic. Or they may believe that a husband has a right to discipline his wife.

The pyramid concept has been important in organizing research and in guiding research. By comparing pyramids and their shapes, there is some basis for comparing different areas of law and different societies. Catherine Albiston, Lauren Edelman, and Joy Milligan, however, have recently criticized the pyramid idea as somewhat too narrow. It puts "adjudication" at the top of the pyramid and emphasizes legal remedies; it "suggests a single linear path through which disputes progress (or not)." In fact, there are many ways to handle or deal with disputes, "multiple normative systems for resolving conflict." Their metaphor is not a pyramid, but a tree with many branches; besides the legal branch, there are also other paths, like ADR (alternative dispute resolution). The tree also produces "flowers" and "fruit." Flowers are "symbolic indicia of justice, such as the public opportunity to be heard" and fruit represents "material remedies such as reinstatement at work or financial compensation for injury."[34] The tree metaphor complicates what is already a complex subject; but it does open the door to a wider study of legal impact than the pyramid metaphor suggests.

Adjustment

Both on the criminal side and on the civil side, what we have called adjustment is an important concept; important, that is, for understanding impact. As mentioned, in tax law, there is a distinction between evasion (a crime) and avoidance (quite legal). *Evasion*, though, is a rather slippery term. The line between evasion and avoidance is blurry and complicated. A whole industry is devoted to tax avoidance. The methods are all forms of adjustment, modifications of behavior designed to minimize taxes. They can be elaborate: parking money in the Cayman Islands or buying a complex "shelter" scheme from an accounting firm. Other adjustments are simple and benign. Indeed, the law encourages them: giving more money to charity, for example, or buying tax-free municipal bonds. Some are responses to (possible) punishments, others to (possible) incentives. Tax advisers and the Internal Revenue Service are engaged in a kind of arms race. The advisers look for "loopholes" or find small ones and try to enlarge them. The IRS fights back with rulings and regulations. Congress, too, may respond by amending the Code, making it tighter or looser.

In the legal system, evasion, avoidance, and adjustment are ubiquitous. The legal history of any society, and any field of law, can be mined for examples. Starting in the late nineteenth century, American law barred the Chinese from immigrating. Also, no Chinese person, even one living legally in the United States, could become a naturalized citizen. Anybody born in the United States, on the other hand, was automatically a citizen, no matter who their parents were, or why they were in the United States at all.[35] (In 2015, federal officials conducted raids, for example, in southern California, and broke up "birth tourism" rings, companies that "arranged for pregnant women to come to the United States on tourist visas to give birth to babies."[36]) A Chinese person arriving by ship in San Francisco would have the right to land if he was a citizen by birth. Consular officials, however, regularly assumed that any Chinese person who made such a claim was lying. In fact, most of them were. Immigrants used various tricks to get around the law. The San Francisco earthquake and fire in 1906 had destroyed local birth records; this was a help. Or a Chinese person who was a citizen by birth could claim a child was born (on a trip to China, for example); this "created a 'slot' that could be sold to someone" who would then enter the United States (apparently) legally.[37] Many Chinese used these "paper families" to frustrate and evade the immigration laws, which were, in any event, racist and unfair. Members of the "paper families" were living a lie; they made stories about themselves, their parents, and adjusted their behavior to conform to these stories. Illegal immigrants—there are millions in the United States—are breaking the law by their very presence, and they adjust their lives in countless ways to avoid getting caught and deported.

The United States is a federal union; each state has its own legal system. This creates rich possibilities for evasion. During the era of strict divorce laws, well-off New Yorkers who wanted a divorce took the train to Nevada, where divorce laws were loose; Nevada made it easy to become a "resident." People also flocked to Nevada to gamble at a time when casinos were illegal at home. Quick and easy marriage was also a Nevada specialty. In Massachusetts at one time, teenage girls needed consent from a parent or the court for an abortion. Massachusetts is a small state; New Hampshire and Connecticut, close by, could oblige them. One New Hampshire facility, in 1982, advertised in the *Yellow Pages* in areas near the border, reminding potential customers that parental consent was not required. They got a good deal of new business.[38] Delaware, a tiny state hanging off the side of Pennsylvania, enacted laws around 1900 that induced corporations to base themselves at least nominally in Delaware. Thousands of companies fly these flags of convenience; they can and do conduct business wherever they please, but they remain "Delaware corporations." And the corporation law of Delaware, including court decisions, has an influence and an impact far beyond what one might expect from this minuscule eastern state.

In a recent study, Sarah Morando Lakhani interviewed immigrants applying for a so-called "U Visa." This United States visa was designed for victims of violent crime who had helped out law enforcement. They were required to be people of good moral character. Lawyers for an organization called Equal Justice of Los Angeles worked with clients who wanted these visas. They "edited clients' accounts," leaving out anything damaging, rephrasing what the clients said, and, in general, shaped the story and the image of their clients to conform to the legal require-ments.[39] Was this evasion? That depended on the particular case, the particular client, and how far the attorney stretched the facts. But this is what lawyers often do. They have a duty to present clients in the best possible light—to adjust their case and, sometimes, their behavior, as well. In this regard, too, lawyers act as intermediaries between govern-ment and citizens. Insurance companies hire claims adjusters; lawyers are claims adjusters for society.

Individuals and businesses today have to cope with the tangle of laws and doctrines and practices that make up the legal environment. *Coping* might be a better word than adjusting. Coping mechanisms make laws work, or not. Coping can make a law a success, can give it the impact it was supposed to have, or it can nullify or pervert a law, twisting the way it operates in a way that frustrates the goals and spirit of the law.

How often do either of these things happen? And under what cir-cumstances? Frequently, no doubt, both on the positive and the negative side. Lauren Edelman and Shauhin Talesh have studied what they call "legal endogeneity." The basic idea is this: businesses mold and reinter-pret regulations to further their own goals rather than the (ostensible) goals of the regulations. The dichotomy between compliance and non-compliance is, in this sense, misleading; instead, "organizations con-struct the meaning of both compliance and law."[40] Not that they flatly disobey legal mandates, but they reformulate, restructure, reinterpret. The result may be far from the spirit or goal of the law. Regulators, they found, tend to accept the business version of compliance, especially when regulations are general or ambiguous.

A number of studies have shown endogeneity in action.[41] Businesses, for example, faced with laws against forms of discrimination, hire ex-perts in "human relations," beef up their staff of in-house lawyers, and set up special grievance procedures. The point is to cocoon the company from lawsuits, bad publicity, and workforce unrest. All this "legaliza-tion" and "institutionalization" helps the company; it vaccinates the company against legal problems. But does it advance the "goals of civil rights laws"? In Edelman and Talesh's opinion, probably not.[42]

Endogeneity, yes; but the question is: How often and to what degree? *Regulation* is a vast ocean, a general term that covers literally thousands of rules and regulations directed at businesses and people in general. The way regulators and the regulated square off varies tremendously. At one end of the scale, there is something close to a state of war; on the other end of the scale, something close to a perpetual honeymoon. The two sides (and there may be more than two sides) often strike some sort of bargain or accommodation. These can be as complicated and variable as marriages—the two sides can be partners, lovers, friends, or anything in between. One side can be more dominant, more submissive, more authoritarian or more democratic, convincing or unconvincing. The two sides can get along or not get along. Or both, depending on the time and the place.

Sharon Gilad did a study of the way British financial firms reacted to an initiative of the Financial Services Authority (FSA). The endogeneity theory did not, she felt, fit in well with what happened in the real world. The FSA, she found, had some success in framing the way firms interpreted the law. The relationship between the regulated and the regulators was something like a partnership; more so, she felt, than endogeneity theory would predict.[43] In short, endogeneity is not an iron law of nature, or of business, or of regulation, but a tendency, a trend. The endogeneity studies at least remind us how complex the concept of compliance can be in the modern world of business regulation. It is one thing to tell drivers not to park in spaces reserved for the handicapped; another thing to tell a huge corporation, with a Byzantine structure, with many branches doing many different kinds of business, and with tens of thousands of employees scattered over the globe, to comply with a blizzard of rules, laws, and regulations on the environment, on the health and safety of workers, on the floating of stock, and on competition and monopoly. Endogeneity is one of many ways of coping. Stockholders, management, suppliers, and employees all have different goals, incentives, and motivations. All of this has an impact on impact.

Regulations are not only a problem for big business. A homeowner who wants to add a bathroom or cut down trees in her backyard might discover that local housing codes or zoning rules can stall or block the process. Nobody likes red tape, but there it is. Both for individuals and businesses, there are also many degrees of compliance. Compliance can be eager, even thoughtful, cooperative, or, at times, even showing enthusiasm and initiative, that is, going beyond what the letter of the law requires. Or, in the opposite direction, grudging, ritualistic, or downright rebellious. It may not even be clear (to a business) whether it is complying or not. In a study of food safety regulation in the United Kingdom, researchers found that businesses commonly thought they were in compliance; then inspectors came around and pointed out that, in fact, they were not.[44] And the reader will recall the problems of communication discussed in earlier chapters: what messages did the businesses get and how did they understand them.

Cases like *United States v. Hilton Hotels* (1972) raise a fundamental issue about compliance and adjustment in large organizations.[45] Hilton, of course, is a giant hotel chain. The government accused Hilton of violating the Sherman Anti-Trust Act. In Portland, Oregon, the manager of a Hilton Hotel joined a scheme (with other hotels and restaurants) to lure convention business. Suppliers were asked to make contributions to the hotel and restaurant group, and the group agreed not to do business with suppliers who did not make the payments. This scheme, the court felt, clearly violated the Sherman Act. As to that, there was no doubt.

But this was a criminal action, and the defendant was Hilton itself, not the manager of the hotel in Portland, Oregon. The Portland manager, Hilton said, had violated company policy. Indeed, management had specifically told the locals not to take part in the scheme. Nonetheless, the court held Hilton liable. "[G]eneral policy statements" were "no defense." The corporation was responsible for the acts of its agent. This was true even in a criminal case where, normally, the state has to prove an intention to commit the crime—an intention which, Hilton quite plausibly claimed, it simply did not have.

In some ways, the result seems unfair. (Of course, nobody was going to jail; Hilton would simply pay a fine.) But a big, loose-jointed, far-flung company does not "comply" with legal rules simply by issuing "general policy statements." Compliance requires a lot more. It requires structures, procedures, methods—ways to make sure that company policy seeps down into the very marrow of company behavior at the operating level. Holding Hilton liable in this case would force Hilton to devise these structures, procedures, and methods.

Not every court follows this general approach. In *Wal-Mart Stores, Inc. v. Dukes*, decided by the U.S. Supreme Court in 2011,[46] the plaintiffs were women who sued Walmart for sex discrimination in a class action. Walmart was the "nation's largest private employer," with some 3,400 stores and more than a million men and women on the payroll. One of the plaintiffs, for example, worked at a store in California; she asked the manager about management training, "but was brushed off." She claimed she was consistently "denied opportunity for advancement because of her sex." According to the company, local managers had "broad discretion" to make decisions about pay and promotion, discretion that could be exercised "in a largely subjective manner." The company had an "announced policy" against "sex discrimination," which they apparently at least sometimes enforced. The Supreme Court rejected the class action. Each woman would have to bring her own claim of sex discrimination.

Perhaps, technically speaking, the case was defensible or even proper; the law on class actions is complex and involute. But the case does illustrate again the tricky issue of compliance, not just with regard to sex discrimination law, but generally, in these big behemoth companies, and especially those that are radically decentralized. Still, if a company really wants to comply with rules about sex discrimination, it has to do more than issue some general policy statement; has to do more than tell employees to please don't violate the law. It has to have structures in place to make sure that compliance is real. Management cannot hide behind some sort of bland general "policy" and decentralization. That, at least, was the message of the Hilton case; the Walmart case sounds a different note.

A Note about Goals and Purposes

In a law against, say, burglary, it seems quite clear why the law was passed and what the goal of the law is supposed to be. Society wants to keep people and their property safe, discourage burglars, and make burglars pay for their crimes. On the civil side, the goal of a law might be not so much to encourage or discourage as to channel behavior in some specific way. You can dispose of your property at death as you like, but you have to follow the rules (about wills, testamentary trusts, and so on). The law does not encourage or discourage people from planning their estate; but it does say you have to do it the right way or not at all. Marriage laws, quite obviously, are not meant to discourage marriage. If anything, the opposite, but they also insist on certain formalities. Divorce law is certainly not meant to encourage divorce. Here, too, if anything, the aim is the opposite; here, too, the law insists on formalities.

Every law, at least in theory, has some point; every law is expected, in theory, to have an impact on behavior. In this book, we focus on that impact: who gets the message, who reacts to the message, how do they react, and why. But the intent of the law, the goal, the state of affairs it is trying to reach, is also supremely important. That goal is not always easy to figure out. Complicated laws give out mixed messages, or inconsistent messages. Complicated laws get put together in a give-and-take way; they are more like sausages than steaks. A law is "effective" when it achieves its purpose. Sometimes it is easy to know what that is, and to measure it. But it is much harder to tell if a law is effective when its very purpose is unclear.

Why People Obey (or Disobey)

People are not machines or robots. Their behavior in response to law is mostly (though not always) chosen more or less freely. Bradley Canon and Charles Johnson, talking about the impact of judicial decisions, describe a two-step process. First, they say, comes the acceptance decision, "psychological reactions to a judicial policy," acceptance or rejection based on what people think the decision means to them, how strongly these opinions are held, and what they think about the decision-maker. Then comes the behavioral response; that is, what the audience in question actually does as a result.[47] The distinction can be applied more generally to any legal act: a statute, a rule, a regulation, even a command from a police officer.

The acceptance decision obviously depends on communication, on how the person or institution in question understands what is asked of her or it. But that is only a prerequisite, a beginning. What follows? When is there an actual acceptance decision? An acceptance decision is only something at the psychological level. A response might never follow, because of laziness, inertia, habit, or ideology. The actor has to make a conscious decision to obey, disobey, avoid, or adjust. The question is: Why this particular response? What motivates this person? What is it that guides her decision?

The answers are often obscure. Even when we think we have a way to measure impact, we cannot be sure why the impact occurred. To take just one example, some states anxious to cut down on auto accidents have set up a system of graduated licensing. New drivers have to follow special rules: no night driving, for instance; no alcohol whatsoever; no high-speed highway driving. Later, the restrictions fade away. Graduated licensing seemed at least moderately effective—fewer accidents took place. That was good news. But why were there fewer accidents? Why did the law seem to have an impact? What were the drivers thinking, or not thinking? If we do not know the answers, it is hard to learn much from the experiment and hard to plan further steps.[48]

Examples could be multiplied. Notoriously, as this is written (2016), the American crime rate is lower than ever before; the crime rate seemed almost to collapse in the early years of the twenty-first century. Nobody really knows why. A lower crime rate means that thousands of people (young men, mostly) have made concrete decisions: not to break into this house, not to rob this store, and so on. To find out why, we would have to enter into the minds, so to speak, of these young men, and the others, who reacted in other ways; and then aggregate the data. This is not really possible. All we can do is talk about motives in general, and the research that explores these motives. This is the subject that the next chapters take up.

5

REWARDS AND PUNISHMENTS: THE PUNISHMENT SIDE

PEOPLE CAN RESPOND to laws, rules, and orders. They can obey, they can disobey, they can ignore, they can evade. This is clearest in the case of criminal laws. In other areas of law, we can talk in terms of use, nonuse, or misuse; also of avoidance, evasion, coping. All of these terms are, of course, problematic. Obeying the law can refer to an individual or to a group or to an institution; or all of these. Laws, as we pointed out, are directed most of the time to two separate audiences. With regard to criminal laws, one audience consists of ordinary people who are supposed to obey, who are supposed to follow the rules of the code. The other audience is the audience of enforcers. The burglary law is a message to the general public; but also to law enforcers. The same is true of use and nonuse. The law about wills applies, first of all, to people with money who are pondering what to do with their estate when they die. The law also gives directives to clerks and officials of the probate court, among other people. It gives guidance to lawyers who help people plan their estate.

All of this enormously complicates the question of obedience (or use). Nonetheless, I—along with other scholars—think there are general comments worth making. Why do people respond to law as they do? What are their motives or reasons? There is obviously no simple, general, universal answer. Motivation varies from time to time and place to place; audience A is not the same as audience B. But, generally speaking, we can divide peoples' motives into three types, or rather, three clusters of types. The impact of a law, rule, or doctrine, generally speaking, depends on one or more of these types.

The first type is the subject of this chapter: rewards and punishments. This is, in a way, the most obvious. Rapists and armed robbers face long years in prison. A murderer, in many American states (and in China, Saudi Arabia, and Iran), can even be put to death. The point of strict laws is deterrence. Society puts a heavy price tag on criminal behavior. There are also punishments—perhaps the better term is disincentives— outside the criminal justice system. Money damages, for example. If you commit a tort—by rear-ending your neighbor's car, let us say—it can cost you hard money. If your work for the Department of Agri- culture is slow and sloppy, the Department will pass you over for pro- motion, deny you a raise, and, in the worst case, let you go.

Rewards seem, on the surface, less obvious than punishments. But they are everywhere in the legal system. Tax breaks, for example, or juicy government contracts awarded to an eager bidder. If tort law de- fines you as a victim (it was your car, not your neighbor's, that was rear- ended), you stand to get money from the system. If our worker for the Department of Agriculture is fast and efficient, she may get her promo- tion, or higher pay. And for police officers, members of the Navy, and civil servants in general, there is a government pension at the end of the road. Most workers who retire will get Social Security payments, or the equivalent pension in France or Poland. The whole system is shot through with incentives. We will take this up in more detail in Chapter 6.

Deterrence

Incentives may be everywhere in the system, but scholarship, unless I am wrong, has tended to focus on deterrence.[1] Deterrence is a key concept in any discussion of impact. Scholars distinguish between general and specific deterrence. If you punish Mr. X for picking pockets, this might persuade him to stop picking pockets. This would be specific deterrence. But also, if we punish Mr. X and Mr. Z and Ms. Y, along with many other people, observe this and are deterred from picking pockets, this is general deterrence. General deterrence is sometimes referred to as "vicarious punishment." Punishing a company for fraud or business malfeasance, and doing this with a lot of noise, will have an impact, presumably, on other companies. Such a punishment also has "great informational value." It tells other firms "what types of behavior are permitted or prohibited," what types are subject to punishment.[2] This "signaling" effect is an important aspect of general deterrence.[3]

Mark Stafford and Mark Warr have argued that we can also talk about specific and general nondeterrence. When a pickpocket gets away with his crime, presumably he is more likely to do it again. This is specific nondeterrence. And if other people see that pickpockets are rarely caught and punished, the result might be general nondeterrence. If word gets around that nobody has ever gotten a ticket for parking overtime on Elm Street, I might be more likely to park there and break the rules. Stafford and Warr argue that general and specific deterrence can both affect people at the same time. They define general deterrence as the effect of "indirect experience with punishment and punishment avoidance," and specific deterrence as the effect of "direct experience with punishment and punishment avoidance." Both can "operate for any given person or in any population."[4]

Scholars also talk about incapacitation.[5] Hanging Mr. X for murder absolutely guarantees that his murdering days are over; this is the ultimate in specific deterrence.[6] Putting burglars in prison is a pretty sure way to keep them from burglarizing, at least as long as they stay behind bars. Shipping noncitizens back home if they commit crime incapacitates them, at least in one country. Ankle bracelets and similar devices also, in a sense, incapacitate. There is a good deal of argument (and research) on the actual effect of incapacitation.[7] One issue is whether the supply of criminals is elastic. A drug dealer in prison cannot deal drugs (we hope), but somebody may easily fill his shoes in the outside world. This replacement point, on the other hand, is not true for rapists; and not true for murderers, with the possible exception of contract killers. Incapacitation works differently for different crimes. Moreover, locking people up has side effects: on their families, their children, perhaps even their communities. These side effects might, in fact, nullify any gains achieved from getting these people off the streets.

How significant is incapacitation? Some scholars think locking people up has a real and significant effect on the crime rate. Others find only a small effect, or no effect. One study, in the 1970s, of "dangerous offenders" came to the conclusion that incapacitation accomplished little or nothing. One reason was this: most people arrested were first offenders. Incapacitation could not have prevented their crimes. Also, the typical offender committed violent crime "infrequently," or, at least, was "arrested infrequently." Because of these factors, they argued, incapacitation was an ineffective tool for fighting crime.[8] But by no means is this the consensus among scholars. Steven Levitt, for one, thinks the explosion in the prison population deserves at least some of the credit for the dramatic drop in the crime rate in the 1990s.[9]

Another point. We talk about punishments and rewards as if what the state imposes is either one or the other. A year in jail is certainly punishment; the Nobel Prize is certainly a reward. But suppose we force drunk drivers to undergo some sort of training program. Is this a punishment? What about rehabilitation programs in general? These are (arguably) "punishment," in the sense that the offenders (usually) did not choose them for themselves; they are something that a person is forced to undergo. But education and training are hardly "punishment" in the same sense as a term in prison or a stiff fine or loss of a driver's license. Are diversion programs punishment? In Ontario, Canada, under a 1998 law, drunk drivers who wanted their licenses back were required to go through a program called Back on Track.[10] The program was, apparently, quite successful. Some participants gave up alcohol completely. It is not clear if it was the program itself that produced these happy results. Our question is a bit different: Was Back on Track a form of punishment, or was it something else—some sort of in between?

Criminal Careers

Punishing people—specific deterrence—in theory ought to discourage them from doing the same wrong thing again. And in practice, no doubt, it does—to an extent. Yet there are criminal careers, people who offend again and again and again. Many of them are also punished again and again and again: drivers who drink and drive repeatedly even after getting caught; burglars who can't or won't stop burgling even after a prison sentence, or two, or three. Why should this be the case? Why are there criminal careers? Why doesn't punishment work?

There are a number of possible reasons. One (minor) reason may be this: what seems like punishment to some people, and a real deterrent, has little or no effect on others. Not everybody considers prison an awful fate. John Cross, who studied the drug trade, argues that many "crack users and low-level distributors" lead miserable disorganized lives. They were "effectively homeless and without stable family networks." They had so little to lose that they "simply do not see jail or prison as a significant threat." Indeed, it would give them "regular meals and . . . a warm dry bed." One drug seller said he was "more relaxed" in prison. Another claimed jail was safer than his job had been when he was a construction worker; also, there were "more drugs in the jails than outside. It's easier to make money."[11] Young men, in particular, might brush off the idea of prison as no big deal. As one career criminal said (much later), "I was young, simple, man. I didn't care, you know. . . . Doing time to me was nothing."[12] Some offenders, too, respond to the thrill or excitement of crime, the rush, the headiness; or succumb to the temptations of easy money. And, of course, a small number of people, for whatever reason, simply cannot help themselves. I will return to this theme in later pages.

Another possible factor in criminal careers is what has been called resetting (or the "gambler's fallacy"). The idea here is that a burglar, say, once he is caught and punished for burglary, "resets" his notion of how likely it is that he'll be caught again. So, "just as card players sometimes increase their bets after losing," these offenders decide that lightning never strikes twice in the same place; their luck will change; they have a greater chance than before of getting away with their crime. And so they continue to offend. There is some (slim) evidence that something of this sort may account for the behavior of at least some offenders.[13] On the other hand, the burnt child (as the saying goes) dreads the fire. A study of student shoplifters in Pennsylvania found that the ones who were caught were more likely to think they would be caught again (this was not, however, a very "powerful" effect).[14]

Career criminals—hard-core criminals—sometimes seem oblivious to risks, and seem also to behave quite irrationally; but even these criminals do modify their behavior to fit the situation. And even they often decide to give up their career altogether after spending long years in prison, or to switch from a greater to a lesser type of crime. As one armed robber said, after a ten-year sentence, "I'm not gonna stick no pistol in nobody's face . . . I'm not gonna strong-arm nobody . . . I'm not gonna go in nobody's house." A burglar was quoted saying he was going to give up burglary and switch to shoplifting; if you get arrested for "boosting" (shoplifting) "it is generally a fine. If worse comes to worst, you're going to have to do a year in the county jail."[15] Burglary, of course, carries a heavier penalty.

The Anatomy of Punishment

Punishment, so the theory goes, or the threat of punishment, is a powerful deterrent. Some skepticism is in order, so long as it is not too much. The basic assumptions behind deterrence theory make sense, including empirical sense. People on the whole will bend behavior toward benefits and away from whatever is costly or painful. This seems obviously true. Deterrence theory has a particular attraction for economists, who tend to have a rather cynical or, if you will, mechanical take on human behavior. A criminal commits a crime when the expected gains outweigh the expected costs. The economics of crime, like the economics of everything else, is based on this notion.

It is easy to sneer at this idea. To be sure, it tells us almost nothing useful about why burglars burglarize and why people respond or don't respond to incentives. Yet the theory surely explains a good deal of behavior. Nobody races down the highway at 100 miles per hour when there are police cars around. Even our burglar "casing" a house makes at least some crude sort of calculation. If he sees police nearby, and nosy neighbors sitting on a neighboring porch, he decides there is too much danger of getting caught; he passes this house by. Obviously, the burglar does not take out a pad of paper and start figuring risks and benefits. But he uses common sense. If the house seems like an easy mark, and full of jewelry, cash, and other goods, the reward side may overwhelm the risk side.[16] Robbers in the Netherlands "choose moments when they expect most money at the target site," for example, at banks "when the night safe is emptied." Thieves are more active in winter, because of the darkness. They ask themselves: Is the target guarded, or not?[17] Burglars and other thieves, in other words, do adjust their behavior under the influence of risk and reward, costs and benefits.

Clearly, if crime did not pay at all, or paid too little, there would be a lot less crime. For many people at the bottom of the social order, crime seems to pay better than flipping hamburgers at McDonald's. Moreover, concepts such as gains, losses, costs, benefits, and the like mean different things to different people. "Punishment," too, is a complex concept. When we use the word, we usually think of fines, jail sentences, maybe even the death penalty. There are others, too: ostracism and shunning, for example. Or banishment or deportation. Loss of privileges, like forfeiting a driver's license. Whipping and flogging. Torture. Mutilation, which was once commonly used: cutting off ears, branding with a hot iron, castration.

Punishment has a long and colorful history. In the colonial period in the United States, punishment was always carried out in public. Whipping was a common form of punishment, carried out in the public square, in front of everybody. The colonists also used stigma and shame: putting people in the stocks, or making an adulteress wear the "scarlet letter" made famous by Nathaniel Hawthorne. Branding with a hot iron or cutting off a criminal's ears was a form of punishment that left a permanent mark on the offender.[18] The ultimate punishment was hanging. And this, too, was carried out in public; the whole town, perhaps, would gather to see the convict dangle from the end of a rope. In the nineteenth century, there was a revulsion against bodily punishments, at least officially; imprisonment replaced the whip (and, to some extent, the gallows) as a major form of punishment. In the first half of the nineteenth century, the penitentiary was born: huge, walled, austere buildings, heavily guarded, in which prisoners, once punished in public, now suffered in total isolation from the rest of society.

Penal codes can be read as a kind of catalog of punishments. These are texts that fix the price, so to speak, for each class of offenses. But punishment, of course, is not just words. Punishment is a system. Imagine, for example, a driver pulled over by the police, accused of drunk driving, and hauled into court. The arrest, the arraignment, the whole procedure—all this is unpleasant, disruptive, most likely humiliating, and perhaps psychologically harmful. Even if the driver is ultimately let go, he has already suffered. Malcolm Feeley's well-known study of a lower court bore the provocative title *The Process Is the Punishment*.[19] The phrase has a great deal of resonance. Moreover, the punishment does not end with release. Take a man convicted of a felony. He serves a term of years in the penitentiary. Then he comes out. He has, as the phrase goes, paid his debt to society. But has he finished paying? In many regards, he keeps on paying. Convicted felons, as Joan Petersilia has pointed out, "lose many essential rights of citizenship." In some states, they no longer have the right to vote. An ex-con may have trouble getting a job. His prospects in life are generally poor. His family relations may have suffered. He has almost certainly incurred what has been called "attachment costs."[20] His situation, to be sure, is worse in the United States than in, say, France. Debt to society seems never to be paid in full. Society is a harsh creditor, and whole clusters of "invisible punishments" remain in effect.[21]

Think, too, of a businessman, arrested and charged with a white-collar crime—say, insider trading. Suppose he is tried and the jury acquits him. A good result, of course. But by then, he will have spent a fortune on lawyers. He may have suffered sleepless nights; his name has been in the newspapers; his reputation was dragged through the mud. Whatever the outcome, he has been through an ordeal. Acquittal is, of course, much better than conviction, but it comes at the end of a long, hard, and punitive process. His career may never recover. Or his reputation. Many people will think: where there's smoke, there's fire. The jury let him go, but was he really so innocent as all that? On the other hand, the impact of a fine of, say, a thousand dollars would be almost nothing to a millionaire; for a poor man, it might be a crushing blow. The effect on people and businesses of indirect or consequential punishments varies greatly; the effects depend on who, and what, and how.

All these indirect forms of punishment shape part of the system of deterrence. For the innocent, of course, there is nothing to deter. But this leaves general deterrence on the table. Potential lawbreakers might think twice about what they might do; even the chance of getting arrested and what this brings with it might deter. But "process" punishment might also chill innocent or even socially useful behavior if that behavior comes close to the line of illegality. And a middle-class person has more to lose (socially and otherwise) from process punishment than perhaps a young gang member. And a jolt in prison, similarly, has a differential effect on people. For some repeat criminals, a prison term, though regrettable, is almost part of the normal lifecycle of his career.

Moreover, when we say "five years in prison," we haven't described the actual punishment. What kind of prison is it? What are conditions like in the prison? Is the prison a dangerous place, full of gangs, where prisoners get beaten, by guards or each other? Is it a place where prisoners get raped? Is it a "super-max," where prisoners are locked up for twenty-three out of twenty-four hours? Is it a local jail with cockroaches and blistering heat in summer? Or is it a "country club," a relatively milder prison? If the thought of going to prison is a deterrent, the true deterrent effect surely depends on what the prison is like (or what people think it is like). In one intriguing study in Florida, researchers tried to measure the impact of arrest on men accused of domestic violence.[22] The men had been taken into custody, fingerprinted, held for a while, and then either released or put on trial. Were these men—arrested for, say, beating their wives—likely to repeat these offenses, or was entanglement in the web of criminal justice an effective deterrent? Men who had jobs were deterred by the experience; the unemployed were not. The deterrent effect, in short, was greater for men with more to lose. Or was this because they were more subject to stigma and shame—a subject I will deal with later.

Deterrence theory assumes at least some sort of rational calculation. Obviously, the typical criminal (or potential criminal) has no way of doing this with any precision. The burglar looking up at an apartment has no real clue about what he is likely to find in the house. If there is very little loot, the job is hardly worth the risk of getting caught. But gains and losses are not just matters of dollars and cents. For many burglars, burglary is all they know how to do; they have no real alternative, or at least none that they can see. Burglary is a job, a profession, a way of life. For some crimes, as I mentioned, there is an element of thrill, of excitement—take joy riding, for example. Or even burglary. Burglars, in a study of English burglars, were motivated by money, for the most part; but some said they robbed houses "when we were bored 'cos we had nothing to do" or "just for the fun of it."[23] Under some circumstances, making behavior a crime might actually stimulate rather than deter behavior: the "forbidden fruit" phenomenon. As we mentioned before, blue-nosed censorship in Boston turned banned books into best sellers.[24] A law can increase criminality in another sense (a fairly obvious one): any new crime, unless it stamps out what it outlaws entirely (which never happens), in a sense, increases criminality. The more behavior gets labeled as deviant, the more there is deviant behavior.

The Deterrence Curve

As a general rule, the more severe the punishment, or the more lavish the incentive, the greater the impact might be. This seems intuitively right. It is also the sort of proposition dear to the hearts of economists. The higher the price of a product, the less people will buy (other things being equal). But the relationship between severity and actual deterrence, though certainly real and significant, is not a linear relationship. Ironically, the more serious the crime, the less likely it is that jacking up the punishment will have a major effect. This is because, for really serious crimes, like murder, the threat of punishment is not the chief deterrent. Moral considerations are.

There are a massive number of studies on the death penalty—on whether or not it deters. Death is the ultimate punishment, the most severe, the punishment of punishments. But why are the studies so ambivalent? Why are they so inconsistent? Why do they come out now this way, now that? Why is it so hard to tell whether capital punishment acts as a deterrent or not, and if it does, by how much?

We can analyze the problem in terms of what I like to call the deterrence curve. Suppose the sentence for burglary is five years in prison. Suppose we increase it to ten years in prison (and the enforcement level stays the same). The harsher sentence might have an effect. But doubling the typical sentence will almost certainly not double the impact, that is, cut burglary rates in half. The deterrence curve is the curve that describes the actual relationship between severity and impact of punishment. The point may be easiest to see for minor crimes. Suppose the fine for overtime parking on Main Street is $1, and two out of ten violators are caught. Many people, in a hurry, will risk the fine. After all, $1 isn't much and parking space might be scarce. Then the fine is raised to

$100 (and two out of ten violators are still caught). Most drivers will now think twice about parking overtime. A few, out of desperation or whatever, still take a chance. Now raise the fine to $200; this might have some impact, but it will certainly not cut the number of violators in half, if for no other reason than that very few violators are left. (The fine for parking in a handicapped spot without a sticker is huge, and most people scrupulously avoid those spots.) Back on Main Street, the city, in addition to the fines, now starts ruthlessly towing cars away. This might make some small difference. But it cannot make a big difference; most people are already deterred. The deterrence curve has flattened out.[25]

There is, no doubt, a deterrence curve for every crime. Take murder, for example. Most people are not potential killers; moral factors are enough to do the job of preventing murder. For the few potential killers, severe punishments are already in place—life imprisonment, for example, or a very long sentence in prison. Now suppose we add the possibility of a death sentence. How much of a deterrent would it add? Not much—not because deterrence theory is wrong, but because the curve has already flattened out. Perhaps not entirely, but so significantly, I suspect, that the death penalty might give us little or no extra deterrent power.

The curve has also, no doubt, flattened out for most serious crimes. Kenneth D. Tunnell interviewed prisoners who had committed burglary or armed robbery.[26] He found that they simply did not think much about the risks. As one of them said, "I never really thought about getting caught until, pow, you're in jail." Tunnell decided, on the basis of his interviews, that harsh punishments would have a "dubious" effect on frequent offenders.[27] In other words, the curve for these crimes had flattened out. A small club of habitual offenders were left, men who, for one reason or another, failed to respond to threats—like the few overtime parkers willing to run the risk of the tow truck.

What is it that flattens out the curve? First of all, moral considerations—strong norms against murder, rape, armed robbery. There may be other reasons. Each crime, as we said, has its own deterrence curve. It is an empirical question, to determine what the curve looks like for such crimes as burglary or rape or embezzlement or gambling or for running a Ponzi scheme. Or for shoplifting or drunk driving. Probably no two curves are the same. The curve will be determined by all sorts of factors: the type of punishment, its severity, the level of enforcement; also local culture, the personalities of people who violate and people who don't, and whether the forbidden act is intensely desirable or not.

Who are the survivors—the undeterrables, the few people left when the curve has flattened out? This, of course, varies from situation to situation. Perhaps the survivors have nothing to lose; they are in a situation where breaking the rules is an absolute necessity. A man facing a firing squad is in this position. He will do anything, risk anything, try anything—even though all resistance is forbidden. In some totalitarian societies, the atmosphere may be so punitive, so arbitrary and dangerous, that people violate rules out of sheer desperation; their curve has flattened out. A Nazi death camp was worse than Dante's hell; it was a "legal no-man's land," where inmates were stripped of all rights and all humanity.[28] When life and death are in the hands of sadists and tyrants, revolution is less of a risk than submission. The Jews in the Warsaw Ghetto knew they were doomed; they fought, in part because they had no other choice. In a classic prison study, Gresham Sykes made a similar point.[29] Guards and other officials were in constant battle with disorderly, rebellious inmates. This was, Sykes thought, because the officials were "dangerously close to the point where the stock of legitimate punishments" had been "exhausted," and the remaining punishments "had lost their potency." In this prison, then, the curve had not only flattened out; it had perhaps begun to move downward, at least to a degree.

Or consider the passengers on United Flight 93, on 9/11/2001. They realized the plane had been hijacked, the hijackers, they knew, were on a suicide mission; they were all going to die. No threats from the hijackers could have stopped the passengers from trying anything, no matter how risky, in a desperate attempt to save their lives. They failed, but at least they thwarted the plans of the hijackers.

It is hard to deter people who are fatalistic, or who don't care, or who are simply incapable of planning for the future. You have to wonder about men who run Ponzi schemes. They must know that sooner or later the party is going to end. Which it does. Bernard Madoff, who ran a Ponzi scheme on an enormous scale, is now spending the rest of his life in prison.[30] But while the fun lasted, he was rich, powerful, honored in his community; he lived the high life. Did he wonder how long this life would last? Did he have an exit strategy? Or did he feel, maybe, that it was all worthwhile, that the trip was worth it, no matter what happened later on? For Madoff, apparently, the curve had not flattened out.

William Chambliss, in a well-known article, drew a distinction between "expressive" and "instrumental" crimes.[31] A crime is expressive if it is done for its own sake, that is, the act itself is pleasurable. He mentions rape and drug addiction as examples. On the other hand, an instrumental crime, like embezzlement or income tax evasion, is only a means to an end. Chambliss argues that instrumental crimes are easier to deter than expressive ones. The psychological drive to commit expressive crimes is stronger, less resistible, than the drive to commit instrumental crimes. The two types of crime would, therefore, have rather different deterrence curves.

But this is not necessarily true. Suppose I see a beautiful flower in a quiet meadow. I want it for a bouquet. Picking the flower would be an expressive act, but if the flower is rare and endangered, it would also be a crime. Most people, I think, would keep their hands off the plant if they knew that they could be in serious trouble if they picked the flower. And embezzlers, con men, and others who commit instrumental crimes might be supporting a gambling habit or a drug addiction. Or the embezzler might be so bedazzled by what seems to be easy money that he dips his hand into the till time and again. As we mentioned, the men who run Ponzi schemes must know that some day the music will stop. For all such people, the game is apparently worth it. People live in the present, not the future. It is easier to spend than to save. It is easier to eat potato chips than to diet. Deterrence depends on a kind of rational calculus that many people, in many situations, simply do not make. Or cannot make. The distinction between expressive and instrumental crimes as a key to understanding where deterrence works best does not hold up very well.

To take another instance, it is hard to think of anything more expressive than sex. Sex, of course, is not a crime, but societies regulate sexual behavior, or try to, fairly heavily. Teenage sex would seem to be particularly "visceral or emotional," leaving little room for "reason and calculation." Suppose a law requires young girls to get parental approval before they are allowed to have an abortion. Would this law lead to a decrease in "risky sex" (risky in the sense that the girl is likely to get pregnant)? Apparently, yes. Rates of gonorrhea among a cohort that was studied declined by a significant amount.[32] Many teenagers surely went right on indulging in risky sex, but at least some of them either stopped or took more precautions.

Another scholar, John Gallo, has drawn a line between "white-collar" crime and violent crime. He argues that it is easy to deter white-collar crimes and hard to deter violent crimes.[33] White-collar criminals are more rational than violent criminals. The punishment message tends to work. By way of contrast, he asks us to think of drug "mules," couriers who deliver cocaine to buyers and collect the money. These couriers are not paid very much and, if caught, face horrendous penalties—a huge fine, and years and years in prison. No "rational actor would . . . take on the risk of such severe penalties for such a meager reward."[34] The conclusion, of course, is that the mule is not acting rationally. White-collar criminals, on the other hand, are "generally rational, informed individuals." Enforcement of the laws will have a strong deterrent effect. The violent "do not act rationally," and, often, they are "unaware of the punishment for their conduct."[35] Again, we have to ask, are white-collar criminals really that rational? Some of them seem, on the contrary, to be wild risk-takers, high-flying wheeler-dealers. And then there is Bernie Madoff to consider.

Professional criminals might think and act differently from amateurs— for example, members of a car-stealing ring versus kids who steal a car for a joy ride. Professional criminals are "experts at controlling or minimizing risks"; they also know how to manipulate the legal system, how to get in touch with a fence, and other information that the amateur may not have. Commercial theft is likely to be planned in advance, a "stick-up" less so. Experienced criminals have different and better ways to assess opportunities and more "information about strategies and actions."[36]

But the type of crime does make a difference, on the whole. It seems a lot easier, in theory, to stop jaywalking than to get people to kick a drug habit. Yet people do give up drug habits, and it is hard to get people to stop jaywalking. They see nothing (morally) wrong with it, and enforcement is typically weak. If punishments for drug use become very severe and enforcement gets tight and rigorous, a certain number of drug addicts will force themselves to quit; some will enter drug programs voluntarily and make great efforts to free themselves of their habit. Sweden, in 1998, passed a law that criminalized "johns." Under the law, buying sex became a crime. The idea was to end prostitution, which victimized women. Getting at the customers looked like a winning strategy. One might have thought that buying sex was the very epitome of expressive behavior. Still, the Swedish law (accompanied, to be sure, with a massive education campaign) seemed to make a difference; prostitution apparently declined.[37]

To repeat a point, there is no doubt a different deterrence curve for every crime. Perhaps also for every crime in every society. What works in Sweden might not work somewhere else. Or might not have worked in Sweden in the past, or in the future. Expressive and instrumental crimes might, as a general rule, have different deterrence curves, though, as I said, this idea can be carried too far. The curve for embezzlement (a white-collar crime) is probably different from the curve for rape. The curve for rape is probably different from the curve for armed robbery. Armed robbers are, after all, in it for the money; rapists are not. Rapists, according to a study, commit this crime out of "desperation and emotional turmoil." A rapist rapes as a "last desperate attempt to deal with stresses which he feel will otherwise destroy him; he often fears that he is losing control and may go insane."[38] This study paints a depressing picture of the rapist—depressing not only because of the terrible impact of the rapist on his victims, but also because it describes rapists as men with violent and unthinking impulses, men clearly not easy to deter (or to cure).

Still, the shape of the deterrence curve is always an empirical question. Some rapists, to be sure, cannot be deterred at any level of punishment. This may be especially true of rapists who are brutal and who prey on strangers. Date rape, and the kind of rape that takes place at drunken frat-house parties, might be more responsive—to punishment, to education, to campaigns that insist that no means no. Universities are struggling to deal with violence against women on their campuses; they certainly assume that something can be done, that some combination of education and sanctions might work.[39] Changing the culture of young males on campus, especially fraternity culture and (male) athletic culture, would not be easy, but the attempt is worthwhile and might just succeed.

A study published in 1992 was a rare attempt to test whether a "deterrence/rational choice" theory could work with sexual offenders.[40] The subjects were ninety-four male college students who were taking a social science course at a state university in New England. Most of them were young freshmen. They were given various "scenarios," all involving Lori, a twenty-year-old female, and Tom, a twenty-two-year-old male. In the scenarios, Tom has sex with Lori, but against her wishes. The facts vary from scenario to scenario. Is Tom a guy she has been dating, or not? Did she just say no; did she push him to try to get him to stop; did he threaten to beat her; did she scream and cry or not; was she bruised or psychologically damaged; and so on. The students were asked if they could imagine themselves doing any of the things Tom did, and they were also asked whether they thought they would be punished. The punishments could be expulsion from school or actual arrest. They were asked also whether they thought Tom's behavior was wrong, on a scale from "Not Wrong" (0) to "Very Wrong" (10). It turned out that those who were at the Very Wrong end of the scale were unlikely to be influenced by any threat of punishment, but these were (naturally) people who tended to say they would absolutely never behave like Tom in the first place. For the others, though, the "perceived risk of formal sanctions did have a significant deterrent effect."[41]

Of course, these male students were not actual rapists, as far as we know. Just under half of them could imagine themselves as a brute like Tom (though not necessarily at the most violent level). The subjects were asked to make predictions about their own future behavior. The authors claim such predictions can be trusted. This might or might not be true. And this was a narrow case study of a narrow group responding to a narrow set of scenarios. It is, in a way, a study of the deterrence curve for (potential) sex offenders. It seems likely that most men are deterred both by fear of punishment and by their own inner gyroscope of values. The curve flattens out quickly for extreme cases—committing violent rape on strangers. For less extreme cases, the curve takes longer to flatten out. Changes in the law of rape and the rising voice of women in our times might make a difference in the deterrence curve for less violent forms of sexual predation—for guys who, like Tom in some of the scenarios, are slow to take no for an answer but who would probably call a halt if their date screamed or fought back. There is also, of course, the question of whether paper-and-pencil exercises really tell us much about the real world of action. Smoking, like drug addiction, is expressive. Indeed, it is a form of addiction. Governments have used all sorts of tactics to get people to stop smoking: civil and criminal laws; restrictions on advertising; heavy taxes; rules that outlaw smoking in restaurants, airports, and many other places; and educational campaigns, inside and outside government. On the whole, the crusade against smoking has had real results. Smoking in developed countries has gone down dramatically (it has, however, actually increased in some less-developed countries, including China). But at some point, the curve flattens out. Most people have stopped smoking. Doubling the tax, say, or heaping on more restrictions might not produce much of an impact. It is harder and harder to get the surviving smokers to quit. In the United States, "smoking among adults stabilized between 2006 and 2008," and in Europe, a point was reached "from which it will be difficult to show further decline" without heroic measures.[42]

Deterrence Theory: Severity versus Certainty

In the vast sea of studies on deterrence, there is considerable debate about the exact role of its two main components: severity and certainty. Severity is the actual, formal punishment, say, five years in prison for burglary. Certainty is the likelihood that a burglar will get caught, say, one time out of six. There are studies that claim that certainty is more important than severity;[43] and findings of this sort can be quoted from some studies.[44] Greg Pogarsky, however, studying the usual suspects (college students), has cast doubt on these findings. They are based, he says, on surveys that are too broad. They include people who will never violate the law, no matter what. If you eliminate these people, severity does make a difference. The students in his study were given a scenario: imagine you go to a bar, about ten miles from your house, and proceed to get drunk. You have to be at work the next morning. Do you drive home drunk or try to find some alternative way to get home? Leaving the car behind would be awkward and bothersome. If you subtract from the study those who absolutely will not drink and drive, and look only at the "deterrable" subjects (those who might or might not drink and drive), certainty no longer dominates severity.[45]

Pogarsky is cautious. As usual, this is one study, of one particular offense, with one type of subject. I think skepticism of another kind is in order. I do not see how one can weigh certainty against severity. The two factors are never found in isolation. How can you separate them? Neither term has any meaning apart from the other. The punishment for drunk driving might be quite severe on paper, but (suppose) only one out of a thousand drunk drivers ever gets caught (and drivers know this). The true severity, if we wanted to express it mathematically, would not be the legal punishment (say, six months in prison), but six months subject to a heavy discount. In short, the whole notion of severity includes—has to include—some sort of notion of certainty; that is, how often in reality the severe punishment is actually imposed. The impact of a punishment can be expressed, mathematically, as the product of severity and certainty. A one in ten chance of a $100 fine is not the same as a one in twenty chance. But the relationship is not linear. There is no way, actually, to multiply severity and certainty and come out with a meaningful number. But one thing is clear: if nobody enforces a law, and people know this, then it has no impact, no matter how loud the thunder from the pages of the penal code. Zero times anything else is still zero. If severity is zero (there is no actual punishment), then it hardly matters that nobody gets caught.

Probably most of us have done things that are at least technically illegal because we were sure we wouldn't be caught: an illegal U-turn, for example, when no police car is likely to be around. Certainty is zero, as far as we are concerned; in this case, severity hardly matters. Of course, certainty is rarely actually zero. Most drunk drivers, for example, never get caught. But a few of them do, along with a few people who make illegal U-turns. But it can be vanishingly low. Your chances of getting caught are like your chances of winning the lottery. Jaywalking or littering may be normally in this category.

A third factor, besides certainty and severity, is celerity. When is punishment likely to come? Is the process fast or slow?

The effect of celerity on deterrence, like so many impact issues, is not very obvious.[46] Relatively little work has been done on this question. One exception was a study of drunk drivers in New York by Jiang Yu.[47] Drunk drivers could be fined, they could lose their licenses, or both; and the punishments could come quickly or slowly. Yu's data suggested that "swift punishment" might "deter the general public and first-time offenders but not multiple offenders."[48] Loss of license, by the way, seemed to have little or no effect; the drunks kept right on driving, with or without a license. Normally, we would consider losing a license a stronger deterrent than a fine. But Yu's study suggests otherwise. Some men and women are addicted to alcohol; they have a drinking problem they apparently cannot control or, more accurately, a drinking-and-driving problem they cannot or do not control. For these hard-core survivors, the curve has flattened out. But why did fines make a difference? A heavy fine "always creates a financial burden." You can drive without a license, but you can't live without money. Another study of bad drivers—this time in Portugal—also looked at celerity. Portugal not only jacked up punishments; it also adopted an "on-the-spot" policy of assessing fines. But this policy did not seem to add much to the impact of the other enforcement strategies. Perhaps here, too, the curve had flattened out.[49]

Does the Death Penalty Deter? The Time Element

In theory, it should make a difference whether punishment is fast or slow in coming; and, as I mentioned, there has been at least some research on this factor of celerity.[50] In some situations, and with regard to some forms of punishment, a person might want to "get it over with quickly." In this case, celerity would make punishment less effective. A person might prefer ten lashes on the back compared to a jolt in prison (modern law does not give you this option). A few prisoners on death row have practically begged for quick execution, which they preferred over years rotting away on death row. Timothy McVeigh, for example, who was sentenced to death for bombing a federal building in Oklahoma, dropped his appeals at one point; he said he preferred it that way.[51]

Punishment for murder is fairly certain, in the sense that fewer murderers get away with it compared to (say) rapists or pickpockets or drunk drivers. In many American states, the death penalty is available for first-degree murder. Not all states, of course; and, indeed, there is something of a trend against it. Nineteen states now lack the death penalty. A few have never had it (Wisconsin, Michigan); some have recently gotten rid of it (New York, New Mexico). Connecticut is a recent convert. Many states use it only rarely: California, for example. A few states, however, mostly in the South (and above all the great state of Texas), use it more frequently. Of the thirty-five executions in 2014, ten were in Texas. This one state accounted for almost a third of all the executions in the United States, but this was hardly an avalanche of executions.[52]

Even in Texas, years and years, even decades, go by between sentencing and execution. Quick or immediate punishment might be a better deterrent, compared to an event that will happen, if at all, far, far off in the future. At one time, the lag between sentence and execution was fairly short. On February 15, 1933, Giuseppe Zangara tried to assassinate the president-elect, Franklin Delano Roosevelt; instead, his bullets killed Anton Cermak, the mayor of Chicago. Zangara was executed just over a month later, on March 20, 1933.[53] This is no longer even remotely possible.

Modern death penalty laws date from the 1970s. In 1972, in *Furman v. Georgia*, the Supreme Court struck down all existing death penalty statutes; this was a narrow, five-to-four decision.[54] The majority based its decision on the Eighth Amendment to the Constitution, which forbids cruel and unusual punishment. Two justices thought the death penalty was cruel and unusual in itself; the other three justices on the majority side did not go this far, but agreed that all existing laws were defective. Four justices dissented. Clearly, this decision did not close the door on the death penalty once and for all. States that wanted to keep the death penalty tried to remodel their laws to satisfy the Supreme Court. And, indeed, four years later, in 1976, the Supreme Court did approve one model, the new law in Georgia.[55] Most states then redid their own laws, more or less along the lines approved of in the Georgia case. Death penalty cases now have two phases. First is the guilt phase. Then comes the penalty phase. Here, the jury must find, beyond a reasonable doubt, at least one aggravating factor (for example, killing more than one person). Aggravating factors have to outweigh any mitigating factors. The Georgia law also called for automatic review of all death sentences.[56] All this became standard in death penalty states.

Public opinion on the subject seems to vacillate. People, on the whole, apparently favor the death penalty. But if we look at the way the system actually behaves, we might reach a more nuanced conclusion. The process is uncommon, slow, and subject to special, complex, and niggling rules. The system, in operation, suggests a deeply divided country. Some people favor it, some do not; but even those who like it seem satisfied if it is rare, and hedged about with all sorts of procedures and exceptions.[57]

The long, slow, but steady decline in executions supports this view. Public hanging is history. The electric chair is history. The method today is lethal injection.[58] No member of the European Union has the death penalty. It exists in Japan, but is not used very much. It flourishes in authoritarian states (China, Iran) that are not bashful about using it. Indonesia puts drug dealers to death. Polls show that support is fading a bit in the United States. The public reads about DNA evidence and innocence projects. People are told about false convictions.[59] The future of this most final of punishments is cloudy.

■ ■ ■

And does it work? There are, it is said, literally hundreds of studies on this question: Does the death penalty deter? I have already suggested why capital punishment might make little practical difference, whatever its theoretical effect. This is because the deterrence curve has almost completely flattened out. But in addition, to compute impact, you would have to apply a drastic time discount. Zangara, the man who was executed so quickly in 1933, would today spend years and years on death row. The process today seems to stretch out endlessly. There are, to begin with, mandatory appeals. There is a good chance an appeals court will overturn the sentence and order a new trial. But even when this doesn't happen, writs, processes, and actions, of all sorts and flavors, consume more and more years. Partly this is because these cases are complicated, partly because qualified lawyers for death case appeals are in short supply. But whatever the reasons, the years go by. A prisoner can figure on a minimum of ten years before he is put to death. Some men have been on death row for twenty years, and quite a few even longer. When Askari Muhammad, age sixty-two, was executed in Florida in January 2014, thirty years had gone by since he was sentenced; and eleven others who were executed that year had been on death row twenty years or more.[60] Thousands of murders are committed every year; but the number of death penalties is a tiny fraction of this figure, and the number of actual executions, even fewer. The highest figure in any year since 1976, the year the death penalty was reinstated, was ninety-eight executions; the figure for 2014 was thirty-five. In that year, there were over 16,000 homicides, of which a fair number (it is impossible to know how many) would at least be eligible for the death penalty. About 750 men and women are on death row in California at this writing; California has not executed anyone in years.

We have to ask, then, how much added deterrence does the death penalty give you, compared, say, to life imprisonment. After all, the men and women on death row are already undergoing punishment. But the final walk to the death chamber? That is far, far off. A killer on trial might know that the death penalty is possible. But it is never certain. Not every murderer is sentenced to death. Even when this happens, the chances on appeal are fairly good in a surprising percentage of the case. Execution may not come, and if it does, it will be far off in the future. (And, of course, whether killers calculate these chances, or do any calculating at all, is another question entirely.)

In the last paragraph, I deliberately talked about the death penalty as an added deterrent. If you ask whether the death penalty deters, as an abstract matter, the obvious answer is yes. It clearly does. Or would. Or might. But the real question is: deters compared to what? Compared to getting away scot-free? Surely. As Michael Tonry put it, society is safer because of criminal sanctions rather than not having them; but that is simply not the issue. The issue is marginal changes. Do they make a difference? And the consensus is, they do not.[61] This is not to deny that the death penalty can be extremely powerful in the hands of the state. Tyrants have used it to crush dissent and dispose of enemies; they use it to terrify people into submission. Ruthlessness works. Ian Kershaw tried to puzzle out why Germany kept on fighting during the Second World War long after it was clear to everybody (including the Germans) that the war was totally lost. But the regime was absolutely merciless toward dissidents and deserters; it was willing to execute quickly and brutally anybody who showed the slightest signs of disaffection. Germany executed 20,000 soldiers for desertion or other offenses in the war. The British executed a grand total of forty. Although Kershaw thinks there were other, perhaps more powerful, reasons for Germany's dogged struggle, terror certainly played a role.[62]

Ruthlessness works, alas. But in our society, the death penalty, compared to life without possibility of parole, or even a conventional life sentence, is not that much harsher; especially since, as I pointed out, the death penalty is simply not imposed that often; and even when it is, execution will be carried out, if at all, ten, twenty, or even more years after sentencing.

The Death Penalty and Deterrence: What the Research Shows

Despite all the considerations mentioned that complicate the issue of deterrence, scholars have still spent (or wasted) an incredible amount of time, money, and effort trying to figure out whether the death penalty in the United States does or does not deter.

And what do these studies show? The results, to be honest, are inconclusive. Some studies fail to find any deterrent effect.[63] A few claim the opposite. Economists, in particular, are attracted to the idea that the death penalty works; it fits in with their general mind-set. After all, the more severe the punishment, the more it should deter; when a price goes up, all else held constant, sales of a product should go down. Death, the most severe punishment, should pack the most powerful bang. Economists also tend to be conservative, politically speaking; and conservatives, for whatever reason, like the death penalty more than liberals do.[64]

A paper by Isaac Ehrlich, which appeared in 1972, argued that about eight murders were deterred by each execution. Fans of the death penalty seized on this paper as scientific proof that capital punishment worked.[65] Other scholars entered the field and returned fire, with heavy attacks on Ehrlich's methods and statistics. They demonstrated, pretty effectively, that Ehrlich's brash conclusions were something of a statistical red herring.[66] In the years afterward, there was a veritable blizzard of studies, some with impressive econometric and statistical apparatus. They go every which way. A careful review by John Donohue and Justin Wolfers makes a valiant effort to sum matters up. They conclude that "the . . . evidence for deterrence is surprisingly fragile." The death penalty in the United States has, at most, a very small effect. And it is not even clear if that effect is positive or negative. Nor is it likely, they claim, that "existing data can resolve this uncertainty."[67]

Some economists (and many political figures), not to mention members of the general public, remained unconvinced. They think the death penalty works. More important, perhaps, many people seem to think it ought to work. They think the men and women on death row mostly deserve to die. Some crimes are so awful that they call for nothing less than death. Some people argue executions are good for the victim's family: it gives them "closure."[68] Sociologists, and some members of the public, tend to dislike the death penalty. They glom on to studies that argue that capital punishment is too expensive, or even claim that capital punishment does more harm than good—that it actually increases the homicide rate. How could this be? Because, it is said, of the brutalization factor. The argument is this: the death penalty, a cruel and savage practice, devalues human life, and in so doing, it legitimates murderous behavior, vengeance, and the like. One study, published in 1980, claimed to find evidence for a brutalizing effect. A before-and-after study of executions showed more murders after the execution compared to the number before. The authors made the rather extravagant claim that, if the states were to execute all the people on death row, hundreds of innocent lives would be lost.[69]

A study published in 1994 tried to test both the deterrence and the brutalization thesis.[70] In 1990, Oklahoma executed Charles Troy Coleman; this was the first execution in the state in twenty-five years. Using the most sophisticated statistical tools they could muster, the scholars studied murders in the state before and after the execution. They distinguished between felony-murders (killing a store clerk during an armed robbery, for example) and other murders (murders inside the family; or deaths during barroom brawls), which rarely get the death penalty. They found absolutely no deterrent effect. Indeed, their figures suggested the opposite: "an abrupt and lasting increase" in homicides in Oklahoma. But if you thought the increase would be in murders that qualify for the death penalty—brutal murder of a store clerk, for example—you would be wrong. The increase was in homicides in other situations, especially those "where the offender perceives having been wronged"; the paradigm case would be homicide stemming from a fight between two guys in a barroom.[71] Their study, they thought, gave some support to the brutalization thesis. Presumably executions act as some sort of a catalyst, unleashing dark and dangerous impulses, in at least a few people.

Both sides bring up heavy statistical artillery. Yet, in this vast society, murder is a rare event, and neither hypothesis seems convincing. To me, the death penalty seems morally repulsive. I find the brutalization thesis attractive—but (to be honest) not particularly plausible. Perhaps more American states will join the civilized world and the nineteen abolition states, and get rid of the death penalty once and for all. In any event, for all the reasons suggested, it is hard to believe that the current U.S. system has much impact at all, either as a deterrent or a brutalizer; that is, if you compare it to the rather harsh alternatives, like life imprisonment without parole. The current death penalty system is also "costly and inefficient." Arguably, it wastes "resources that could be expended on crime-fighting measures," like hiring more police.[72] The incredibly slow pace of executions reduces any possible deterrence, perhaps enough to make it meaningless. And, above all, the death penalty seems to make little difference; the deterrence curve for murder has basically flattened out.

The Role of Perception

So far, we have talked about deterrence (and incentives) as if what matters is what the law actually provides: so and so many years for burglary, such and such a bounty or reward for blowing the whistle, and so on. But, realistically, what deters people, or gives them incentives, is not the actual risk of getting caught and punished, or the actual chance of getting some kind of reward. Rather, it is perceived risks and benefits.

This point wouldn't matter if, say, perceived risk were the same as the actual risk. But this is probably almost never the case; some sort of gap, big or small, will almost always divide the two.[73] Recall the discussion about knowledge of law—or, for the most part, lack of knowledge. People (including me) simply do not know how many tax returns are audited and what happens to people who cheat. Pickpockets probably have no knowledge about how many pickpockets get caught and go to jail. A doctor surely has little or no idea (or the wrong idea) about how often patients bring malpractice cases; or how often plaintiffs win or lose; and what kind of damages are awarded. And different people undoubtedly have different perceptions of risk. People about to commit a crime, or thinking of it, may be more likely to feel they can get away with it than members of the law-abiding public. And, in fact, they might be right.

A great many people drink and drive. Only a tiny percentage get caught. Do drinking drivers know this? Perhaps they do. One study of college students showed that the subjects felt their chances of getting caught and arrested were very small.[74] On the other hand, did they know how the law defines "drunk"? In California, a blood alcohol level of 0.08 makes you (legally) drunk. Of course, nobody carries around equipment to measure blood alcohol levels. Still, if a person is very drunk, this fact must be obvious to him and to the rest of the world.

Perceptions can be changed or manipulated. When a city announces a crackdown on drunk driving or on drug pushers in a blaze of publicity, the campaign, at first, will usually produce results. The publicity tells drivers and pushers that the risks have gone up. But the studies also show that the effect peters out after a while.[75] The campaigns run out of steam, for one thing. The drivers and pushers begin to realize that the campaign is basically over. They readjust their perception of risk. If the back-off is less garishly obvious than the crackdown, there might be a residual effect, a long-term change in risk perception, which leads to a long-term deterrent effect.[76]

Drunk driving is a crime that, alas, millions of people commit. It is also a crime for amateurs. There are career burglars and career armed robbers, but nobody makes a living out of drunk driving (though there are, of course, repeat offenders). Professionals and amateurs tend to have different perceptions of risk. Professional criminals may dismiss or underestimate or ignore the risks of capture. The first-time shop-lifter may be terrified of capture and smell danger everywhere. The professional has a more realistic notion of risk. Not that amateurs are always the timid ones. Heavy smokers ignore or underestimate chances of lung cancer, emphysema, heart disease. Teenagers often dismiss or ignore risks of pregnancy or sexually transmitted diseases. Or perceptions of benefits (of cigarettes, or sex) outweigh any of the perceived risks. Perceptions of benefits are just as important as perceptions of risk. And they also may vary systematically. The nerd and the daredevil may both see very clearly the risks of hang-gliding or climbing Mount Everest. But they see the benefits with very different eyes.

Risk is not the same as uncertainty. Uncertainly can be a stronger deterrent than risk. Burglar A thinks it is risky to break into the house on Main Street. Burglar B simply has no idea what the risk might be. Burglar A might be more willing to go ahead than Burglar B. In many situations, people face total uncertainty, rather than some sort of calibration of risk. A campaign against drunk driving might increase perceptions of risk, or perceptions of gross uncertainty, or both. Drivers realize a crackdown is going on; but how serious will it be? How many police will be swarming on the streets? How many drivers will be caught? They have no idea.

In any event, perception is a crucial factor in determining impact. Perceptions of risk. Perceptions of benefits. This is true for burglars; for people who would like to cheat on their income tax; for drivers at a party considering another shot of whiskey; for everyone deciding whether to cross the bridge into a zone of illegality. The relationship between the "objective and subjective properties of punishment" is "one of the most crucial links in the deterrence process," but because it is not easy to get at, "it is the one we know the least about." There is, in fact, a growing but somewhat bewildering body of research on perceptions, mostly criminal perceptions.[77] Studies show a good deal of uncertainty and misinformation. In California, for example, "the public does not know very much about the maximum and minimum punishments . . . for different offenses"; prison inmates "were only slightly more informed" than the general public.[78] In one study, college students in Florida were asked whether they thought people who smoked marijuana were liable to be caught, and what the penalties were; they were also asked if they themselves smoked. The ones who didn't smoke thought the risks were higher than those who did.[79] David A. Anderson interviewed prison inmates in North Carolina and Kentucky between 1997 and 1999. Presumably all of them were guilty of a crime. The results are startling. Sixty-three percent "either did not think they would be apprehended or did not think about the possibility." Fifty-three percent "either did not know what the punishment would be if they were convicted or did not think about it." If you put these two groups together, you came out with 76 percent who lacked "at least one of the necessary conditions for making a rational response to punishment," and this does not include those whose behavior had not been rational because of "drugs, rage, psychosis, or heat-of-the-moment impulses."[80]

Kenneth D. Tunnell interviewed burglars and armed robbers who were doing time. These men too had had no clue about chances of getting caught or what the punishment might be. Nor did they spend much time thinking about these issues. Sixty percent of the juveniles and 56.7 percent of the young adults "never or occasionally worried about arrest." (Older adults were more savvy.) The subjects were equally naïve about punishment. One burglar, when asked, "Did you know you could get some time as a juvenile for burglary?" gave this as an answer: "Everybody told me . . . 'Hey, all they're going to give you [is] probation.'"[81] For offenders of this sort, it is not much use increasing punishment on paper (or even in practice); they either do not know or do not care. One study found "no significant association between perceptions of punishment levels and actual levels." The conclusion was (again) that either raising or lowering the (paper) punishment would have little or no impact on behavior.[82] But it is important to remember that actual burglars, armed robbers, and persistent drunk drivers, the subjects of these studies, are a kind of residue; the deterrence curve has flattened out, and they are all that is left.

Not all criminals, of course, are incorrigible, and not all are as ignorant as some studies suggest. Men and women who get caught, tried, convicted, and sent to prison undergo a kind of learning process. They find out, for example, what the "going rate" might be for certain crimes. Neal Shover studied career criminals; experience, he found, taught them quite a lot about the "definitions and penalty tables at the heart of the criminal code." As one prisoner put it, in jail "you learn a lot of things." Prisoners tell each other what the law can do to you, and what the law had done to them.[83]

Two Canadian criminologists conducted a telephone survey of some 1,900 people in Ontario, Canada.[84] They rather boldly asked people about violations of tax laws. For example, had they ever failed to report rental income on their returns? Or had they improperly deducted home office expenses? A fair number of people—a little less than one out of five—admitted doing at least one type of tax evasion. Then people were asked: Did they think tax evaders were likely to be caught? People who evaded taxes themselves (or at least admitted it) were more optimistic about their chances. They assessed the risks lower than the people who said they were clean. The non-evaders were also more likely to think they would suffer real punishment if caught.

It is not easy to know what to make of this type of study. You could conclude, for example, that the way you perceive certainty and severity has an effect on whether you are likely to go ahead and violate the law. But which way do the causal arrows go? These perceptions might be simply a story that tax evaders tell themselves (nobody will catch me); that is, the behavior molds the perceptions, and not the other way around. Same for the non-evaders. They think they might be caught and punished. Is this what deters them? Or are these perceptions the way they explain why they are so clean and law-abiding? A study of students in Pennsylvania (in the 1970s) that asked about shoplifting found that students who admitted shoplifting (and were not, in fact, caught) were also those who perceived "the least risk associated with shoplifting," that is, the least chance of getting caught and the least danger of getting serious punishment.[85] This fits in nicely with the Canadian study but, again, one wonders about the direction of the causal arrows.

In any event, exactly what are "perceptions" of risk? Do people really think about risk systematically? Do they actually make calculations of costs and benefits? What goes on in the heads of real burglars or armed robbers? Richard Wright and Scott Decker studied armed robbers in St. Louis. These robbers knew they ran a risk of capture and punishment, but they were mostly able to "push this thought out of their minds." Some were fatalistic. One of them, for example, said, "Well, if I go to prison, then I just go to prison." Others felt they were more or less safe. "Nine times out of ten you not gonna get caught." Still others felt trapped; they saw nothing else for them to do. Some would get high on liquor or drugs to avoid thinking about getting caught; the best way to avoid an "uncomfortably high level of mental anguish" was to "forget about the risk and leave matters to fate."[86] One "stick-up man" said he didn't "dwell on" the future: what was important to him was "getting mine" now; after all, "One day I might not wake up."[87]

Perceptions of risk may also vary by criminal "occupation." In David Anderson's study of inmates, he found that people who committed crimes likely to be repeated—burglary, for example—were more aware of risks than violent criminals, murderers, rapists, and the like, whose criminal acts were not in any sense a career.[88] Or, to put it another way, the less "rational" the crime, the more likely that the criminal did not know the risk, or didn't care, or discounted it. The deterrence curves for these crimes have already flattened out to a considerable degree. That means, of course, that most of us have already been deterred, or (more likely) that most of us would never dream of becoming a burglar or an arsonist or a rapist. For most of us, risk perception makes very little difference. It might matter for jaywalking or pulling the tag off a mattress, but not for major crimes. Even if the state decided not to punish armed robbery, most of us (I hope) would not get a gun and rush out to clean out the till of the nearest convenience store.

Where do perceptions of risk come from? As we said, for people with criminal records, some of it might come from bitter experience. For many of us, what we read about or see on television or on the web might be one source. In a way, this is unfortunate because, as we pointed out, the media systematically distort news about the legal system. On deterrence and perception of risk, it is hard to know which way the distortion works. Publicity exaggerates the number and result of malpractice cases and trumpets the few huge verdicts; this may have a real effect on the minds of doctors. They wildly exaggerate the number of claims and lawsuits. A study showed that only 4 percent of injuries led to malpractice claims; doctors thought the percentage was 45 percent. Perhaps this perception might lead doctors to practice "defensive medicine" or avoid high-risk procedures or high-risk patients.[89] The misperceptions, however, surely helped nurture the "tort reform" movement, which had some notable successes in state legislatures.[90] News reports may lead people to think that more criminals are caught and punished than is actually the case; or, conversely, that many criminals escape punishment because the law is slow or inefficient, or because criminal defendants have too many "rights," and so on.

Risk perceptions also change over time, both in general and for particular individuals and groups. They can get updated. I have already mentioned the process of resetting.[91] "Criminally naïve individuals" assess their chances of getting caught higher than "experienced offenders." If these "naïve individuals" go on to have a "criminal career," they can adjust their perceptions upward or downward: upward if they get caught; downward if they find that the risk of getting caught "is lower than they initially expected." Perceptions, then, can vacillate, wobbling up and down, depending on the way a life of crime turns out.[92]

Phantom Deterrence

Deterrence, as we pointed out, is a matter of perception. The actual threat is not as important as the perceived threat. In the 1970s, New York tried to reduce crime on the subways by throwing more police at the problem. A study of this campaign also found a "phantom effect," meaning "deterrence caused by a police activity that is not actually present." Crime decreased even when the extra police were not around, because people thought they were there; they had an "incorrect perception of the threat of apprehension."[93] Homeowners sometimes try to enlist the phantom effect: they post signs warning of burglar alarms (or dogs). Burglars, they hope, will not bother to test whether the signs are telling the truth.

The phantom effect is probably more common than one would imagine. After all, most of us—almost all of us, in fact—have no idea how often drunk drivers are arrested, how often pickpockets are caught, how many tax returns are audited every year. What people think about their chances of getting caught and punished is, as we have seen, extremely variable; the ignorance factor is enormous. The Internal Revenue Service, with a lot of noise and publicity, sometimes cracks down on a few taxpayers to give the rest of us an exaggerated idea of IRS muscle and the frequency of audit. In Senegal, in the battle against female genital mutilation, the phantom effect made a difference. People who were interviewed could not cite any cases of actual enforcement, but "rumors or imaginings of enforceability generated fear of prosecution."[94] The phantom effect is probably relatively unstable. When the truth comes out, if it does, the effect will tend to disappear.

Plain, ordinary bluffing can produce a kind of phantom effect. Keith Hawkins, in a study of pollution control in England, found that field officers, faced with polluters who do not cooperate, can threaten to use "procedures or sanctions they do not intend to employ" or that "are not theirs—legally—to use." Bluffing works, too, because the polluters really do not know or understand the law or what the actual penalties are. This allows the development of a "socially manufactured form of deterrence."[95] These field inspectors are surely not the only regulators who take advantage of the fact that their subjects are ignorant of the law; this ignorance opens the door to rich possibilities for bluffing.

Punishment: The Delivery Systems

The technology of enforcement obviously makes a big difference in fighting crime, and with regard to business regulation. Enforcement is heavily dependent on institutional arrangements. When we think about impact, we think about enforcement; and when we think about enforcement, we think about the police, detectives, jails, trials, and the whole vast apparatus of criminal justice. On the civil side, we think about lawsuits, administrative agencies and their inspectors, auditors, field staff, and the like. Laws do not enforce themselves. This last statement needs to be qualified a bit. In a sense, they do—insofar as people voluntarily submit themselves to the yoke of law. I talked about three clusters of motives that mediate and influence impact. The first was rewards and punishments; the second is the influence of the peer group; the third, the internal sense of right and wrong. "Voluntary submission" will come under the second or the third cluster of motives. Later chapters will take these matters up. These factors—peer group and moral sense—are extremely significant. No modern society depends entirely or even mostly on force to get people to obey the rules. But, by the same token, no modern society can do without some sort of police force or the equivalent, or without inspectors and at least spot checks to make sure businesses behave.

In fact, every modern society has a vast army of inspectors who swarm over the legal landscape monitoring and enforcing an enormous regulatory apparatus: food and drug laws; clean water and clean air laws; occupational safety and health laws; building codes; securities laws; transportation safety rules; licensing of doctors, lawyers, architects, accountants, and many other occupations. And every major regulatory law has its criminal side. Willful or blatant violators can be punished. The main enforcement thrust is through noncriminal means, but the threat of criminal process remains a possibility.

Criminal justice today is also heavily dependent on forensic technology: fingerprints, analysis of blood and fibers, ballistic science, radar, breathalyzer tests, DNA, and so on.[96] These can be, in some cases, decisive: DNA in criminal cases, or on issues of paternity. Societies decide how much to invest in enforcement. They can hire more policemen or make do with less. Governments can invest in forensic labs or not. It can employ thousands of tax auditors or cut back on this investment. There is a tremendous amount of private investment, too. Much of this is deterrent and preventive: locks, burglar alarms, bright lights, encryption. Everywhere, too, there are private security guards, usually big, overweight men who stand around in jewelry stores and other places that think they need protection. There are gated communities; there are buildings with doormen; not to mention metal detectors in banks, office buildings, airports, and courthouses. Both public and private investment levels are, of course, not static. In the 1950s, panic over violent crime led to massive increases in money spent on enforcement, public and private. Money poured into police budgets and for private security guards. There was a period of frenzied construction of prisons and more prisons. In the world of today, governments spend billions of dollars in the struggle against terrorists and terrorism. Many billions are spent on airports alone, to prevent terrorists from hijacking airplanes.[97]

It is very difficult—maybe impossible—to know the real impact of all this investment on the crime rate. That rate, notoriously, goes up and down like the stock market. In the United States, there was a bulge in violent crime from the 1950s into the 1990s, but the rate has been falling in recent years—dramatically so, in New York City and other places.[98] The exact causes are completely obscure. But then again, the spike in violent crime, in the second half of the twentieth century, had been equally mysterious.

The criminal justice system in the United States is quite severe, compared to other developed countries—Europe, Japan, Australia, and New Zealand. No European country still has the death penalty. Even American states without the death penalty hand out long, draconian sentences to convicted criminals. Conditions are harsh in many American prisons. American convicts are, in general, treated worse than prisoners in, say, Sweden or Germany.[99] And punishment, as we saw, continues when the prisoner gets out: ex-cons lose privileges (like voting); and they have a tough time recycling into respectable society.

Still, many people in the United States are sure that the system, if anything, is too mild; too much mollycoddling of prisoners. Technical rules, ideas about due process, doctrines like the Miranda warning, and so on: these are not popular (insofar as people know about them at all). Misguided Supreme Court decisions and toothless law enforcement are blamed by some people for what they see as an epidemic of high crime.[100] Actually, the impact of, say, the Miranda rule, is extremely hard to measure. It is almost surely less than most people assume, either way—that is, whether it opened the door to more crime and tied the hands of the police or whether it led to better and more humane interrogation methods. Perhaps it had little or no effect at all.[101] As anybody who has read this far is aware, it is hard enough to figure out the direct impact of a rule like *Miranda*; and, for the indirect impact, almost impossible.

The Miranda warning is still somewhat controversial. But so is police behavior in general—in particular, the treatment of minorities, especially African Americans. This is at the bottom of the dispute over "stop and frisk" techniques, that is, the "controversial practice of stop, question and search," which began in New York City in 2002, but is surely older and more widespread.[102] In recent years, there has been scandal after scandal over the use of excessive force, sometimes deadly force, against African Americans who seemed to pose no real threat to the police. Outrage in the African American community led to the Black Lives Matter movement and to demands for change in many cities. That the police in many cities engage in racial profiling and unfairly target members of minority groups seems clear. And the excessive use of force also seems clear. Police officers tend to be clannish, to stick together, to resent outside interference, and they react defensively to criticism, whether by courts, politicians, independent review boards—or by the public. No question, of course, that the police play a vital role in enforcing the law. But there are costs and side effects that flow from police misbehavior, in the United States and surely in other countries as well.

Recently, the technology of surveillance has gotten dramatically— some would say catastrophically—better. What can be done, and is done, in real life goes beyond some of the worst nightmares of science fiction. Yet, on the whole, people put up with surveillance, even in staunchly democratic societies, and despite the rising power of norms of privacy and autonomy. People accept metal detectors in courthouses and government buildings, security lines in airports; by now, these are simply part of the landscape. They also accept the beady eyes of cameras watching, watching, watching, on street corners and in banks, and in the lobbies of apartment buildings. They even accept—though this is more controversial—scanning and tracking of email, phone conversations, and Internet traffic. All this in the name of "wars" on terror and crime—especially the "war" on terror. The attack on the World Trade Center in New York in 2001 was something of a turning point. Since then, the perceived threat of terror has ebbed and flowed, but it hangs in the air like a bad smell. This is, of course, not only or even primarily an American issue. There were terrorist attacks in Bali, in Madrid, in London, in Mumbai, and elsewhere; most recently (November 2015) in Paris and (March 2016) in Brussels. England outdoes the United States in its passion for surveillance cameras. Every developed country is fighting its own version of the war on terror, and many less-developed countries as well, Nigeria and Kenya, for example.

Technology is an eye that never sleeps. It can record every flutter of a butterfly's wing. There are tiny local "bugs" and miniature cameras; satellites patrol the sky. Perhaps in the future, cameras will track the progress of every car driving on streets and highways. They will pick up and record all violations of the speed limit, and every drunk driver. They will photograph every license plate and check the film against a computerized record. A computer will spit out a notice, automatically imposing a fine, and automatically mail it to the address of the driver in question. All this, perhaps, without any human input. Other cameras or devices might note every time a driver is parked even one minute overtime at a parking meter. Technology would make possible something undreamt of before, 100 percent enforcement of certain rules.

Whether people would like living in this kind of society is another question. We are used to a world of imperfect impact, where, most of the time, we can get away with minor infractions. Technology can give us a regime of total impact; an era in which noncompliance with certain rules becomes downright impossible. Most people, I imagine, will not think of this as Utopia.

Personality and Impact

Earlier, we mentioned the work of William Chambliss, who drew a distinction between expressive and instrumental acts. Chambliss's work focused on the nature of the crime. But one could also focus on the actor, the criminal himself. Some violators simply seem wildly irrational. Some crimes occur on the spur of the moment. A barroom brawl erupts, both parties are more or less drunk, a gun is drawn, or a knife; somebody needlessly dies. Anger is an emotion that can bring out the worst in a person: "thoughts of future consequences vanish under high emotional arousal."[103] Alcohol and drugs, too, are deadly enemies of any "thoughts of future consequences." Some violators, however, plan their acts meticulously: cold-blooded killers, professional hit men, crafty embezzlers who carefully disguise their thievery. Or even an armed robber, who stalks what looks like good prey.

Criminologists often emphasize how personality type relates to criminal behavior. This even crops up in the work of Gary Becker, whose 1968 article is a kind of classic on the economics of crime. Becker talks about "risk preferrers" and "risk avoiders."[104] Michael Gottfredson and Travis Hirschi, in an important book,[105] argue that criminals are, on the whole, impulsive people, people with low self-control, people who live in the present, people who are not rational calculators (at least with regard to anything past the immediate present). Criminal acts, they argue, provide "immediate gratification of desires." Many crimes are risky, exciting; they take little skill in planning, and they provide "few or meager long-term benefits."[106] A person who fits the profile—impulsive, with low self-control—is obviously harder to deter than a cautious, guarded person, someone who looks before he leaps. These impulsive men and women are the ones who still misbehave, even when the deterrence curve has largely flattened out.

The theories of Gottfredson and Hirschi have been much discussed by other scholars (sometimes quite critically). Their notions have a certain appeal. People come in all shapes and sizes, psychologically speaking. That the impact of a rule, law, or directive varies depending on personality type, as well as by time, place, and culture, seems almost too obvious. The problem is where to go with this notion. And how far to go. Gottfredson and Hirschi call their book *A General Theory of Crime*. No doubt low self-control explains a lot, but surely not everything. Per-Olof Wikström and Kye Treiber argue that "the ability to exercise self-control" is relevant only for people who are thinking about whether or not to commit a crime. Most people never consider breaking the law; others "commit some acts of crime out of habit (without deliberating)."[107] A person does not need self-control to avoid eating eggplant if she can't stand eggplant; she needs self-control only when faced with, say, ice cream. Moral considerations (our third cluster of motives for compliance), rather than self-control, explain much more than impulsiveness, self-control, inability to defer gratification. Gottfredson and Hirschi also dismiss the idea of peer pressure as a causal factor, say, in adolescent crime, but there is evidence that peers are a significant factor.[108] Gottfredson and Hirschi insist that their theory is "general," but how well does it fit most white-collar criminals?[109]

Sally Simpson and Nicole Leeper Piquero, in a study of MBA students and executives attending an MBA program, tried to test the Gottfredson and Hirschi theory, as applied to business offenders. Their conclusion (based on responses to vignettes) was contrary to the "image of the corporate criminal as someone who is impulsive, risk-taking, and shortsighted." Rather, he was a "rational calculator" who commits his crimes "to achieve personal and organization gains," and is aware of the risks. Moreover, the organization is a site of "socialization," where people learn how to "fit in, go along to get along, and succeed."[110] This sounds plausible but, of course, this was not a study of actual behavior.

The Gottfredson–Hirschi theory is a theory of personality. One can ask, how do claims about the role of personality fit in with claims about the role of "culture." *Culture* is a troublesome word, with many meanings, some of them controversial. I use the term here in the sense of a bundle of traits that are old, deep-seated, and mark a particular society or group like a tattoo etched into their very skin. People claim, for example, that Americans are litigious, and that the Japanese avoid conflict and love harmony and mediation. Statements of this sort are not only about culture; they are statements, too, about impact in particular societies. If, for "cultural" reasons, people do or do not "stick up for their rights," this has an important effect on the impact of the law creating those rights. It is perfectly clear that cultures do vary; the French are not like the English, or the Japanese, in many ways (though similar in other ways). But it is easy to carry arguments from culture too far. Is it really true that the Japanese, because of their culture, shy away from litigation, and prefer mediation, compromise, conciliation? Perhaps, but some scholars scoff at this notion. Litigation rates in Japan, they argue, are held down artificially by legal structures and institutions, and not by anything that deserves the name of *culture*.[111] And whether Americans are actually "litigious" (whatever that might mean) is exceedingly doubtful.

The realities are also important; that is, whether legal institutions (courts, for example) are honest and efficient or otherwise. Even a "litigious" person will avoid a corrupt court that she feels will rule against her. Kathryn Hendley used focus groups to study urban Russians, who faced various problems—for example, people who lived in apartment buildings with water that leaked into their flats from a neighbor's place.[112] Obviously, there are many ways to respond to this problem. You can ignore the leak. You can try to work things out with the neighbor (a form of self-help). There are also lawyers, courts, and housing authorities. In Russia, people distrust the courts (probably for good reason), but they also use them from time to time. People also know that clout matters—whom you know and where their influence lies. Some people will try to attack the problem vigorously, using whatever means they have at hand. Others give up and let it slide. There is no single pattern of response. Structure, culture—and personality—determine the response; also, what rung you are on in the social ladder. And all of these factors, though analytically distinct, are clearly interrelated. After all, the structures of a society (its political and legal system) are profoundly influenced by the society's culture, and vice versa.

Gottfredson and Hirschi do not claim that low self-control explains everything. They also stress opportunity. A careless person leaves the keys in his car, plainly visible. Mr. Low-Self-Control passes by, looks in the car window, and decides to steal the car. The empty house with an open window invites the local burglar. Low-hanging fruit, but not everybody will pluck it from a neighbor's tree. Still, on the whole, Gottfredson and Hirschi put their money on a particular cluster of psychological traits. Surely psychology makes a difference; some people are timid, some are aggressive, some are passive, some are active. Some are risk-averse; some are not. Some are impulsive; some are not. Some think in long-range terms, planning their futures; some (especially young people) live only in the present. Floyd Feeney's study of California robbers found that more than half "did no planning at all" before embarking on robberies; the crimes for these men were "impulsive, spur-of-the-moment" events.[113] Personality may be important in civil cases, too. Neil Vidmar and Regina Schuller did a series of studies in Canada. They tried to measure clusters of traits (aggressiveness, for example, and a taste for risk) that they bundled together into a score for "claim propensity." People with high "claim propensity" in their psychic makeup did, in fact, make more claims than people without these traits.[114]

Greg Pogarsky and others, discussing deterrence, range people along a kind of continuum. At one end are "acute conformists"; these are the ones who will comply with the law, come hell or high water. At the other end are the "incorrigibles"; these people will be violators, willy-nilly. In the middle are the "deterrables," who could go either way. Deterrence, so the argument goes, only works on this middle group.[115] The trick, of course, is to find out who falls into each group. And one can ask: What is it that makes the "acute conformist" so law-abiding? Not fear of punishment—at least not fear of punishment alone. Crucial factors might be peer pressure, or the inward bite of conscience; the second and third of our three clusters, which we will deal with separately.

How far can we take Gottfredson and Hirschi's theory, or any of the other theories about the sources of criminality? Whether a general, universal theory of criminality is feasible at all is an open question. In any event, any general theory has to be able to solve four puzzles. The first is why crime is something men do, and women (on the whole) do not. In developed countries, today, women have caught up with men in college attendance; they are doctors, lawyers, members of Congress. A woman president is a distinct possibility. But a woman burglar is (generally speaking) not in the cards. Why are women so far behind in crime? The second puzzle is: Why is crime, on the whole, a young man's game? Most crimes do not require physical strength or youthful vigor. Many career criminals even give up crime as they age, but why? The third puzzle is the historical puzzle: Why do crime rates (insofar as we can measure them) vary so much over time? Violent crime went down in the nineteenth century, slowly up in the twentieth, jumped fantastically from the 1950s to the 1990s, then started coming down: for what reason? This pattern seemed to hold in a number of countries—Sweden, for example—and not just the United States.[116] The fourth is the geographical puzzle or, if you will, the culture puzzle. Why does Finland (for example) have so much less violent crime than the United States?

Do any of the theories floating about solve the four puzzles mentioned? With regard to age, the issue is not the "biological process of aging" (unless you want to argue about testosterone levels), but rather the "socially constructed and negotiated changes in perspectives which accompany aging."[117] Often enough, men decide to give up crime as they get older, a decision "triggered by a shock of some sort." One ex-prisoner, when interviewed, indicated he gave up the life when a rain of police bullets killed his partner. Wives and jobs account for some of these decisions; wives and jobs give ex-cons emotional and financial alternatives to crime. Some men simply realize that "they are wasting time and ruining their lives."[118] Some offenders get religion. The lives of some men spin downward, but their pathologies no longer include crime. Some of the street people Mark Fleisher studied had become totally addicted to drugs and alcohol and, more or less, gave up on life. For homeless alcoholics, going to prison is a "serious deterrent." They cannot "risk being deprived of access to alcohol and drugs."[119]

Attempts have been made to solve the puzzle of the gender gap in terms of Gottfredson and Hirschi's theory. Women in many societies are (for whatever reason) less impulsive than men, more in control of themselves; in addition, men exert control over women, so that women have fewer chances to go wrong. Women could hardly contribute much to the crime rate in Saudi Arabia, where they cannot even drive cars. Teresa LaGrange and Robert Silverman studied young people in the Canadian city of Edmonton. They could explain a lot of the differences between the tendency of men to deviate, and the tendency of women, in terms of variables that measured self-control, opportunity, and the interaction between these factors. A lot, but not all, of the differences. The authors felt "there is something about being male or female that persists in predicting real and substantial differences in behavior."[120] This is quite possibly correct. I suspect, though, that the differences that count are cultural, not genetic or biological.

The other puzzles are, I think, even more difficult to solve. The United States is a relatively violent country. You hear talk about the frontier tradition as a possible explanation. But why Dodge City, Kansas, and Tombstone, Arizona, should have an impact on crime rates today in Detroit, Michigan, is hard for me to see. And England and Japan, to pick two examples, were at one time very violent societies; at some point, the violence simply stopped. So much for the history puzzle. The culture puzzle is also difficult to solve. Some people think men are naturally more violent because of the Y chromosome; but this explanation, whatever its virtue, founders on the rock of national culture. There is, after all, the same chromosome in the bodies of men in Helsinki as in New York—or Caracas. Hard to argue, too, that some personality traits are so fundamentally criminogenic that they apply across the board, to all societies, all cultures.[121]

Probably no current theory can solve our four riddles. Crime rates are too complex to lend themselves to prediction. We can maybe say some things about why some crimes occur at some times, or some places, or the impact of criminal justice systems here and there. Possibly we could explain why Honduras is so violent today, and why modern Japan, despite the samurai past (and the rape of Nanking), is so nonviolent. But to go further is a little bit like the task of predicting next year's weather, or the next big earthquake; that is, beyond our present capabilities.

Deterrence: Some Summary Thoughts

What have we learned from the reams of studies on deterrence? The basic theory seems solid. It fits economic theory, not to mention common sense. Raise the level of punishment, and more compliance follows. Jack up the level of incentives, and you get a better response. But the evidence is weaker than the theory. Daniel S. Nagin summed up the scholarship in a long and learned article published in 2013. His conclusion: deterrence is real, but its effects are terrifically variable, "ranging in size from seemingly null to very large." Existing studies are often flawed, statistically or otherwise; and, despite the huge volume of work, there are still important gaps in both theory and research.[122]

We might ask: Why has so much effort produced so little consensus? What accounts for the disarray? One answer is the deterrence curve. I used overtime parking to describe the curve. Here was a pure form of deterrence. Nobody, after all, thinks overtime parking is a crime of moral turpitude, and there is no peer-group effect worth mentioning.

There is, as we said, a deterrence curve for every crime or offense. The curve for rape is quite different from the curve for overtime parking. Most men in modern societies are (we hope) "acute conformists." They do not and will not rape women; they consider rape an unspeakable crime. The punishment is, thus, pretty much irrelevant to the vast majority, except (maybe) as a statement that society takes rape quite seriously.[123] The same is true for murder, arson, and armed robbery. These are, for most people, indefensible, horrendous, and, therefore, unthinkable. Even before we tinker with actual levels of punishment, the curve has pretty much flattened out. In this society at least; and in most developed countries.

This, then, is the second general conclusion: deterrence works, when it works, only on people who might conceivably commit some particular crime. These are the "deterrables," the folks in the middle of the continuum between the undeterrables and the total conformists. Most people, in fact, "refrain from crime . . . not because they fear the consequences but because they do not see crime . . . as an 'action alternative.'" People start out with a menu of "action alternatives"; only afterward do they "make their choices."[124] And crime may not be (for most people) an "action alternative." What to do Saturday night? A movie, maybe, or watching TV, or making love. But robbing a convenience store, no. It is not a viable "action alternative."

The words quoted in the last paragraph come from a study that actually tried to examine this continuum. The subjects were young people in the city of Peterborough (United Kingdom). They were asked about "self-reported criminality" (for example, had they "punched, stabbed, kicked or head-butted someone" in the last year). They were also asked whether they felt tempted to do these acts, or some other offenses. Some of the subjects were "crime prone," and some were "crime averse." Deterrence had no relevance to those who were "crime averse." It worked, if it worked at all, only on those who were "crime prone." And for these "crime prone" people, it worked if they thought there was a high risk of getting caught and punished.

All this seems rather obvious; and, indeed, it is. For the worst and most grievous crimes, the deterrence curve flattens out fairly quickly; most people are "crime averse" to begin with. These stellar crimes are, at the same time, both easiest and hardest to deter. Easiest, in that social norms and moral issues have already done most of the work. Hardest, because reaching the few who are still undeterred is a daunting task. Murderers are a rare breed. Terror bombers are even rarer. Plane hijackers probably the rarest of all. Rare, but hard to identify, reach, and deter. Perhaps, in the end, impossible.

This does not mean that the murder rate, say, is flat; that it never changes. It changes a great deal. It goes up, it goes down. Currently, in the United States, the murder rate is down—dramatically, in some cities. In Honduras or Venezuela, on the other hand, the rate has gone through the roof. But in each case, causes and effects are complex, and sometimes unknowable.

6

REWARDS AND PUNISHMENTS: INCENTIVES AND THE CIVIL SIDE

THE REWARD HALF of the team of rewards and punishment seems on the surface not to loom as large in the law as punishments. But this might be, and probably is, an illusion. Thousands of studies of crime and punishment talk about deterrence. Studies about the rest of the law, the noncriminal part of law, dwarf the studies on the criminal side. But my impression is that studies on this side talk less about rewards and punishments, at least explicitly, and least of all about incentives. But these are everywhere. They come in all sorts of forms. The most obvious incentive is money—cold, hard cash. During the nineteenth century, Colorado (for example) gave a bounty to anybody who killed a wolf: $1.25, to be exact. To collect, you needed to bring in the scalp with the ears intact.[1] That was in the bad old days, before there were laws about endangered species. (Today, killing a wolf is probably generally a crime.) Money rewards are sprinkled throughout the codes of law. But not all incentives are money. A soldier can win a medal for bravery. A scientist can win the Nobel Prize. Drugstore employees who work hard can be named "employee of the month" and have their picture displayed on the wall. Civil servants who do well get promoted; and they might get the corner office, the one with the windows, as well.

Very often, saving money is the incentive, or at least not paying it out. A tax credit is a common policy device. In the United States, Canada, and the United Kingdom, gifts to charities result in tax breaks. In the United States, taxpayers can deduct these gifts from income on their tax returns, and charitable gifts are exempt from estate tax on death. All this almost surely stimulates gifts to charity. A homeowner can deduct mortgage payments (unlike rent) from his tax return; this subsidy is worth billions to homeowners, homebuilders, homebuyers, not to mention the indirect benefit to carpenters, masons, and plumbers. Health is another powerful benefit. Safety rules save lives. People buckle up their seat belts and quit smoking to safeguard their health.

Practically any rule in the legal system can be analyzed in terms of incentives or disincentives. American companies have to carry workers' compensation insurance; the more accidents they avoid, the lower the premiums. Seat belt rules, and traffic laws in general, stimulate careful driving and lead (one hopes) to fewer accidents. On the other hand, a plaintiff in a tort case, if she has to go to court, faces all sorts of technical barriers (and costs). These are real disincentives. They are one reason why the tip of the tort pyramid is so pointy. A zoning ordinance in a city stops a landowner from making big money by selling his land to a leather-tanning factory. But it helps keep up the value of the land of the landowner's neighbors. No-fault divorce makes divorce cheaper and easier to get. But it is not, after all, absolutely free; and for some people, even a small fee is beyond their means.

Rules of law, in general, channel behavior along certain lines. If you want to leave your money to a favorite nephew, or to a charity, or a friend, you have to make out a will (or use some functional equivalent). The law specifies how to make out a will—what formalities to follow. The same for divorce, for buying a house, for patenting your invention. You need to follow the rules. Whether the rules actually work as incentives or disincentives is (as always) an empirical question. Do medical malpractice rules cause "defensive" medicine and the overuse of CAT scans?[2] Do easy divorce laws hurt family structure? (Probably not.) Do patent laws actually stimulate innovation? Do copyright laws stifle or promote creativity?

On the literal use of incentives, there has been a certain amount of research. Some researchers have tried, experimentally, to see if incentives in schools can get students to study harder or get better grades.

Paying kids money seems to make a difference, in the short run at least.[3] But is giving the incentives to teachers more potent than giving the incentive to the students? And do girls respond differently from boys? Nobody doubts the power of incentives—especially big ones. For a million dollars, we would do all sorts of things that we would not do otherwise. Government could clearly spend its way to greater compliance, but how much would it cost, and compliance with what rules? Students in a psych experiment might respond to the lure of a dollar or two; getting people to stop smoking or to lose fifty pounds is another matter.

Incentives are also used to encourage "whistle-blowing." People who "blow the whistle" and report illegal behavior can win a money reward. Under the federal False Claims Act, if someone reveals that government contractors are making fraudulent claims, she is entitled to a slice of the money the government can claw back from the contractor.[4] The Internal Revenue Service has a bounty program for whistle-blowers. For a century or so, the bounty was quite stingy; few people collected. The law was changed in 2006; now whistle-blowers get between 15 and 30 percent of the proceeds, at least for big recoveries (more than $2 million). Bounties for smaller recoveries are at the discretion of the Service.[5] Whistle-blowers might be employees of a company or agency, or members of the general public. To avoid disincentives, bounty laws try to protect whistle-blowers from retaliation by their bosses.

Even so, a whistle-blower's life is not always easy. His job might be precarious. Fellow workers might consider him a snitch. Are there cultural propensities to blow the whistle, or not? Yuval Feldman and Orly Lobel have suggested that Americans are more willing to report illegal conduct than Israelis; this might be, they thought, because the ethos of Americans is more "individualistic." Gender was also a factor in their study.[6] In close-knit groups—a sports team, for example, or a youth gang—"the stigma as a traitor . . . is more powerful than the instinct to do what's right."[7] "Going outside" the group is deeply resented. The same is true for groups like the Amish, or the ultra-Orthodox Jewish community in New York, or, for that matter, the hierarchy in the Catholic Church.

Whistle-blowing can be controversial and, at times, even dangerous. Particularly dangerous, to be sure, in autocratic or corrupt societies. But not only there. Edward Snowden blew the whistle on what he considered government misconduct in the United States, in June 2013—illegal surveillance, for example. Some people consider him a hero. The government insists he broke the law. It has branded him a traitor, and accused him of treasonous behavior. He is currently a fugitive, living in Russia.[8] Moreover, rewards for whistle-blowing can even, at times, be counterproductive—by virtue of the so-called "crowding out" effect, which I discuss later.[9] There is also, of course, a powerful norm in many situations against "snitching." The norm is strongest, no doubt, between social equals: snitching on another kid in class will complicate life for the snitch. In prison, the snitch is a hated figure; an inmate who snitches on another inmate is unlikely to live very long. Also, as I suggested, fellow workers in a business might not appreciate a whistle-blower, especially if scandal might threaten their jobs.

Offering a reward for informing also tempts people to tell lies to get the reward. This problem plagues and contaminates the use of informants in the criminal justice system. Prosecutors often offer a deal to one suspect if he will testify against another suspect—a chance to "walk away," or face a lesser charge.[10] Prosecutors benefit—they get more convictions; but at what cost? False convictions can come out of this kind of jailhouse tattling. Yet law enforcement relies heavily on snitches, men who "rat" on offenders and help out the prosecution. They are notoriously unreliable, but they earn rich rewards, including massive reductions in sentences.[11]

Despite these issues, societies do make use of rewards for citizen complaints—against businesses, or against the government itself. In China, for example, some local authorities began to reward locals who gave tipoffs about polluters. In China, law enforcement has been notoriously weak; powerful business interests can make a mockery of food safety laws, rules about air and water pollution, and the like. The reward program seemed successful, so much so that it went national, with a system of "hotlines." The central government "introduced a general rewards system" for citizens who submitted "valid complaints and comments."[12]

A newspaper account in April 2014 describes a scheme in Slovakia to improve enforcement of rules about value-added taxes. The government enlisted consumers in the battle to make merchants comply with the rules.[13] Ordinary citizens were asked to collect receipts for products they bought, and register these receipts with the government. Registration was a kind of lottery ticket; citizens who registered receipts had a chance to win a car, or a big bundle of cash (10,000 euros in awards each month), or an appearance on a popular TV show. Citizens registered millions of receipts. The point was to find out which sellers were tax-cheaters. And, in fact, tax collection went up in Slovakia, perhaps because of the lottery. Other countries—Portugal is one—are planning or using similar schemes.

Studies in behavioral economics suggest that people respond differently to the risk of losing, compared to the chance of winning. People "hate losses. . . . Roughly speaking, losing something makes you twice as miserable as gaining the same thing makes you happy." This has been corroborated in lab experiments.[14] The idea, of course, suggests that incentives and disincentives influence impact in different ways. Another powerful influence on impact is the so-called default position. An employer offers dental benefits for, say, $30 per month. If the employee does nothing, he is automatically enrolled. But if she wants out, she has to fill out a form. Most workers take the benefit. A different employer takes the opposite position: to enroll, you have to fill out a form; otherwise, you do not get the benefit. Here, fewer workers will be covered. Richard Thaler and Cass Sunstein, in their study of "nudges," illustrate the point with the case of magazine subscriptions. If renewal is "automatic, many people will subscribe . . . to magazines they don't read."[15]

Can your organs be harvested after you die? This is up to you, but the default rule makes a huge difference. If the law says your body parts can be harvested after your death unless you opt out, more kidneys and corneas will be available than if you have to opt in.[16] A store can quote the price of some object with sales tax included in the asking price; or announce the pre-tax price, and add the sales tax later. People pay less attention if the tax has "low salience" (it gets added on after the sale); if the tax goes up, they do not change their buying habits. "High salience" has the opposite effect.[17] Of course, "salience" has no effect on the real after-tax price, but it has an influence on consumer behavior.

Default positions are, in fact, ubiquitous in the legal system. Take the issue of disposing of your assets when you die. The probate code instructs people on making out a will. It also contains an intestacy statute:

this is the default position. If you fail to make out a will (or some legal equivalent), the property will go according to the statutory scheme. Everybody, then, who makes out a valid will is choosing to use the law and turning down the default position. Anybody who executes a deed, or, for that matter, anybody who writes out a check is choosing to follow the forms. A couple that applies for a marriage license, or a person who files for divorce, is bypassing a default position; default positions strongly influence the choices people make.

You can, of course, analyze default provisions in terms of punishments (or disincentives). Unless you get a marriage license and go through the formalities, you cannot have the legal benefits of marriage. The same is true for the benefits of a will, a copyright for your novel, or a patent for your ingenious new gimmick. Or you can talk in terms of ways to channel behavior, or in terms of use and nonuse. But in any case, the results are the same: defaults are powerful tools that influence impact. After all, people are careless, forgetful, and subject to the drag of inertia. A rich man without a will may be a man who somehow "never got around to it," or kept thinking, I will do it mañana. That tomorrow never comes.

Carrots and Sticks

A complex modern legal system has at its disposal a whole menu of carrots and sticks. In the hundreds and hundreds of pages of the Internal Revenue Code, for example, are dozens and dozens of tax breaks, loopholes, exceptions, and exceptions to exceptions. Governments award contracts to low bidders (or to favored companies). They also award medals and prizes. There are pensions for civil servants, and for retired members of the armed forces. The welfare state offers all sorts of benefits: unemployment compensation, pensions, education, medical care. Bankruptcy laws hold the promise of second chances. It would be hard to argue that a modern legal system uses more sticks than carrots. The modern state also provides important benefits, like public education, health care, and unemployment compensation.

The civil side, of course, is not just about incentives. It is about detriments, as well; one might as well call these punishments. Punishments increase the cost of behavior. The civil side of the law is full of disincentives, rules, and doctrines that, deliberately or not, discourage certain behavior. So-called Pigovian taxes are meant to cut down demand for bad products by making them more expensive. A heavy tax on cigarettes or whiskey would (hopefully) reduce the number of smokers or drinkers. A pollution tax might have a similar effect on pollution. Behavior can also be "punished," in a way, by making it slow and difficult. Red tape and bureaucratic hassle are powerful disincentives, whether or not this is the actual intention.

It is not always easy to tell the difference between a carrot and a stick. The difference, in fact, might be nothing more than the manner of framing or wording. Suppose there is a rule, in Country X, that all noncitizens living in the country must register at a state office on or before April 1. Those who register late will have to pay a fee of $100. But the order could also be phrased this way: noncitizens must register and pay a fee of $100; those who register on or before April 1 are excused from paying the fee. From an economic standpoint, these two arrangements are exactly the same. One uses a carrot, one uses a stick, or so it seems. In fact, the two arrangements might not feel the same; people are likely to look more kindly at the discount than at the fee.

As mentioned, studies suggest strongly that people might look differently at alternative ways of stating a rule. This is not just as a matter of "framing." Punishment, we are often told, does not work as well as "positive reinforcement," which is not necessarily money. Of course, this is a tendency, not an iron law of nature. A very harsh punishment might overwhelm a skinny incentive and have more impact. How a reward or a punishment feels is, of course, an important factor in determining impact. A masochist might enjoy twenty lashes on his bare back; most people would hate this. Going to jail is not a reward, although on a subzero day in Minnesota, a homeless person might prefer a jail cell to life on the streets. A study of male felons in Texas, in 1998, found that two-thirds of them, somewhat surprisingly, would choose a year in prison over ten years' probation.[18] I would have guessed that any spell in prison would seem worse than probation, no matter how long the probation lasted, but apparently not. The results, I would also guess, might be different for a sample of white-collar embezzlers compared to members of a juvenile gang. A $500 fine is nothing at all to a millionaire, but crushing to the poor. Damages in a tort case might convey a less punitive feeling, social and psychologically, than the same amount labeled as a fine in a criminal case. Of course, this is not just because of the money: a criminal record can damage life and career. On the other hand, losing a tort case—for medical malpractice, for example—can also carry with it very bad consequences far beyond the money damages.

The Law of Small Numbers

In the discussion of communication, I mentioned what I called the law of small numbers: the fewer the people you need to reach, the more likely the message will get through. The law of small numbers applies to impact itself. You need fewer guards to watch over ten people than to supervise ten thousand. The design of the system also matters. Think of the architecture of a prison, for example. Normally, the prisoners outnumber the guards. But some guards are armed; the prisoners are not. The prisoners are locked in cells and held within walls; the guards are not. The first true penitentiaries in the United States, in the first half of the nineteenth century, were organized on the silent system. The prisoners were housed one to a cell, and they were not allowed to speak. In this realm of silence, it was virtually impossible to organize, to start riots, to rebel, or to plan for an escape.[19]

For rule-makers, the trick is to structure a system that makes it hard to avoid or evade the rules. Try to find bottlenecks, choke points. Look for devices that need as few people as possible to comply. Suppose the goal is to cut down on street accidents. Jaywalking is dangerous, but is hard to control. Every pedestrian is a potential jaywalker; millions of pedestrians are actual jaywalkers. It is also hard to turn bad drivers into good drivers. You can try, with driver training, educational campaigns, more traffic police, and so on. But there are millions of bad drivers, and always will be. It is also hard to do anything about drunk driving; that is, anything with lasting impact. As we saw, crackdowns, campaigns, and the like do work, at least in the short run. But even during crackdowns, only some small fraction of drunk drivers will actually get caught (at least with the technology of today).

The law of small numbers, then, suggests that it might make more sense to work on the cars themselves—to make them safer. Only a handful of companies build cars. These companies are big and powerful and have lots of political clout, but once safety measures are on the statute books, government can concentrate on these few actual players. Making manufacturers install air bags will be more effective (at least in the short run) than persuading millions of drivers to fasten seat belts. Similarly, meat regulation is best done at the level of packing plants rather than at the level of butcher shops and supermarkets. This is, of course, not an argument against inspecting these shops.

Much the same point can be made for the other two clusters of motives—peer pressure and the inner voice of conscience or morality. Suppose you wanted to get serious about sex discrimination in corporations. Take a giant retail chain, say, Walmart. An effort to get top management to take effective action might make more of a difference than a campaign at the level of the individual store, its managers, its workers. Of course, in the end, the war on sex discrimination will be won or lost at that lower level.

The Cloverleaf Effect

Karl Llewellyn, among the most prominent legal scholars of the twentieth century, used to talk about what he called the cloverleaf effect.[20] On the highway, drivers go very fast; but we want them to slow down when they leave the highway. Exit ramps are designed to force them to do this. These ramps are shaped like cloverleafs, and they are sharply banked and curved.

A cloverleaf, then, is a device that forces behavior into a certain, desirable groove. You could, theoretically, make drivers slow down when they leave the highway by imposing fines, or even (theoretically) by handing out free candy and cookies to drivers. You could mount an educational campaign. The cloverleaf takes a different tack: it more or less compels the driver to obey. The cloverleaf, in short, makes compliance easier than noncompliance. A fairly reckless but skillful driver can, of course, ignore the cloverleaf and zoom at full speed off the highway, but this is quite dangerous. Most drivers will react to the cloverleaf as expected; that is, by slowing down.[21]

The legal system is full of cloverleafs: arrangements and devices that force compliance or make violation more difficult. The withholding system, in tax law, is a powerful and prominent cloverleaf. The worker gets a paycheck with taxes already deducted. Of course, people still cheat on their taxes, but they surely cheat less than if withholding disappeared and they had to pay a lump sum once a year. People who are paid in cash (waiters who pocket tips, moonlighting painters and plumbers, cleaning ladies) probably cheat at a higher rate than workers who get paychecks.

It is a known fact that, in the United States, young people, the poor, and members of minority groups tend to vote for the Democratic party; it is also well known that these groups do not turn out at the polls at the same rate as, say, elderly white folks. A state can make it easier to register and vote—for example, by letting people register even on Election Day, or by increasing the number of polling places, or by allowing early voting by mail. But state legislatures controlled by Republicans tend to put this machine into reverse. They make registration and voting harder. They get rid of the cloverleafs. They require, for example, some sort of photo ID to register. This is done, they say, to snuff out voter fraud. Many suspect the real reason is to discourage likely Democrats from voting.

Default rules can be a form of cloverleaf. Default rules come into play when the subjects of the rule simply do nothing. Changing the default rule has, very often, a massive impact on impact, as I mentioned earlier. Similarly, suppose you want to disinherit your children. You can do it (under American law) in your will or living trust; otherwise, they claim their share. In civil law countries, disinheriting children is much more difficult. Standard forms for legal documents are an obvious cloverleaf. Checks are an everyday example. The form is absolutely fixed and printed on the check itself. Statute books are full of standard forms and standard contracts. All these are cloverleafs.

Tax law is full of cloverleafs. A sales tax may be included in the price of goods we buy. The withholding system, as I mentioned, is a cloverleaf. In a restaurant, the custom is to leave a tip, and almost everybody does. But there are always some people who leave small tips or no tip at all. For them, it is better if the restaurant attaches a "service charge."

Which, indeed, some restaurants do, often for groups of six or more; occasionally for everybody. Cloverleafs and default rules, and "nudges" of all sorts, do not override other factors when those factors are powerful enough. But for the most part, default rules and cloverleafs have an enormous effect on impact.[22]

The Deterrence Curve: The Civil Side

Earlier, I introduced the concept of the deterrence curve. As punishment gets tougher and more certain, more people are deterred. The curve flattens out, and heaping on more punishment has less effect. This concept was used, for example, to analyze whether the death penalty deters.

There are deterrence curves in civil law, as well. In the campaign to reduce smoking, taxes on cigarettes can be raised. As the price goes up, the smoking curve might flatten out. If whiskey is expensive enough, only rich people will drink. Would more malpractice lawsuits, and higher awards, make doctors more careful? Doubtful. Most doctors want to do a sound and professional job. They follow rules of personal and medical ethics; and they conform to professional standards. Perhaps this curve has already flattened out. No-fault divorce law, as I mentioned, lowers the price of divorce—makes it cheaper and easier to get. Does this increase the number of divorces? Maybe. Most people (I hope) want to stay married. Telling a couple on their honeymoon that divorce is now totally free would have, I suppose, no impact at all. Students learn in Econ 101 that a lower price induces more people to buy. But this only works if they want the commodity. For loving couples, the price has no influence on divorce. Divorce is already, in the no-fault age, fairly easy and fairly cheap. A lower price may sell more cars or washing machines, but not many more divorces.[23] That curve has flattened out.

Do the rules of tort law deter people from doing reckless and careless things? One study, using vignettes (always a bit of a risk), failed to find much effect. (The vignettes included such things as talking on a cell phone in your car.) The researchers reeled off a whole list of possible explanations: one, for example, was that tort liability was "empirically uncertain."[24] But perhaps tort rules (or some of them, at least) have little or no impact because the curve has flattened out. People have incentives not to act recklessly—a reckless driver can get himself killed, along with other people—not to mention moral considerations. If the ranks of reckless drivers have already thinned out, this would blunt the impact of the rules of tort law.

On the incentive side, offering more money, of course, has an impact; but here, too, there are limits. A highly profitable company, which can hardly meet the demand for its product, would be foolish to lower its price. Would a bigger tax break increase gifts to charity? It might. Maybe even a great deal. But if people are already giving all they think they can afford, no change. The actual impact would be, of course, an empirical question.

Self-Regulation

In modern developed societies, regulation of business is pervasive. In addition, many business groups practice self-regulation; that is, they devise and publish codes of their own. Sometimes the idea is to fend off more or more hostile regulation. It is a way to say (to the regime), look, no need to pass a bunch of restrictive laws; we can control our businesses ourselves. These industries engage in what we might call preventive compliance; they act to ward off unwanted laws and regulations. The industry's code anticipates regulation, but on the industry's own terms. A lot of "self-regulation" in industry falls into this category. For example, facing widespread complaints (and a possible blizzard of laws) about sugar-drenched drinks in public schools, the big firms in the American Beverage Association agreed to self-regulate; they promised to phase out soft drinks in the schools.[25]

John Braithwaite has pointed to a practice that he calls "enforced self-regulation."[26] This is neither top-down regulation ("command and control") nor pure self-regulation, where government plays no (overt) role. In "enforced self-regulation," the regulators set out policy objectives; they then leave it up to the companies to do the rest. Companies make the rules and procedures to get them to the goal, and are responsible, too, for putting these rules and procedures into practice.[27]

Does self-regulation work? That depends, of course. On the whole, self-regulation, industry codes, and the like are apt to be less stringent than the formal laws (or feared formal laws); otherwise, why bother? But sometimes the worry is not about too-harsh regulation, but wrong-headed regulation, regulation insensitive to industry needs. There is value, for industries, in trying to act like good citizens. And sometimes there are good competitive reasons. The big beverage companies might be willing to withdraw sugary drinks from the schools because they could deliver other drinks (bottled water, diet drinks, sports drinks), that they also manufacture and market.[28] Self-regulation might some-times be more efficient than government regulation; industry might do a better and quicker job of enforcing rules. Self-regulation also makes for good public relations. Travel, for example, is a sensitive industry; dissatisfied or stranded customers can cause the whole industry to suffer. To avoid problems, the Association of British Travel Agents has a code of rules, and a committee to enforce the code, with power to punish members who break the rules.[29]

The nuclear power industry in the United States is a striking example of self-regulation at work. The industry was badly frightened when a serious accident occurred at Three Mile Island, a nuclear plant in Penn-sylvania. In response, the industry formed an organization, the Insti-tute of Nuclear Power Operations (INPO). INPO has had considerable success in keeping safety standards high and promoting good manage-ment. It has also drawn together the various units in the industry, creating thereby a kind of close-knit "community." In this industry, as Joseph V. Rees has pointed out, power plants are "hostages of each other."[30] A problem at a soap or cement factory does not threaten other soap or cement factories, but a major accident at a nuclear power plant might turn the public against the entire industry.

The nuclear power industry is, of course, rather special. But there are other instances in which sensitive industries have used protective self-regulation. A famous example comes from the history of the movie business. From the 1930s to the 1950s, Hollywood studios subjected themselves to an elaborate and rigid Production Code, which they im-posed on all movies made in the United States.[31] No nudity, no swearing, no overt sex; even married couples had to sleep in twin beds; no crime could go unpunished; adultery could not be shown in a favorable light; no criticism of organized religion. The movie studios put on this strait-jacket themselves. The loose morals of Hollywood movies had given rise to a wave of criticism (not from mass audiences, of course); some states and cities had adopted censorship codes. Movie moguls were deathly afraid of federal regulation and federal control over movies. The industry forced itself to follow rules that had never become law, and perhaps never would have.

7

THE PRESSURE OF PEERS

REWARDS AND PUNISHMENTS explain a lot about human behavior, but clearly not everything. Why do people pay their taxes? To some economists, this is a puzzle. Enforcement is low, lax, slow, costly, and inefficient; punishments are not usually severe. In short, tax evasion, though common enough, should be more common than it actually is (they feel). The cloverleaf idea (withholding, for example) is part of the answer. But clearly other factors are at work, not just the fear of getting caught and punished. Why do people comply with the law even when they do not expect to be caught and punished?

The answers are pretty much obvious. One factor is what we might call peer pressure. Like rewards and punishments, this is not a single, unified factor but, rather, a cluster of factors. The general idea is simple: people want approval from their friends, their family, their group. They want to avoid gossip, scandal, and shame. Friends, family, clans, groups, clubs, organizations we belong to, churches, schools: all of these are important to us and powerfully influence what we think and do. If the peer group wants us to obey the law, we obey. And if the peer group says disobey, this, too, may bend our behavior.

As I've already suggested, there are all sorts of peers; they might be mother and father, or other relatives, or close friends, or your group, your gang, a tribe, an occupational group, or, simply, people in general. Johannes Feest studied the behavior of drivers in northern California. He hid at the side of the road and watched cars as they approached a stop sign. No police were in sight. Some people made a complete stop, some made a so-called rolling stop, and some drove right on through. One thing struck Feest: drivers who were alone in the car violated the rule more often than drivers who had somebody with them.[1] Would pedestrians in New York—the subject of another study—cross the street even when a sign said "Don't walk"? Less likely if a person (actually hired by the experimenter) stood on the corner and obeyed the rule. If the hired person, on the other hand, broke the rule and crossed the street illegally, other people tended to do the same.[2]

Peer pressure can be an extremely powerful force. Custom, habit, and tradition determine much of our behavior. Whatever economists might think, not much of what we do in a day is the product of rational calculation. Nobody goes through life with a giant cost–benefit meter implanted in their brains. Customs and habits are transmitted by mothers and fathers, by schoolteachers, by religious leaders, and by friends and neighbors. Human beings are social animals. They need connection. Total isolation is an abnormal state. Legal behavior, like all other forms of behavior, reflects this fundamental fact. Social connections, to be sure, can be strong or weak. Church membership can be everything to some people, little or nothing for others. The same is true even for family connections.

Societies, especially modern societies, are complex organisms. All major societies are pluralistic; they are never moral monoliths. They all have subcultures. And the subcultures have their own norms, their own forms of peer pressure. Subcultural pressures may or may not mesh with the pressures and norms of the majority. Majority norms, of course, are the major source of law, but these norms can and do conflict with subcultural norms. Such conflicts are everywhere in the legal system. Gang members respond to what gang leaders suggest, even when it means breaking the law. Devout members of religious groups follow their faith out of deep convictions; other people, born into the same faith, obey the rules because they feel they are supposed to, because breaking the rules might lead to social disapproval, or ostracism, or banishment, or worse.

Family relationships are among the most powerful "peer" pressures of all: parents, brothers and sisters, and wives, husbands, or long-term partners. A study in Oregon looked at men with criminal records: married men were less likely to fall back into criminal ways (at least as measured by arrests) compared to men who remained lone wolves.[3] Is this because of the pressure a partner exerts, either openly or through some sort of silent signal? This seems likely. Also, married men, or men in committed relationships, tend to be busy and involved with family affairs; crime work somehow drops by the wayside. But maybe the chain of causation runs the other way. Some ex-cons are more likely to marry or form attachments than others. Perhaps these are the types that would not have gone back to a life of crime in any event. Still, there is no reason to doubt that special, intimate peers have tremendous power over what a person thinks and does.

Peer pressure, as we said, can work both ways. In the Oregon study just mentioned, if the wife or lover was herself "antisocial," that is, a lawbreaker in her own right, the relationship lost its "protective" features.[4] The same might be true of the influence of friends. They can have a "protective" function; but in gangs, friends might encourage (or even force) new recruits to break the law or go along with others who do. The scholarship on delinquency makes much of this feature of gang life. Young people who have violent friends, and who see and experience violence, are more likely to be drawn into a culture of violence.[5] Here, the peers are a direct source of deviant behavior. One study of young people tried to measure risk-taking (through experimental use of a video game called "Chicken"); the study found that young people "took more risks during the risk-taking game" when peers were with them, compared to the risks they took when they were alone.[6]

But, as I suggested, one can question what is cause and what is effect in these studies. Birds of a feather flock together. An adolescent male whose personality might tilt him toward delinquency could gravitate toward like-minded males, who, then, all influence each other. Young men who join gangs might differ systematically from non-joiners. Choirboys and computer geeks avoid these gangs, if they can get away with it. Personality likely makes a difference. Also family structure. And the social context.

Gangs flourish in poor neighborhoods, where choirboys and computer geeks are a rarity. Pressure to join a gang can be almost overwhelming; once somebody joins, there is pressure to go along with gang behavior.[7] That gangs in big cities breed violence is an obvious fact. So is the appeal of the gangs. Mark Fleisher interviewed young delinquents; his subjects, he found, "were motivated to band together with other rejected and neglected children." Their depression and "gnawing feelings of low mental health were assuaged by the temporary excitement of the ritual process of deviant behavior . . . and the numbing high of drugs and alcohol."[8] A study of drug use also concluded that friends introduced young people into the world of delinquency, but "selection factors" also played a key role in the process.[9] It is hard to separate the two factors. Is it the peer group that does the motivating; or is the kid drawn to the gang like a moth to a flame? There is a third possibility—that both ideas are correct; what the gang does is a kind of "enhancement," that is, "new gang members are recruited from a pool of individuals who show propensity to engage in crime and violence." This propensity is intensified once they join, "because the gang provides a structure that encourages crime and violence."[10]

There is a strong taboo against killing, especially killing the innocent, in most societies. Yet in the sad times we live in, the newspapers tell us time and again about suicide bombers, young people who blow themselves (and other people) up, who wear explosive belts and dispatch their young lives into eternity. There are violent organizations that recruit these young people, that draw them in and brainwash them, groups that have no compunctions against slaughtering "infidels."[11] The suicide bombers, men (and a few women) who blow themselves to bits in the name of the cause, are foot soldiers in a radical and violent army of terror. The selection factor comes in here, too; the recruits are young, disaffected, searching for a goal in life, and seduced into a radical form of religion. Ideology, circumstances, and peer pressure (particularly after recruitment) are a toxic brew that help a boiling pot of emotions.

The "armies" of jihadists are, in one regard, not that different from armies in general. Armies depend to a degree on stern and severe discipline, but they also need and demand the powerful magnetic force of peer pressure. Comradeship is crucial to the armed forces. Cowardice is not only shameful and criminal; it also means letting your buddies down. Armies can and do punish deserters severely, even with death sentences. But no army could sustain itself if desertion became a habit, and if soldiers laid down their arms en masse (which happens, often enough, in a defeated and demoralized army). What makes an army function is group morale, camaraderie, a sense of belonging, and the presence of fellow soldiers.

Peers also perform an educational function, as it were. The delinquent gang teaches delinquency to members, especially the raw recruits; they may be eager to learn but, nonetheless, a socialization process takes place. Prisons are said to be notorious colleges of crime. Quite a few crimes are "social crimes," in which older and more experienced practitioners teach the newbies. This is true, for example, of auto theft. Novices start out in the "lookout" role; the peer group turns these novices into experienced auto thieves. They learn how to "effect entry and bypass the ignition," they learn which cars to target, how to avoid the police, and so on: "It was sort of like an initiation type of thing."[12]

There are many studies of gangs, as far back as Thrasher's classic study in the 1920s.[13] Thrasher's gangs of kids in Chicago—stealing, skipping school, staying out all night—seem almost benign compared to more recent and more violent gangs. Gang life today is a symptom of widespread social disorganization. It is also, more broadly, a reflex (pathological, to be sure) of what I have elsewhere called the horizontal society.[14] Modern life has become much more horizontal. That is, in recent times, the vertical power of parents, leaders, chiefs, has weakened, compared to the power of peers. Stations and statuses in life are no longer quite so fixed and invariable. People orient themselves to those on the same horizontal level, whether this is the kids at school or those who hang out in the neighborhood, or people who share your hobbies, religion, habits; groups consisting of anything from fellow stamp-collectors to members of your deeply demanding cult. Horizontal life is as dominant for middle-class kids as it is for ghetto kids and gang members, but the herd behavior of the middle class does not, for the most part, erupt into crime.

Obedience and Its Discontents

Peers can also insulate a person from other influences. This was true in the famous (or infamous) Milgram experiment. Stanley Milgram, a social psychologist, set up an experiment that was, supposedly, a study of memory; at least, this was the cover story. The experimenter, an authority figure, was (apparently) in charge of this study. The innocent subjects he recruited were supposed to administer electric shocks to a "learner," when the learner made mistakes. The learner was actually an actor, but the subjects did not know this. The idea was to give stronger and stronger shocks to the learner as more mistakes were made. There were, in fact, no shocks at all, but the learner pretended he was suffering, sometimes even banging on a wall and showing signs of great pain. This made the innocent subjects nervous and uncomfortable, but the experimenter, stony-faced, told them to continue. Surprisingly, the subjects, for the most part, kept right on obeying, despite their own distaste and misgivings.[15]

Milgram was trying to prove a point: blind obedience to apparent authority. His subjects seemed to act out the great line from King Lear: "a dog's obeyed in office." Obedience to authority is an aspect of our third cluster (the moral or mental element). But at this point, something else is worth noting. When Milgram varied the experiment by bringing in (apparent) "peers" to join the innocent subject and these peers (who were, of course, part of the study) defied the experimenter, the innocent subject, too, was more likely to stop and refuse to administer more shocks.[16]

For the peer factor, too, there is probably a kind of curve, similar to the deterrence curve. The stronger the pressure from peers, the more effective peer pressure is likely to be. But it is never completely effective. In a powerful and cohesive group—a gang, a religious sect—peer pressure is enough to keep almost everybody in line. But in any group, there might be some who cannot and will not conform: the free spirits, the deviants, the defiant ones, the ones who leave the Amish community, the women who drive cars in defiance of the government of Saudi Arabia, the civil disobedients, and so on. There is a point at which the peer pressure curve flattens out.

Stigma and Shame

Stigma refers to an external marker or label identifying or marking a person who broke some norm or rule. *Shame* is a feeling of guilt and embarrassment; it is what stigma, or some other form of labeling, can evoke in the person who is stigmatized. Stigma is a strong punishment, and shame is a powerful influence on behavior. A small child put in the corner in school with a dunce cap on his head is unlikely to find this an uplifting experience. But stigma and shame do not work the same way with everybody. What one person feels shamed by, another might consider a badge of honor. Imagine a group of young people protesting against this or that war or this or that government action. They block highways, they shout, they carry banners. They build barricades. The police move in and arrest them. For some, there is no shame in the arrest, the arraignment, the nights in prison, which a middle-class person, arrested for shoplifting, might feel.

Stigma and shame work best under definite social conditions. The American colonies, especially the Puritan colonies of New England, made constant and dramatic use of stigma and shame. Everybody knows about the famous scarlet letter, the badge for adultery which provided the title of a famous novel by Nathaniel Hawthorne. The scarlet letter was not a creation of fiction. A New Hampshire statute of 1701 ordered adulterers to "weare a Capitall Letter A of two inches long and proportionable in Bignesse," to be sewed on their "Upper Garments."[17] Tourists today visiting Williamsburg, Virginia, find the stocks amusing; they pose with their heads in the stocks while their friends take photographs. But it was no laughing matter in the seventeenth century. It held a person up to shame in front of the whole community. A servant who stole a "pair of breeches" in Virginia in 1638 had to sit in the stocks on Sunday, with a pair of breeches around his neck.[18] In Maine in 1671, a woman named Sarah Morgan, who had struck her husband, was ordered "to stand with a gag in her Mouth halfe an houre . . . at a Public Town meeting & the cause of her offence writ upon her forhead."[19] The scarlet letter was, of course, a more permanent sign of misconduct than a few hours in the stocks. For burglary, according to the Laws and Liberties of Massachusetts (1648), punishment could include loss of an ear, not only painful, but also stigmatic: it marked the offender for life.[20]

In these colonies, punishment was always a public affair. Whipping was one of the most common punishments, and it was carried out in the town square. Whipping was physically painful, of course; but it was also shameful. Leaders and clergymen in old Massachusetts used stigma and shame deliberately. They were, they believed, powerful and effective deterrents. The communities were small, they were relatively homogeneous, religiously at least, and it was hard to escape from the massive power of public opinion. In the New England towns, there was, most probably, a great deal of consensus about the norms, the moral values, the religious ideals. It takes this kind of consensus to make shame punishments work effectively. Public punishment also educated; it acted as a kind of didactic theater, teaching moral lessons to the community. Hanging was also carried out in the public square. Sometimes, the condemned man even made a speech in the shadow of the gallows, talking about the sins and errors that had led him to this sorry state and warning the audience not to follow in his path.[21]

Later on, by the time of the nineteenth century, shaming punishments fell out of favor. In big, diverse cities, you could no longer assume that they worked as didactic theater. People were no longer locked into small communities; it was easy to leave town, escape local pressure, or simply melt into the urban mass. Public hangings, in particular, no longer seemed beneficial, no longer seemed vehicles for moral education. Now, in the crowded cities, they seemed, instead, to incite the blood lust of the mob, and they were abolished in state after state.

Stigma and shame still work best in tiny, ingrown communities, or perhaps in societies like Japan, where the country sometimes seems to act like one big family, at least in the opinion of some people who study Japanese society. Stigma and shame also still work within tight-knit groups like the military; "admonition or reprimand" is a sanction mentioned in the Uniform Code of Military Justice, and this is surely felt as a real punishment.[22] Religious sects, like the Amish, make heavy use of stigma and shame. In theory, stigma and shame should not work well in complex modern societies, where there is less consensus about norms and where it is easy to escape from the heavy weight of peer group

opinion. For this reason, like-minded people tend to cluster in particular communities or spaces—villages dominated by Orthodox Jews or
the Amish, or gay neighborhoods in big cities like San Francisco—where
residents could find fellowship and safety, and avoid discrimination and
rejection.

Some scholars see a wider role for stigma and shame, even in our
societies, and even in big, heterogeneous cities. Some judges seem to
agree. In Alabama in 2007, a judge imposed a shaming punishment on
a woman who had shoplifted from Walmart. He made her stand outside the store with a sandwich board that said "I am a thief; I stole from
Wal-Mart." A man in Colorado, who drove in the carpool lane with a
dummy in the passenger seat, was forced to stand at an intersection with
the dummy and a sign that said that the carpool lane "Is Not for Dum-
mies." Under a Tennessee law, drunk drivers have been ordered to pick
up trash at the side of highways, wearing orange jumpsuits carrying the
slogan "I am a drunk driver."[23] No doubt the Walmart woman, the Colorado man, and the trash collectors hated these tactics; but was there
any broader impact? On their future behavior? On the wider public? The
answer may depend in part on the degree to which the wider public
thinks shoplifting, cheating the carpool lane, or even drunk driving are
truly shameful. Shaming, however, does not need to involve a wide
public. Shaming can be painful and hurtful to a person because of what
friends, family, and colleagues might think.

There is an old Broadway slogan that no publicity is bad publicity. This
may work for plays on Broadway, but it is definitely not true for people.
Some states publish lists of people who "skip out of taxes." In three states,
according to a newspaper account, one group of taxpayers got letters
telling them they were on an online list of delinquents. For another
group, the authorities tried a more focused form of shaming: the list of
names was given to "other people from the same community," and this
was, apparently, more effective.[24] In some towns, the identity of "johns"
who patronize prostitutes is made public. The lists of sex offenders, under
"Megan's Law," was meant to protect the neighbors, but the stigmatic effect is blatant and obvious, and has serious consequences.

Apparently, then, even though we live in big, heterogeneous communities and not small, inbred villages, the legal order still has a place for

stigma and shame. Public housing in the United States is clearly labeled as such; Pruitt-Igoe in St. Louis, Missouri, and the Robert Taylor homes in Chicago, to take two notorious examples. This labeling was surely deliberate. It was surely meant to stigmatize poor families who lived in "the projects." This fact might have contributed to the decay of public housing, its unpopularity, its descent into pathology. The classical American poorhouse of the nineteenth century was also meant to stigmatize and shame the inmates. In many communities, "paupers" had to enter the poor house to get relief; there was no other way. The aim was clear: to make sure that only the truly desperate would go on the dole. Historically, life had to be made hard for the "undeserving" poor; making welfare stigmatic was a deliberate strategy. This strategy has never been quite given up. If you label the "projects" clearly, everybody will know that the tenants are poor and live in public housing. "Council housing" in England, for example, is not labeled as such, and living in council housing is probably less stigmatic than living in American "projects."

Explicit attempts to use shame as a weapon surely have some impact, though much probably depends on the tactics and who the "victims" are. An Ohio law, the Traffic Law Reform Act of 2004, enlisted shame as a weapon in the battle against drunk driving. Under this law, cars driven by convicted drunk drivers required a special license plate: bright yellow, with red letters. This presumably told the world that convicted drunk drivers were behind the wheel. Lauren Porter studied the impact of the law. The use of the plates led to fewer license suspensions; they worked on some drivers, but only up to a point. The results were hardly overwhelming. The plates, she concluded, "were marginally effective at controlling rates of drunk driving."[25] Probably the effect depended on how other people reacted to the plates, what place the drivers had in their community, and the response of the driver's peers.

James Q. Whitman has argued, forcefully, that even "in a modern, anonymous, urban society," shame sanctions have potential.[26] It all depends on the circumstances. An old study contrasted the stigma of a prison record with the effect of malpractice lawsuits on doctors' careers. The lawsuits had a much smaller effect.[27] But a cluster of well-publicized malpractice cases would surely hurt a doctor's reputation and his practice. Publishing a list of "johns" would embarrass most middle-class men; and for a minister of the gospel, it might be devastating. Saying shameful things about a business can definitely hurt the bottom line. How many customers would go to a restaurant if a big sign in the window said the place had rats, cockroaches, and poor sanitation? What if the sign said: "The owner of this restaurant beats his wife"? Whitman is not very worried about the effect of stigma and shame on the "victim"; the "victim" might not even care. The problem, rather, is that shaming techniques enlist the public, the audience. Stigma works, when it works, because it evokes a community reaction. It is, therefore, a (milder) form of lynch law; it incites and recruits the public.[28] And it can get easily out of control. It lends itself to a "politics of stirring up demons," to oppression, to the tactics of dictatorships. It "invites the public to rummage in some of the ugliest corners of the human heart."[29]

Shame and stigma are, thus, still powerful weapons. They are particularly powerful nowadays. In this age of mass media, social networks, YouTube, and other devices, rumors, gossip, and criticisms can spread with the speed of light. Punishments for minor misdeeds can be wildly disproportionate to the "crime." The unfortunate "dog poop" girl of Korea is an example. This unlucky young woman refused to clean up after her dog defecated in a subway car. What she did was certainly not laudable; but it was hardly a capital offense. Unfortunately for her, blogs and videos spread the word about her sin and she became an object of scorn and derision to millions of people.[30] People have lost their jobs, their friends, their self-respect after getting shamed in social networks.[31] This is also the age of "revenge porn": nude or revealing pictures of ex-girlfriends (or boyfriends) displayed on the Internet for the edification of millions of people.[32]

Each society has its own menu of events, words, and situations that are considered shameful. In some societies, going to court is avoided because the community frowns on it. Bankruptcy may be shameful, at least mildly so, even in modern, developed societies. Divorce was once quite shameful; much less so today. Shamefulness surely influenced rates of bankruptcy or divorce. In the age of cohabitation and the sexual revolution, premarital sex is no longer a scandal in most segments of society, and in most developed countries. In the United States, between

1970 and 2000 the number of couples who live together ("cohabit") without bothering to get married increased tenfold, to 5.5 million; by now, this is the "majority experience among cohorts of marriageable age."[33] The same is also more and more the case in Europe, especially in northern European countries, like Sweden, and in parts of Latin America. These couples produce children who are, of course, "illegitimate." But the stigma of illegitimacy, both socially and legally, has almost entirely disappeared.[34]

Shame is an emotion, but it can impact businesses, even big businesses, as well as individuals.[35] Corporations have no souls (the Supreme Court seems to think otherwise), but the people who run them do have souls. Corporations cannot blush, but executives can. Stigma and shame can work even on companies much larger than the restaurants we mentioned earlier. If you damage the reputation of a company by exposing shameful behavior, you embarrass company officials; profits and sales might suffer as a result. Whether these consequences occur is, of course, an empirical question. As Judith Van Erp points out, most "regulatory disclosure initiatives" do not "evoke strong or consistent consumer reactions." This is so for a number of reasons. The consumers may not understand the situation, especially if the business committed some technical violation of, say, pollution laws. Or the message may be lost in the vast noise and clamor of news and information that bombards people day in and day out. Or violations may be small enough or sporadic enough that consumers simply do not hear about them.[36]

There is, in general, a lively debate about the role of shaming techniques: whether they should work, whether they can work. Part of the problem is that shaming is not a simple phenomenon. Shaming can degrade and humiliate; it can be an instrument of cruelty, profoundly dehumanizing. Many modern examples use shaming as a form of degradation, as punishment, and also as a deterrent (both general and special). But the Puritan way of shaming was meant, on the whole, to be different. For the Puritans, shaming could be part of a process of reintegration. The scarlet letter, branding, cutting off ears: yes, these were permanent or long lasting. But sitting in the stocks or wearing a sign one day in church: these were transient. Their goal was to teach a lesson, both to the offender and to the community. In the end, the offender was supposed to rejoin the flock. Shaming, then, was part of a positive process, a way to reintegrate offenders. That is, shame was followed by forgiveness; shame taught a lesson. Shame was one step in a journey back from sin or crime into the sheltering folds of the community.

Modern American criminal process is, on the whole, designed to degrade, and not to integrate. Think of prison uniforms, handcuffing, the "perp walk," harsh prison conditions. Some European systems aim much less at degradation, and more at rehabilitating prisoners.[37] The Japanese system tries hard to use integrative shaming. In Japan, the police, when they catch young offenders, particularly those who have committed minor offenses, will lecture the offender, warning him to straighten up. They may make him sign an apology and promise not to do bad things again. They may call in family members, employers, or others, and ask them to keep an eye on the offender, and even to sign an agreement, in writing, promising to supervise that offender. The authorities also try to convince the offender to make restitution to the victim. There is at least some evidence that these tactics work, at least in Japan.[38] There are, of course, so many differences between systems and societies—between the United States, Japan, and, say, France—that it is hard to make a definitive judgment about techniques and modes of penology. The vast expansion of the American carceral state, the long, long sentences, the harshness of prison life: have these paid off? Have they lowered the crime rates? The huge army of prisoners in the United States is, of course, "incapacitated," and this, perhaps, may reduce certain crimes a bit.[39] The evidence, as we saw, is weak. Yet for the most part, the public seemed to feel that toughness is all. At this writing (2016), attitudes may have changed—at least a little.

In any event, it is a question. Would reintegrative tactics work—would they even be possible—in the United States? Or France? Or Australia? Or in other societies or contexts? There has been an upsurge of interest in reintegrative shaming, a lot of it due to the work of John Braithwaite.[40] There have been attempts to examine the process empirically, though this is not at all easy.[41] Jon Vagg looked at data in Hong Kong, a society that, in theory, should be receptive to reintegrative shaming (like Japan). Here he found a "strong commitment to labeling and exclusion" and a rush to punish young delinquents, all of which suggest that reintegrating these young people into society would not be easy.[42] In a study of nursing homes in Australia, teams that enforced regulations and used the technique of reintegrative shaming got better compliance than teams that stigmatized.[43]

Shaming is a complex concept, and shame is an emotion with many shades and varieties. Shaming, moreover, as Whitman reminds us, invokes the power of the audience, and this can be a bit like opening Pandora's box. There are definitely dangers and limitations. Even John Braithwaite, the guru of reintegrative shaming, is keenly aware of the problems. He tells the story of an Australian prisoner of war, accused by his mates of stealing money, tried by a "kangaroo court" in the prison camp, convicted, shamed, and "sentenced to Coventry," that is, shunned by the mates. As a result, his health failed and he died within months. At that point, his mates discovered he was totally innocent. Rats had taken the money and used it to construct a nest. Shaming is powerful, but dangerous. It can be used, Braithwaite admits, "to stultify diversity . . . or simply to oppress diversity." It can become the "principal weapon of the tyranny of the majority."[44]

Still, Braithwaite insists that modern societies could make more use of reintegrative shaming in the battle against crime and delinquency. Modern societies—certainly his own society, Australia—are hardly small, face-to-face societies, nothing at all like the Puritan colonies of the seventeenth century, or even modern Japan. Still, everybody is part of some small network or group. Shaming is reintegrative when it operates within a family, a group, or a network; is administered with respect, even love; and holds open the chance to be forgiven and taken back into the group or community. It could be, presumably, part of a package of techniques used to rehabilitate prisoners.

"Restorative justice" is another term found in the scholarly literature. The famous South African Truth and Reconciliation Commission (TRC) is a prime example. The awful era of apartheid had ended. The TRC had the task of exposing the crimes of the apartheid era, giving the victims voice, and reaching some sort of closure, as a substitute—or complement—to actual punishment for crimes committed in the past. The idea, in other words, was to try to bind victims and offenders into a single normative system. Restorative justice invokes the power of the audience, but in a positive way: the power of the community. The offender, for his part, is encouraged to take responsibility, to apologize, and to make restitution. For victims of crime, there is supposed to be a sense of satisfaction, closure, or healing; and they reap the psychological benefits that forgiveness may offer. There is probably also the notion that the offender, even if he does not literally make amends, will have learned from the experience, has had some kind of catharsis, and has renounced his evil ways. The idea spread from South Africa to other countries, other societies, other circumstances; many institutional forms emerged, variations of attempts to achieve restorative justice: for example, the National Commission on the Disappearance of Persons, in Argentina.[45]

Restorative justice probably has to be tested case by case, society by society. The notion has its corps of enthusiasts. They think that, properly used, it can promote social healing and bring offenders back into society. A certain amount of evidence backs them up, with regard to juvenile offenders, for example. Japan, of course, is supposed to be the *locus classicus* of "restorative justice." But its utility there might depend on aspects of Japanese culture (and its system of criminal justice) that are not easy to duplicate elsewhere. It is hardly suitable for certain crimes in modern society—murder, for example. Perhaps it worked in older, more traditional societies, but people today would blanch at the very idea of settling a murder case by transferring cows and horses, or money, from the offender's family to the family of the victim, along with some sort of ceremony. At least one scholar rejects the idea of restorative justice for cases of domestic violence; women, in these cases, need "effective, safe, and just outcomes," not "symbolic reparation such as apology and forgiveness."[46] And a German scholar objects that "restorative justice" is "an attempt to institutionalize premodern models of dispute resolution, under the conditions of modern society," apparently a fatal flaw.[47]

Whether reconciliation actually works, whether it actually accomplishes its goals, is not easy to say. (Indeed, the goals themselves can be fairly murky.) Two scholars studied the tactics of the Australian Taxation Office (ATO). The ATO sent out harsh letters to offenders, demanding payment with interest and penalties. This met with a lot of resentment and anger, and did not bring in much money. The ATO then took a different approach: encouraging settlement, leaving off the penalties, and admitting that the taxpayers might have gotten bad advice from financial advisers. Nice words—and actual forgiveness—made for better results.[48] Tax amnesties and similar devices also seem to have an impact.

In the United States, and a handful of other countries, a victims' rights movement has led to laws allowing so-called victim impact statements.[49] The main political point, no doubt, was to make the system tougher on defendants, that is, more retributive, by allowing the victims to tell their stories of suffering (which were real enough).[50] It was also supposed to provide closure for victims. But (just possibly) some offenders might feel remorse, might accept responsibility; victims' statements might, in other words, play a role in restorative justice. The testimony of victims and their families before the South African TRC was something akin to "impact statements" in the United States or Australia.[51]

There are many studies, mostly by anthropologists, about the ways in which preliterate societies settle disputes.[52] It is hard to sum up these studies, but there are some common themes. These are often small societies, in which everybody knows everybody else; people are connected to each other in networks of "multiplex relationships"; and are, in any event, fated or condemned to keep on living together. Under these conditions, legal process is, and has to be, restorative; it has to be concerned with social harmony. It has to avoid disrupting social networks. The goal of legal process, then, is less to decide who's right and who's wrong, in some legal or quasi-legal sense, than to mend a ripped social fabric, to bring back balance and harmony, and to satisfy the parties, the families, and the community as a whole that justice has been done. In these societies, peer pressure plays a critical role in resolving disputes.

Asian societies, one is told, are more close-knit than Western societies, which are more individualistic. The group and the extended family count for more than in the West, especially in those societies—China, Japan, Singapore, Korea—where the so-called Confucian tradition is strong. The West—the United States perhaps most of all—is supposed to be more atomic and anomic, more free-floating, more a society of lone wolves than a social cluster. I am frankly skeptical about an argument that assumes a vast cultural influence, based on a thinker who lived more than two thousand years ago. If Confucius really does count more than, say, Plato and Aristotle in the West, it is because of political and cultural use made of his work centuries after he died and perhaps not relevant today. In any event, China, Japan, Singapore, and Korea are quite different from each other—in forms of government, in manners and morals, in religion, and in ways of life. And each of these societies is clearly becoming more "individualistic" in our times. Japan and Korea are functioning democracies. Three of these countries are rich and highly developed, and the fourth (China) is on the way. People in Europe, in the Middle Ages, lived mostly in small communities; kings, popes, emperors—and family ties—demanded deference as strongly as in any "Confucian" society. What loosened these ties was the rise of market economies, democratic institutions, the urban-industrial revolution, the scientific and technological revolution, and all of the other factors that come with the modern, developed world.

How strong is the influence of parents on, say, adolescents? Weaker, I suspect, than it used to be. And weaker in some societies compared to others. Robert H. Aseltine Jr., studying deviance among adolescents, tried to measure whether parents had more influence on these deviant kids than their friends and peers had. Friends, it turned out, had more influence than parents.[53] As a parent myself (and a resident of the USA) this result does not come as much of a surprise. Parents, after all, are rarely "cool." Yet, not so long ago, a parent's word, even in Western societies, was absolute, iron law. It would have been unthinkable for a child, even a grown-up child, to disobey a parent. For complicated reasons, this is no longer the case in many or most developed countries. And it is weakening, probably, everywhere. More and more, as I mentioned, we live in a horizontal society.

Whatever one feels about reintegrative shaming, it clearly depends on context and culture. Shaming is a weapon that is at times too strong, at times too weak. Perhaps it would be best to forget the shaming part and focus on reintegration, at least as a way to battle deviance and crime. Theories of rehabilitation assume that carrots work better than sticks. The United States has on its books severe punishments for drug offenses, but many scholars would argue that Draconian measures will not help solve the problem of the drug trade and drug addiction. In some communities, there are special drug courts, which serve as an alternative to naked harshness. These courts have as their goal the reformation of offenders; they provide counseling, vocational advice, mental health services, and the like. In two counties in Florida, according to a study, graduates of drug courts had better outcomes in the follow-up phase of the study than offenders who went the ordinary route.[54] Education and training for convicts apparently cuts down on recidivism. Reintegration, in short, can work, when given a chance.

To Succeed in Business

Much of the scholarship on peer pressure is about ordinary people, especially young people, youth gangs, adolescents, students. But peer pressure is not just a young man's game. Peer pressure is everywhere; it bears down on businesspeople as well as, say, rough kids in gangs. *Homo economicus* is not immune to the influence of peers.

In a famous study, Stewart Macaulay interviewed businesspeople in Wisconsin. Macaulay is an expert on the law of contracts. He was investigating the contract behavior of these men of affairs. He found that they ignored many formal doctrines of contract law. They were hardly sticklers for their contractual rights. This was not pure altruism. Making claims and bringing lawsuits is disruptive and costly. More important, to these businesspeople, long-term relationships—between, say, suppliers and buyers—were ethically and economically valuable. Strictly adhering to the rules of the (contracts) game could disrupt valuable connections and destroy key networks. It would also violate norms and understandings among people who are, in an important sense, a peer group. Macaulay's study is usually cited for his point about the nonuse of contract doctrine, and properly so. But his study also pointed to situations where businesspeople did, in fact, use contract doctrine: mostly when long-term relationships broke down—for example, if one of the partners to a deal went bankrupt. Happy marriages have no particular use for the law of divorce; broken marriages do.

Macaulay's businesspeople were also concerned with their business reputation; reputation was important, and was also economically valuable. But *reputation* is just another word for what peers think of you. A company, other things being equal, does not want to be known as a stickler for rules, or as unreasonably tough on suppliers and buyers. Still, only a cynic would see profit margins as the only reason why people in business "do the right thing." They are also human beings; they care what their peers think of them—their friends, the people in their country club, in their trade association, the people they have lunch with.

Joseph V. Rees, in his study of the nuclear power industry,[55] which I have mentioned before, showed that peer pressure had a massive effect on plant managers. This pressure was exerted through and by means of the Institute of Nuclear Power Operations (INPO), a private body the industry set up to monitor, control, and regulate nuclear power plants. The nuclear disaster at the plant at Three Mile Island exposed some critical industry problems. The nuclear energy industry is, of course, heavily regulated by the federal government. Before INPO was established, plants usually complied with government regulations, but at the minimal level, and without any consideration of what might be "best practices." INPO breathed life into the regulatory scheme; it multiplied the impact of state regulation. Self-regulation of businesses is often a dud, but INPO is not one of the duds. It has had a powerful impact, on management, on safety, on the governance of nuclear plants in general. In Rees's view, as we have seen, one reason was that the plants were "hostages" of each other. A nuclear disaster at one plant could be politically disastrous to the other nuclear plants. This chain, then, was only as strong as its weakest link. This is one reason why INPO has been a success, but the way it achieved that success is telling. The nuclear energy business, thanks in large part to INPO, now forms a kind of community; indeed, a rather small and closely knit community, in which reputation is crucial, and the ratings and standards emanating from INPO are important elements in the construction of reputation.

Every example of self-regulation contains an element of peer pressure. Studies of business behavior, quite generally, find that the opinion of business peers is important for compliance. For example, builders, in a study of homebuilders in western Washington State, claimed that the strongest motive for compliance with codes and regulations was concern about reputation among customers and fellow members of the trade.[56] Reputation among customers is vital, of course, but businesses also form communities. And public corporations have stockholders. Firms that are fined for violations of this or that law might suffer, in addition, a lowering of their stock price. This, to be sure, might come mostly from fear that the bottom line will suffer. And this result, apparently, does not happen—that is, there is no "market sanction"—when firms are punished "for regulatory violations involving noncontracting third parties or convicted of an environmental violation."[57] But this might be precisely because, in these cases, there is no reputational damage; customers and others either do not know or do not care.

Where there is some sort of "community," community is important. It mattered for Macaulay's businesspeople in Wisconsin, for nuclear power plants, and in many other businesses and organizations. Of course, you cannot expect "community" among thousands of barbershops or pizza parlors or auto dealers, but nonetheless, reputation always counts for something. All of these businesses have customers, and they depend on their reputation among these customers. Word-of-mouth is life and death for restaurants. And today, the mouth has become technological. It includes the voices of thousands who write reviews on the Internet. Restaurants and stores can sink or swim according to the tenor of these online reviews.

Taming the Tiger: Regulating Modern Business

In an interesting study, Marco Verweij looked at two systems of pollution control in two different places: one, the Rhine River area in Europe; and the other, the Great Lakes region of the United States. The Rhine controls were much more successful, and Verweij wondered why.[58] Not that the Great Lakes project was a complete failure; companies now discharge less toxic stuff than before into the lakes. But the Rhine River project has done much better.

Verweij considers a number of factors. He singles out and emphasizes one of them: the mode of enforcement (or, if you will, the administrative style of enforcement). The American approach was more adversarial than the European approach. The Europeans stressed cooperation, working together, consensual tactics. Rhine firms, probably as a result, "have made extensive investments in water protection measures that have gone beyond existing legal norms."[59] Tourists floating down the Rhine can enjoy the castles, the Lorelei, the landscape, without dead, bloated fish and toxic junk. This is a definite success story. The Great Lakes, less so.

Verweij feels his case study has wider implications. Ecological issues are complex; they tend to cross boundaries ("both territorial and scientific"), and their complexity means that "their resolution needs the cooperation of all involved organizations."[60] This, he feels, calls for the approach that worked so well on the Rhine.

Modern regulatory schemes, including rules of pollution control, can be fiendishly complex. Rigorous enforcement may not be the best way forward. Making controls work takes cooperation. Businesses fight tooth and nail to stay profitable. This is a given. But they also have the power to cooperate, to compromise, to play within the rules. Their leaders have emotions, hopes, desires. American administrative law is often tough, afflicted with what Robert Kagan has called "adversarial legalism."[61] A kinder, gentler approach might clean up rivers, air, environments more effectively. It worked on the Rhine.

Robert Kagan and associates studied "environment performance" in fourteen pulp and paper mills, in British Columbia, New Zealand, Australia, and two states in the United States.[62] They interviewed managers and staff people who dealt with environmental issues. The work of these people was subject to three constraints (the authors called them "licenses"). The first was the need to make a profit ("economic license"). The second, the "legal license," consisted of the rules and laws that applied to the business; and the third was "social license," that is, "pressures for responsible environmental performance" from neighbors, employees, community groups, advocacy groups, and the media. The "intensity" of the "social license" made a difference; in short, a kind of peer group effect. Big firms did better at complying than small firms. They were "usually more closely monitored," but they were also more jealous of their brand name and reputation. Some even went "beyond compliance"; that is, they did much more than they were required to do.

Kagan and associates also drew some interesting conclusions on the "interaction of fear and duty." Companies that comply like to know that violators (other companies) actually get punished. Enforcement "is a key to building a culture of compliance and keeping a sense of duty alive."[63] If everybody is cheating in an industry except for one or two good guys, the good guys are likely to feel like fools and, more significantly, are likely to lose money. Hearing about violators and what happened to them also serves as a "reminder" if not an actual threat; it leads companies to review their own environmental programs or the like.

Styles of regulatory enforcement, and the impact of those styles, is a frequent topic of scholarly discussion. Styles "can be arrayed along a continuum." At one end is strict or punitive or formalistic enforcement; at the other end are "accommodative" or "conciliatory" styles of enforcement. There are also many intermediate styles; flexible at times, tough at other times.[64] Jonas Talberg, studying the impact of directives issued by the European Union, distinguishes between "enforcement" (coercion) and a more "managerial" style.[65] Styles, according to scholars in the field, may also vary with national cultures. American regulation is supposed to lean toward the punitive end of the scale. In Robert Kagan's opinion, American administrative process generally uses "more complex and detailed bodies of rules; more frequent recourse to formal legal methods of implementing policy and resolving disputes; more adversarial and expensive forms of legal contestation; more punitive legal sanctions . . . more frequent judicial review, revision, and delay. . . . [and] more malleability and unpredictability," compared to the styles used elsewhere.[66]

In the chapter on communication, I referred to a study of industrial waste management in Japan and the United States.[67] The study focused on a multinational company that had plants in both countries. In the United States, there was a labyrinth of rules and regulations; enforcement was stringent and hostile; lawyers swarmed like bees; and management became sullen, resistant, and hostile. The Japanese style was entirely different: conciliatory, open-ended, a matter of "administrative guidance" rather than tough enforcement and litigation, and with an emphasis on "performance standards" instead of tight, specific rules.

The authors did mention factors that made direct comparison difficult. The American plants produced for the domestic market, while the Japanese plant was mostly for export; the Japanese plant was profitable, the American plants only marginally so. This meant that the Japanese plant could better afford to pay close attention to environmental issues. Still, the authors felt that "differences in regulatory structures and styles" were "substantial independent forces."[68] The American system, with its "prescriptive rules, adversarial and legalistic enforcement, and harsh penalties," brought about "antiregulation sentiments and suspicion of regulatory authority"; and this "impedes the acceptance of regulatory norms and perpetuates the system's reliance on legalistic regulation and punitive enforcement." The system, in short, is "costly, complex, and cumbersome."[69]

In general, the studies seem to agree that some sort of carrot-and-stick mixture works better than pure stick. But this is a crude summary of a vast body of research. The studies begin, as they must, with the obvious fact of massive and complex regulation of business in the modern state. The state regulates environmental issues, health and welfare issues, monopoly and cartel issues, banking issues, stock exchange issues, and more. Big government also is up against big and very big business. To get an impact, the rule-maker cannot rely on brute force. To begin with, there is never enough money and staff for that, never enough inspectors and regulators to see to it that everybody pays taxes and toes the line. Voluntary compliance is always crucial.

Cooperation, then, from whatever motive, is more effective than using a bludgeon. Businesses that fail to obey the rules fall into three categories, according to Robert Kagan and John Scholz. The first consists of "amoral calculators," who do a kind of cost-benefit analysis and decide that compliance is just not worth it. They are after profit, plain and simple. They do what they can get away with. The second group consists of "political citizens," who respond to the "perceived reasonableness or unreasonableness of regulatory orders." If they fail to comply, it might be because they disapprove of the rules. The third group is made up of "organizationally incompetent" businesses. They fail to comply because they simply can't comply; they have poor management or they do not know or understand what is required.[70]

Ian Ayres and John Braithwaite, among others, argue that the best way to get results is through "responsive regulation." "Punitive enforcement" of rules "engenders a game of regulatory cat-and-mouse"; firms "defy the spirit of the law by exploiting loopholes, and the state writes more and more specific rules to cover the loopholes." The result is a jumble of incoherent rules, and a "barren legalism" that stresses open violations of rules "to the neglect of underlying systemic problems."[71] This strikes one as a good description of the Internal Revenue Code in the United States: a daunting jungle of jargon; a wilderness of inter-locking, sometimes inconsistent provisions; a swamp of legalese. Of course, whole armies of lobbyists have worked for years to squeeze spe-cial tax deals from Congress. Much of the complexity is due to the arms race between the government, on one side, trying desperately to feed Leviathan's appetite for revenue, and on the other side, nimble lawyers and accountants looking for weak spots in the sea monster's hide. And, of course, lobbyists swarm like wasps in Washington, DC, trying to get tax breaks for their clients.

In the last chapter, we mentioned what John Braithwaite has called "enforced self-regulation."[72] A regulator tells business what is expected; the business itself finds ways to reach the goal. Each company has to "write a set of rules tailored to the unique set of contingencies facing that firm." The regulatory agency will approve those rules (or suggest changes). Then the company carries out the plan it devised for itself. This part is "self-regulation," but it is enforced, since violations of the "privately written and publicly ratified rules would be punishable by law." Under this kind of system, "the role of enforcement changes from discovering contraventions of rules designed to reduce risk, to assessing the systems in place for risk management."[73] Another name for this technique is "performance-based regulation." This is basically the same idea. Regulators do not lay down rules. Rather, they set goals for busi-nesses (reduction of pollution, for example, or getting grocery stores to sell healthier food).[74] The business can then try to reach the goal by whatever method works for them. Regulators and the regulated form a kind of community, doing business with each other, each side mindful of the values and opinions of the other.

Does this approach work? It is not, of course, a magic bullet; results would depend on the circumstances.[75] Each particular study of an agency or industry where "enforced self-regulation" is tried out would probably show some variation. Robyn Fairman and Charlotte Yapp looked at businesses in England that were subject to food safety rules. The businesses were small or medium-size. Styles of regulation—did in-spectors try to "educate" or did they threaten—varied from one local authority to another. These businesses, typically, did not have "systems in place for risk management." Compliance was an "outcome." When inspectors came around, the businesspeople "negotiated" terms with these inspectors. The inspectors would drop in, they would point out something wrong; the businesses would fix it. The businesses, in short, were entirely reactive. To them, compliance meant doing what the inspector told them to do.[76] Hazel Genn came to the same conclusion in an earlier study of health and safety regulation in England: the behavior of smaller firms was "largely reactive," limited to the precise action "demanded by inspectors on their generally infrequent visits." Larger firms, on the other hand, were much more "proactive"; they gave health and safety a "high profile."[77] In Japan, regulators enforcing the Water Pollution Control Act would make their rounds testing water for pollution. In about 10 percent of the instances, they found a problem. They would then issue an "Administrative Guidance," that is, a "non-legally binding warning letter," and follow it up to see if the problem was corrected. Compliance occurred almost all the time.[78]

As is clear by now, styles of regulation, and their success or failure, have generated a large volume of research. Large, and rather confusing. In addition to responsive regulation, there is so-called "smart regulation," "risk-based regulation," and even "really responsive regulation."[79] These all basically accept the idea behind responsive regulation, that is, a rejection of punitive, command-and-control regulation, which does not (apparently) work. Robert Baldwin and Julia Black, who advocate "really responsive regulation" (as opposed, one imagines, to "sort-of responsive regulation"), criticize what they consider the crude theoretical basis of many of the studies. Research should cover "five . . . elements or tasks" of enforcement: "*detecting* undesirable or noncompliant behavior, developing tools and strategies for *responding* to that behavior, *enforcing* those tools and strategies on the ground, *assessing* their success or failure and *modifying* approaches accordingly."[80] This is, no doubt, a useful checklist. It does not, however, avoid the underlying problem, which is that regulation (of business) is a giant jigsaw puzzle, with hundreds of pieces of different sizes and shapes. It is hard, and perhaps impossible, to put them together into a single picture.

Take the first element: detecting violations. This can be hard or easy. Baldwin and Black are writing about regulation of fisheries in the United Kingdom. Oceans are awfully big, fishermen are mobile, there are a huge number of landing sites in the United Kingdom, "inspection at sea is very resource intensive," and there are too many ways to avoid getting caught.[81] This is a problem, too, as they point out, with control of tax evasion—there are just too many taxpayers, and too many gimmicks; the same is true for attempts to regulate butcher shops and barbers. Contrast all this, for example, with the problem of regulating car manufacturers or inspecting nuclear power plants.

The scholars who write about the theory of regulatory impact remind me, in short, of the famous story of the blind men and the elephant; they are groping at different parts of the beast and drawing conclusions accordingly. Can we say anything useful about the research as a whole? Researchers all seem to agree that a pure stick approach (punishment) does not usually get good results. Carrots, or perhaps lollipops, can do better. Beyond that, all seems to depend on the industry, the situation, the regulators themselves, perhaps even on the style and text of the law, not to mention national cultures and styles.

Much of the scholarly work on regulation has zeroed in on the techniques the regulators use—that is, on the relationship between the agency and the businesses or individuals subject to that agency. But there is a difference between the impact of a law on the public and the impact on the regulators. Food and drug regulation has an impact on the pharmaceutical industry, perhaps also on doctors and patients. But we can also ask: What is the impact of the statutory rules on the agency itself, the staff, the civil servants who work for the FDA? How do they behave, and why?[82] We can use the same tools of analysis we used to discuss the behavior of the subjects: discussions of rewards and punishment; of what peers think and do; of their notions of ethics and conscience. Hardheaded scholars may sneer, but regulators are people, and they have ordinary human emotions. The reaction of the regulated industry also has, of course, a huge impact on the regulators. The subjects of regulation can "capture" the regulators—a sort of Stockholm syndrome for government regulation; the industry more or less dominates and takes over, like aliens from outer space seizing and inhabiting human bodies. "Capture," if and when it occurs—and it surely does occur—obviously blunts the impact of regulation. Powerful industries that deal with an agency day in and day out will certainly have a bigger effect than, say, members of a diffuse and largely indifferent public.[83] In any event, when the rules are expensive and difficult to comply with, or unduly complex, violations will occur more often. And, if so, the situation may get out of control. It is hard to get a grip on behavior if everybody (or almost everybody) is breaking the rules.

As we saw, styles of regulation vary greatly along a dimension from totally punitive to one of cooperation and collaboration. But clearly, punishment cannot be given up entirely. It has to be used on industry rogues, on companies like Volkswagen who cheat egregiously, whose behavior still violates the rules after all the other methods have been used and after the curve has at least somewhat flattened out.

Corruption

Perhaps in Japan or Finland, gentler methods of enforcing regulations work better than tightness and toughness. But both methods assume that regulation, whatever its problems, will basically do the job, or at least some kind of job. We can, more or less, ignore the role of gross corruption (although scandals occur in every society, including Japan).[84] Some societies, unfortunately, are impossibly corrupt; high- and low-level thievery is everywhere, so much so that corruption can be said to dissipate the impact of formal law. In some societies, bribes have to be given to get anything done at all. Many of the rules on the books might as well not be there, and the chief impact of a law might simply be the chance for officials, up and down the scale, to line their own pockets and the pockets of their friends and relatives. In Bulgaria, supposedly the most corrupt country in Europe (though surely not in the world), a think tank based in Sofia claimed in 2014 that 158,000 corrupt transactions were carried out every month. As a result, law enforcement (this was the claim) was positively paralyzed.[85] Transparency International ranks countries on a corruption scale: the least corrupt countries (in 2013) were Denmark and New Zealand; the most corrupt (of 175 countries) were Sudan, Afghanistan, North Korea, and Somalia. When corruption reaches a certain point, as it probably has in the countries at the bottom of the list, the fight against corruption becomes almost hopeless. An honest civil servant feels isolated; his virtue seems pointless, and he feels enormous pressure to join the (corrupt) crowd.

Corruption is unpopular politically; nobody likes it, except the people who profit by it (which can be quite a large group). New regimes in high-corruption countries are perpetually announcing wars against corruption. The Chinese government regularly makes this announcement. The Muhammadu Buhari regime in Nigeria (he was elected in April 2015) claims this as one of its major goals.[86] These campaigns usually go nowhere. In some rare cases, a government does succeed in getting rid of corruption. Singapore is a classic example. In many countries, ordinary citizens try to make a difference, by complaining, monitoring, making noise, writing letters, blowing whistles, and begging, cajoling, demonstrating, or demanding action. In China, for example, we hear about "barefoot inspectors."[87] Factories were dumping polluted material at night, knowing that government inspectors never came around after hours. But local peasants "became full-time quasi-inspectors, spending night after night on their mopeds moving from factory to factory to catch illegal discharges."[88] This kind of bottom-up pressure for enforcement can be, one supposes, at least locally effective. The problem in many countries is that corruption, like a tapeworm, has burrowed deep inside the body politic. It is no easy task to get rid of it, especially since the people who get the job of fighting corruption may be corrupt themselves, or have elite ties to corrupt authorities.

Corruption, like everything else, is a social phenomenon. It has many causes. In some societies, kinship ties are strong; other attachments—to the state, the public at large, and civil society in general—are extremely weak. Edward Banfield coined the phrase "amoral familism" in his study of southern Italy.[89] There (and in many other places), people feel no particular loyalty or duty to society as a whole. A person with power, money, or influence will use that power, money, or influence on behalf of his family, his group, his tribe or clan. If a cousin asks a civil servant for a favor, the cousin expects to get what he asked for. Blood ties are thicker than the watery ties to the general society.[90]

Some situations, of course, are more prone to corruption than others. Fear is one motive. Drug cartels in Latin America corrupt judges by threatening them; they have to choose between *plata* (silver) or *plomo* (lead). It is no surprise that many judges take the silver. Money, of course, is the most common motive. Money joined with a certain amount of power is a potent combination. A building inspector, who is pretty low in the scale of civil service and is, no doubt, poorly paid, can make decisions that matter greatly to builders, contractors, and developers. The temptation to take a bribe becomes almost overwhelming. Hence all the scandals, in China and elsewhere, for example, when buildings made out of shoddy materials collapse and bury human beings in the rubble. Singapore has hit on the solution: civil servants are very well paid. Supreme Court judges make over a million dollars a year. But then, Singapore is a very rich country.

A Note on Vigilantes

Private enforcers, popular movements (more or less organized) that aim to enforce what is otherwise unenforced or badly enforced, spring up from time to time in many societies. One form is so-called "vigilante" action. The name comes from the famous vigilante movement in the American West, in the late nineteenth century. Vigilante movements cropped up in almost every Western state. They differed from each other in all sorts of regards; but one common thread was a belief that law and order had broken down, and that the people (or some of them) had to fill this gap, often with judicious use of the hangman's rope. The vigilantes themselves were obviously breaking the law; they dispatched the bad guys with no attention whatsoever to due process. Indeed, that was the point. They had (and still have) their defenders. On the other hand, nobody defends the extreme, murderous, and sadistic lynch mobs in the American South before the civil rights movement. The death squads in countries like Guatemala have something of the same flavor.[91]

What many of these movements have in common is the idea that ordinary legal processes have failed to do the job. They are too weak or too corrupt to have an impact on crime, disorder, leftists, or whoever is defined as an enemy of the people. At least, this is the standard claim. More realistically, the regular legal process is not working the way the vigilantes want it to work, or it does not give off a powerful enough message. In the old South, in the late nineteenth century and deep into the twentieth century, the whole system of criminal justice was grossly unfair to African Americans. The doors of justice were completely closed to them. All court officials, judges, and jurors were white. A black man accused of, say, assaulting a white man (or woman) was absolutely certain to be convicted. Yet even this, apparently, was not terrifying enough, powerful enough, to satisfy the ideology of white supremacy. That required the savagery and sadism of lynch law, carried out in public before jeering crowds.

Join the Crowd

People, as a rule, like to conform. They do not want to be "different," to be labeled as oddballs, other things being equal. They model the behavior of others; they want to do what is normal or common among their peers. In short, peer "pressure" is not necessarily "pressure" at all, at least not in the literal sense. Behavior can be influenced simply by an awareness of what other people do or don't do, think or don't think. In a study published in 1967, psychologists asked students whether they thought it was immoral to be drunk in a public place. Then they were asked the same question but with new "information." One group was told this behavior was illegal; another group was told that other college students had "strong" reactions against the practice. Opinions shifted in both cases, but the information about peers had a bigger impact.[92]

Hotels these days try to convince guests to reuse towels and sheets, which saves energy and water (and saves money for the hotels, one might add). One study tried to find out the best way to run a successful campaign. The study contrasted two ways of appealing to guests. One was a message posted in the rooms appealing to conservation motives: "Help Save the Environment." Guests were told they could "show . . . respect for nature" if they reused towels. In other rooms, the message added another factor: "Join your fellow guests in helping to save the environment." It told new occupants of the room that almost three out of four guests cooperated in the program, and that they could "join . . . fellow guests" in this effort. This message was more successful in getting participation; the invitation to "join the crowd" was successful.[93]

The authors then tried to examine this urge to conform a little more precisely. They varied the signs slightly to produce a number of experimental conditions. Some guests were asked to join "fellow guests" in these conservation efforts; others were asked to join fellow guests "who stayed in this room." In a third condition, "fellow guests" was replaced by "fellow citizens," and in one more, it was "join the men and women who are helping to save the environment" (presumably invoking gender identification as well). Contrary to expectations, the most successful campaign was the one that appealed to guests to join the efforts of those who had stayed in that very room, as if their ghostly presence could still be felt long after they had checked out.

As this and other examples show, the "peer group" can make itself felt in subtle ways. In some situations, the peer group supports violations of law, though indirectly: by treating these violations with indifference. Approval is, if anything, simply tacit. People, for example, jaywalk all the time. The other people on the street may not like jaywalking, and may even disapprove of it. But most people pay no attention. They send off a silent message: jaywalking is not that bad and all of us do it from time to time. If people yelled, wagged their fingers, or expressed disapproval, no doubt there would be less jaywalking; but this does not happen. As we saw earlier, the criminology literature talks about general and specific "nondeterrence" as well as deterrence.[94] A person who sees jaywalkers getting away with it may assume that nobody enforces this law and, therefore, it is safe to do. This can be analyzed either as a deterrence issue or a peer group issue, depending on the mental processes of the jaywalker.

John McMullan and David Perrier, in their study of lobster poaching mentioned in an earlier chapter, found that people in the community failed to think badly of the poachers. The "social reputation of a lobster fisher" was not affected when "large numbers of fishers are also poaching and where communities acquiesce in this type of behavior."[95] In China, music fans routinely violate copyright laws. Everybody does it—that is, they treat music on the Internet as essentially free. The fact that this "crime" is universal snuffs out any sense that the act is immoral.[96] The wholesale violation of anti-liquor laws during Prohibition had a somewhat similar effect in American cities. In many communities in the United States, especially minority communities, people fear and distrust the police. The result, at times, is to give tacit support to drug dealers and others who violate the laws.

I mentioned earlier the strong social norm against snitching; this results in peer support for lawbreakers. It is hard to draw a line between whistle-blowing—reporting misconduct—which people generally approve of, and snitching, which is extremely unpopular in some circles. Dislike of whistle-blowers or, indeed, of anybody who goes to the police, or complains at any level of government, is common in small, close-knit groups. People in these communities condemn members who complain to formal authorities; they may even shun, or banish, whistle-blowers. Group solidarity has a higher value than obedience to law, even when the group approves of the law. A man who reported on sexual abuse in the ultra-Orthodox Jewish community in New York City became a pariah among his peers—an "outcast"—even though nothing in the belief system of the community suggests that sexual abuse is okay.[97]

Many Voices, Many Rooms

Complex societies are pluralistic. Many institutions have the job of making and enforcing rules; only some of these are "legal," that is, part of the official apparatus of the state. What scholars call "legal centralism" is largely or wholly a myth—the idea that the formal system, the system nominally in command, actually runs society, and runs it according to official, central blueprints. Another myth is "magic legalism," that is, the idea that rules from the center translate automatically into behavior.[98] Within society, in fact, systems of rules and enforcement of rules compete (and cooperate) with each other. There are many alternatives to the (formal) legal system. Moreover, the actual effect, or impact, of legal commands can never be taken for granted; impact is always an empirical question: how rules, central or otherwise, affect people's thoughts and actions. Indeed, that is the central focus of this book.

Many subgroups run their own affairs, deliberately avoiding or detouring around the formal legal system. This is the message of studies of small, tight groups—for example, Orthodox Jewish diamond merchants,[99] or the ranchers in Shasta County, California, in Robert Ellickson's famous study.[100] A small, conservative sect, the Amish, in Wisconsin, refused to abide by a rule requiring children to go to high school; education at that level, the Amish said, conflicted with the norms and ideals and ways of life of their group. Somewhat surprisingly, the Supreme Court, in 1972, sided with the Amish against the rules of the state of Wisconsin.[101] The Supreme Court in this case romanticized the traditional, conservative folkways of the Amish. Gangs and crime families, for example, do not enjoy this sort of indulgence.

Some subgroups use their own system because it is cheaper and more convenient. In Eric Feldman's classic study of the "tuna court," Japanese tuna experts, in the great Tokyo fish market, settle disputes every day over the quality of auctioned tuna, and they do it quickly, expeditiously, and in a way that satisfies buyers and sellers alike. The "tuna court" (Feldman's name—not the name the tuna merchants use) is technically governmental, but tuna experts run it, not law experts; its users do not think of it as a court at all. In practice, it functions very much like the tribunals in close-knit groups.[102]

In the case of the diamond merchants, for example, the norms of the group, the peers, act in part as substitutes for formal law. Disputes do arise, of course, but there is strong peer pressure to keep these "within the family." Orthodox Jews insist that disputes must be resolved "inside," and there are mechanisms for doing this. Closed communities divide the world into insiders and outsiders; outsiders are resisted and resented. Members who break community rules do get punished, but only inside the group. They can reprimand or, in serious cases, ostracize. For extreme cases, there is banishment—expulsion from the group. This sanction can be brutally effective. It inflicts shame and stigma; it can also mean loss of jobs and connections—even family relations.

Just as peer group pressure can lead to compliance or noncompliance, peer pressure can lead to use or nonuse of doctrines and procedures of law. Diamond merchants and ranchers in Shasta County do not ignore torts and contracts—they do not even disapprove of the formal rules (when they know them); but they prefer to deal with issues of contract and tort in their own insider ways.

The living law is a buzzing, churning cauldron of ethical and social norms. Behavior follows a complex set of rules, which are not necessarily those of the law as taught in law schools. Stewart Macaulay's classic study of the use of contract law by businessmen in Wisconsin, which we mentioned earlier, is a case in point.[103]

A striking example of the power of peers in a small, closed group comes from an old study of society on a small, lonely, barren island in the Atlantic, Tristan da Cunha. Only a few hundred people lived on the island, growing potatoes and catching fish. A team of scholars visited the island in the 1930s. This was long before TV, satellites, the Internet, and other forms of modern communication; the island was almost totally isolated, shut off from the outside world. The visitors (from Scandinavia) were mostly interested in such things as bird life, but the team included social scientists, who studied community life on the island. They found no trace of anything we would conventionally call a legal system: no police, lawyers, jails, judges, courts. But, by the same token, they also found no trace of behavior that would be considered serious crime in other places—murder or rape, for example. No formal "law" existed; it was (it seems) simply not needed.

What made this place such a model of good behavior? The peer group. The pressure of what we might call public opinion. The islanders were utterly trapped on their island. A boat came by maybe once a year. The islanders were dependent on each other for social life and social support. Everybody on the island knew everybody else. Life on the island was totally transparent; life was governed by the "Argus-eyed vigilance of the community." The informal norms, under these circumstances, the pressures of peers, were simply too powerful to be disobeyed.[104]

Richard Schwartz, in the 1950s, published a now-classic study of two Israeli collective settlements. One of the settlements, the kvutza, was a small, face-to-face community, intensely egalitarian. Goods were owned in common, people ate together in dining halls; even the children were raised communally. In the kvutza, there were no formal legal organizations. Social norms and community opinion were all-powerful. There were certainly "laws" in the kvutza, in the sense of rules and ways of enforcing them, but the "law" in this community was like the law on Tristan da Cunha: completely informal, devastatingly powerful, and almost exclusively enforced through peer pressure and the opinion of the settlers.[105]

Can we generalize from these examples? Yes, to other small groups, like the Amish, or the diamond merchants, or the ranchers in Shasta County. Small, face-to-face communities more or less govern themselves; the power of peers is enough to keep the members in line. But not all of these communities are benign and well-run. Pitcairn Island, with fewer than 100 residents, was as remote and isolated as Tristan da Cunha. But it was, if anything, the very opposite of that island. Pitcairn, it seems, was a boiling pot of sexual violence against women.[106] The isolation of this island made it, in a way, into a kind of prison, and the "prisoners" behaved accordingly. Prisons themselves can be face-to-face communities. Inmates are trapped with each other; life in prison is like life on an island, except that the boat from the outside world never docks at all. The warden and guards are nominally in charge. They set the basic rules and they may crack down heavily on inmates during riots and bouts of disobedience. Nonetheless, in many prisons, the prisoners have a good deal of freedom, within the walls. As a result, some prisons turn into little dictatorships, where the toughest and most ruthless prisoners, often organized into gangs, run the show. In face-to-face communities, "peer pressure" always rules—but circumstances (and the identity of the members) determines whether the group becomes a kvutza or a gang-run prison.

Peer pressure is a powerful weapon, but, as a number of experiments have shown, it can be manipulated. The point is, people want to conform. If they are told that "everybody" is doing something, they are more likely to do it themselves. In today's world, which is strikingly horizontal, peers can be more important than parents and teachers, in many ways and in many circumstances. And the "peers" are not necessarily a flesh and blood group; they can be a generalized sense of what other people think and do, like the unseen hotel guests who occupied a room before the present guest checked in.[107] In Minnesota, authorities trying to increase compliance with tax laws told one group of taxpayers that their taxes were used for solid and beneficial purposes, all in the public interest. Others were told that cheaters could be punished. Still others were told how to get help in filling out returns. And some were "just told that more than 90 percent of Minnesotans already complied, in full, with their obligations under the tax law." It was this last intervention—and only that one—that produced results.[108]

Peer pressure, then, runs the gamut from the unseen hotel guests who stayed in Room 406 of some hotel, to the overwhelming power of other people, in closed communities like Tristan da Cunha. It can be a positive or a negative force. It can promote compliance with the norms of the state or push in the opposite direction. But clearly, peer pressure is a key factor in determining impact, in flattening out the deterrence curve.

8

THE INNER VOICE

THE THIRD CLUSTER of motives that mediate impact is extremely important, but also complex and difficult. It is a grab bag of various inner attitudes and moral issues, including what we often call conscience. There is general agreement that these motives matter, but how much is difficult to determine.

The third cluster explains most legal behavior. Most behavior is law-abiding (in most societies). Rewards and punishments do not explain why this should be so, at least not adequately. The third cluster is what flattens out the curve. It tells us why people pay their taxes, even though the risk of an audit is low. True, there is a cloverleaf factor: withholding. But people mostly pay taxes because they are supposed to: because it is legal; because everybody else is doing it; and because the state needs the money. Lars Feld and Bruno Frey talk about a "psychological tax contract."[1] People enter into this "contract" because they feel they get something for their money. But a sense of duty is primary. Deterrence plays a minor role. And procedures matter—fair procedures, legitimate procedures, even for questions of tax compliance. A study of Swiss cantons found that cantons with procedures that were more clearly "democratic" had lower rates of tax evasion.[2]

The concept of legitimacy is a concept in this third cluster that has attracted a good deal of scholarly attention. This has been an important pillar of the sociology of law, at least since the brilliant and insightful work of Max Weber. A system or institution is legitimate, according to Weber, if it is "endowed with the prestige of exemplariness and obligatoriness."[3] Weber distinguished between three sources of legitimate authority in a society or group. Charismatic authority is a kind of personal authority; it is the authority of a god, a hero, a prophet, a supreme leader. This is a rare but powerful type, the authority of Moses or Mohammed, or Jesus, or Buddha. Closer to home, perhaps, it is the authority of Joseph Smith or Mary Baker Eddy, founders of new religions. The word *charisma* has gone into the language, but in a weakened form. Someone who is popular and has a way with people; someone who lights up a room is said to have charisma. But to say that somebody running for governor of Wyoming has charisma because he has a good speaking voice and looks good on TV is not at all what Weber meant by the term.

Traditional authority, Weber's second type, is the authority of elders, chiefs, and other customary leaders. The Pope might be included in this list, and the Dalai Lama, as well. Individual popes might be men with dramatic personalities—crowds gather to hear them speak and conduct a mass—but the papacy itself is, at best, frozen charisma, institutionalized charisma. A pope, like a president, assumes the mantle of all the leaders who have gone before him, and part of his authority rests on this fact. The same is true of the Dalai Lama, and of tribal leaders in many societies, also some religious leaders. There can be dull popes, and dull presidents, but the papacy and the presidency still exert legitimate authority.

The third type is rational legitimacy; laws are obeyed simply because they are law, because they are consciously and deliberately made, and because they arise through procedures that society accepts. This is, of course, the chief source of legitimate authority in the modern world, although the other two types are by no means extinct. Niklas Luhmann, in his discussion of legitimacy, defines it as producing in people a "generalized willingness to accept decisions whose content is as yet undetermined."[4] Luhmann's definition makes explicit that (modern) legitimacy has a powerful, decisive procedural element. For Luhmann, in other words, legitimacy produces a quality of respect for rules, norms, and laws, not by virtue of their content, or because of the personalities of the lawmakers, but because of the way these rules, norms, or laws came into being: democratic elections, or orderly legal process, or majority vote.

I said "democratic elections," and, of course, in our day, those elections do act as a powerful legitimating factor. And, as Luhmann tells us, the factor has a strong procedural basis. But it is not simply the particular procedure that produces legitimacy. The key factor is that the procedure is itself legitimate. We live in the age of the human rights culture, the culture of equality and freedom, the culture of democracy, the idea of the will of the people, expressed in certain ways and through certain forms. It is these social facts that make the particular procedures of our times so powerfully legitimate. During the Middle Ages, of course, legitimacy rested on quite different pillars: the divine right of kings; the authority of lords, religious authority, and so on. There was, to be sure, a procedural element then, too: dynastic succession for kings, for example, or papal elections by the College of Cardinals. There is no guarantee our particular form of legitimacy will stay frozen in place. History never comes to a screeching halt. To us, it seems as if democratic (procedural) legitimacy is the end point of political evolution, the best and only way to govern society. But not everybody agrees. There are alternative schemes that claim legitimacy. And in some supposedly democratic countries, the legitimacy of the regime and its procedures seems wobbly at best.

One way of rephrasing this last, rather gloomy, caveat is to focus on Luhmann's definition again: legitimacy is a willingness to "accept" certain decisions, decisions that create laws and rules. But individuals and groups can, for one reason or another, decide to withhold this acceptance. Anti-democratic, fringe parties may increase their appeal. Devout members of fundamentalist religions do not accept laws and rules, no matter how they were made, if they contradict basic dogma. Then, also, one can ask: What does "acceptance" mean? It can be grudging or reluctant; it can be enthusiastic or various shades in between.[5] The modern state, perhaps, requires robust acceptance in order to maintain stability.

In any event, in one form or other, something like legitimacy plays an important role in studies of impact. Stig Gezelius and Maria Hauck, studying the regulation of fisheries, invoke the concept of "civic identity." This means that people feel "empowered . . . to participate" and have a sense of "citizenship." "Membership in the state has become part of people's conception of self—their social identity."[6] The state in question, of course, has to be more or less democratic, so that people in general (and fishermen in particular) think they have a stake in society, a voice. They also have to think that the rules of the game are fair, that they arose through legitimate processes, and that, consequently, they ought to be obeyed.

Culture and tradition surely play a role here, and the way the state is structured; also the way the organs of government behave. Swiss people tend to trust their government, probably rightly so. Americans have a lot less trust, but perhaps enough, and they are, on the whole, pretty good about obeying laws—even about paying taxes. Notoriously, people in Italy and Greece (at least by common repute) are much more likely to evade the tax laws. Neither peer pressure nor conscience seems to work, at least as far as taxation is concerned. In the fisheries study, compliance was high in Norway and low in South Africa, where there was "weak civic identity." The result was "high levels of resistance against fisheries laws and high levels of noncompliance."[7]

That legitimacy makes a difference seems at least plausible. Americans, aside from a few on the lunatic fringe, think tax laws, and most other laws, are both legitimate and necessary, whatever they may think of the rascals in Congress or the honesty or fairness of the local police force. We assume that this attitude has an impact on impact; we assume, in other words, that ideas of legitimacy affect law-related behavior. But do we actually know this? Legitimacy is not that easy to define or to study. Its effect on behavior is hard to tease out. I mentioned earlier a Swiss study of taxpaying behavior where, presumably, democratic legitimacy made a difference. In a survey done in the 1970s, people in various European countries were asked whether a person should obey a law even if that person thinks the law is unjust. In Germany, 66 percent of the respondents said yes; in Poland, only 45 percent. Another study of Polish attitudes at the time found that women, older people, better educated people, and white collar workers were more likely to display a general respect for law, compared to men, younger and less educated people, and unskilled workers.[8] Poland, of course, was a member of the Soviet bloc until 1989, and the legitimacy of the government was probably quite low. Tom Tyler's study, in Chicago, found high levels of support for obedience to law. Perhaps this was because of the way the question was framed. Still, it is striking that 82 percent of his respondents agreed with this statement: "People should obey the law even if it goes against what they think is right."[9]

What accounts for this attitude of respect? The answers most people might give would probably not satisfy a philosopher or a political theorist. People might say, "This is a democracy, we have majority rule, and the system wouldn't work if people just did whatever they felt like," or something along those lines. They are, in effect, invoking Weber's third source of legitimacy and, also, in a way, Luhmann's definition. People voted for their legislators; and a majority of the legislators voted for this law. In the United States, jury verdicts are legitimate; indeed, the right to trial by jury is enshrined in the Constitution. Most jury verdicts, moreover, have to be unanimous. And judicial decisions are legitimate because of the way judges are chosen; perhaps because of some notion that judges "follow the law." Note also that Weber speaks of legitimate authority. Authority is, indeed, significant. In society, it is usually an aspect of role. Mothers and fathers have authority over their children. Teachers have authority in the classroom. Judges have authority in the courtroom. The police have authority on the streets.

Authority, like legitimacy, is socially constructed. It rises and falls, becomes more or less potent, and is subject, also, to decay. The authority of parents in the modern world is definitely not what it used to be. The authority of governments varies from country to country. Position in an institutional structure is still crucial; the concept of the boss is a vital aspect of the world of work. One can again quote the great line from King Lear: "A dog's obeyed in office." The Milgram experiment is a prime example of the authority of authority.[10] Though, perhaps, once people realize that the office holder is, in fact, only a dog, the authority of that authority will decline, or vanish altogether.

Scholars generally agree that a sense of legitimacy influences impact, but how much does it actually explain? The question is, how often do people comply with law because of a sense of legitimacy and not because of any other reason? We do know (or think we know) that a system based only on fear, terror, or punishments is unstable; systems need the glue of voluntary obedience. Legitimacy might be one of the ingredients in that glue. But, as was said, it is not easy to prove the point. Tom Tyler's book *Why People Obey the Law* (an enlarged edition appeared in 2006) is one of the best-known attempts to demonstrate the power of legitimacy.[11] Tyler argued, on the basis of his findings, that the concept of legitimacy does help explain compliance, for the subjects of his research.

There has been a good deal of work on the subject since Tyler's book first appeared, some of it by Tyler himself. In an afterword published in 2006, Tyler claims that legitimacy, for his subjects, "was more influential than was the risk of being caught and punished for rule breaking."[12] But this statement goes way past what the evidence justifies. So much depends on what rule we are talking about. For murder, rape, burglary, and other major crimes, morality (the conviction that these acts are just plain wrong), together with fear of severe punishment, surely dwarfs the influence of legitimacy. After all, legitimacy, by definition, means compliance without regard to the content of the law. But the content of the law against murder is crucial. With regard to jaywalking, or shoplifting, matters might be different.

The core idea of legitimacy, in other words, is this: in society, there is a certain amount of obedience that comes from respect for authority rather than from fear of punishment or from feeling that the rule in question is the right thing to do, morally and socially. In recent years, drought plagued my home state of California. I share the sense of crisis and am eager to pitch in and save water. I also obey traffic rules because they make sense; speeding and going through red lights might cause an accident, injuring me, my passengers, or people in somebody else's car. I think people should pay taxes, because how else will we have an army, national parks, highways, and hospitals for veterans? "Legitimacy" explains none of these examples of law-abiding behavior. Legitimacy, pure and simple, means obedience, not for any substantive reason but because legitimate authority ought to be obeyed, willy-nilly. It explains why people followed Milgram's man in a white coat, not why we support, say, the welfare state.[13]

Legitimacy—a sense of the rightfulness of authority—does not come out of nowhere. Institutions are not inherently legitimate or illegitimate; they have to behave in ways that people consider legitimate, or at least seem to be doing this. This is, no doubt, a powerful influence on institutional behavior. Lauren Edelman has studied the growth of grievance procedures in businesses, ways of handling, for example, discrimination complaints. Civil rights laws created a new and tricky environment for business, and setting up procedures inside the companies was more than an attempt to comply with the law; it was also a way to achieve legitimacy. The "legal environment" was "a central determinant of organizational change." Change (in procedures and grievance structures) was the result of a "quest for legitimacy." Of course, keeping the workers happy and avoiding a lot of conflict is important to businesses, and these have an impact on profits as well. But this, Edelman argues, is only a part of the story.[14]

Legitimacy (and its evil twin, illegitimacy) is not the same as a sense of morality, a sense of right and wrong. Moral power is probably a stronger force than the naked sense of legitimacy. Moral power and deterrent power are, in a way, competitors. Ironically, for a big crime like murder, deterrence is important only for a few bad guys, the potential murderers, rather than for the rest of us. A shift in punishment from, say, the death penalty to life in prison has no effect on you and me, because we are simply not about to kill people. Since the curve has flattened out, the people who actually might kill are the hardest to deter; yet, paradoxically, they are the only ones for whom changes in punishment scales might conceivably make a difference.[15]

Blind Obedience?

The famous (or notorious) study by Stanley Milgram, already mentioned, was designed to measure obedience to authority, or to put it another way, the mechanism of obedience.[16] In the experiment, you recall, if the "learner" (an actor, actually) made a mistake, the subject was supposed to give the man a jolt of electricity. As wrong answers increased, the shocks also increased. At some points, the learner would groan and demand to be released from the experiment; ultimately, he would give off an "agonized scream." (All this was, in fact, play-acting.) The poor and unsuspecting subject would squirm and feel uncomfortable, but the experimenter, the man in the white coat, would insist that he go on inflicting pain. And an astonishing number did exactly that. They went on inflicting pain to the bitter end. They could have quit at any point; but few did.

Milgram's experiment was an attempt to explain a puzzling and deeply troubling phenomenon. During the period of the Second World War, the Nazi regime put to death millions of innocent people; this included Gypsies, gays, and anyone who dared voice political dissent. The worst Nazi crime, however, was the slaughter of some six million Jews: men, women, and children. Adolf Hitler and his close associates were ultimately responsible for these unspeakable crimes, but the leaders, of course, did not carry out these killings themselves. The machinery of murder was a huge enterprise. It took thousands of men and women at the operating level, men and women who cooperated and collaborated in senseless, wholesale slaughter—who managed and ran the concentration camps, the killing fields in occupied Polish and Baltic villages, and who operated the gas chambers and the crematoria, where they produced huge mounds of corpses, a kind of assembly line of dead bodies, with cold factory efficiency. In many towns, groups of Germans (and helpers from other nationalities) massacred thousands of innocent people. They destroyed whole communities, killing all the local Jews, from babies up to grizzled old men. For Hitler and his circle, there can be no excuses, no mitigation; their guilt was absolute. But many of the subordinates, the workers in the field, claimed that they were simply obeying orders: legitimate commands from higher authorities.

Milgram's experiment seemed to show that people will blindly follow authority, will obey evil commands, even commands that they find abhorrent. Christopher Browning studied the behavior, during the Second World War, of a group of "ordinary men," members of a German Reserve Police Battalion. They were ordered to murder about 1,500 Jews in a Polish village—women, children, and old men. Almost all of the members followed orders. "To break ranks," Browning argued, "was simply beyond most of the men"; it was "easier for them to shoot." Resisting the orders was an "asocial act vis-à-vis one's comrades." The non-shooters "risked isolation, rejection, and ostracism." Here, the urge to obey authority (and perhaps fear of what might happen to dissidents) linked up with strong peer pressure. A few men refused to go along; these men perhaps lost face, but their higher-ups did not, in fact, punish them.[17]

Milgram and Browning were looking specifically at what Herbert Kelman and Lee Hamilton have called "crimes of obedience,"[18] crimes that arise "from a conflict between two competing duties: the duty to obey and the duty to disobey." The duty to obey "is inherent in the very concept of authority," and it is strongly backed by social norms.[19] During the Vietnam War, villagers in the village of My Lai were massacred. An American army officer, Lieutenant William Calley, was accused of responsibility for the massacre. Calley claimed he was simply following orders; his superior told him, he said, that the villagers were enemies and that he should put them to death. Whether such an order was ever given is dubious. But Calley apparently believed the order had been given; he thus felt justified in doing what he did. Moreover, Calley did not do all the killing himself. Men under his command joined in, in obedience to Calley's orders.

"Obeying orders" is not, in fact, a legal excuse in a criminal case. The Nuremberg Charter, which formed the basis for the Nuremberg trials after the Second World War, specifically provided as much: the "fact that the Defendant acted pursuant to orders of his Government or of a superior shall not free him from responsibility" (Art. 8), though it could be a factor in "mitigation of punishment." But it is not easy for "ordinary men" to disobey what seem to be valid orders. If an officer tells a foot soldier to do something illegal, the poor soldier faces a terrible dilemma. Refusing to carry out an order is itself a military offense. But there is, morally and factually, a difference between an order to violate some minor rule and an order to kill innocent people, where the order itself seems clearly both wrong and illegal.

Milgram's experiment was certainly striking but, of course, it hardly explains "crimes of obedience" in full. Indeed, the word *obedience* seems out of place in any discussion of the crimes of the Nazi regime. It ignores the poisonous ideology that animated that regime and infected thousands of adherents. It ignores the "ordinary men" who eagerly took part in the slaughters. Milgram was studying obedience to legitimate authority. But the more powerful motive in the many genocides that stain human history is blind hatred. Just as morality is a mighty force in society, so, too, is its dark opposite: racism, prejudice, religious fanaticism, beliefs in the right to torture and kill infidels, enemies of the state, and all those who, for whatever reason, are despised and dehumanized.

The Courts

What Weber called rational-legal authority is the pillar of legitimacy in our contemporary world. It has, as was mentioned, a strong procedural element. People in Sweden or Canada or Japan believe in the forms of democracy: free elections, regular Parliamentary procedures.

But what about unelected courts? Especially the powerful constitutional courts of today, the courts that exercise judicial review in practically every developed country, along with the transnational courts, like the European Court of Justice, the European Court of Human Rights, or the Inter-American Court of Human Rights. Their source of legitimacy is what we can call the human rights culture.[20] In other words, in our societies, elections are not the only basis of legitimacy. There are strong beliefs among most citizens about basic, fundamental rights, rights that belong to every man, woman, and child. And people think of these rights as inherent, and as (more or less) absolute.

This is not a matter of political theory or philosophy. The human rights culture is a popular social fact. The precise menu of rights, socially and in legal terms, varies somewhat from place to place and from group to group; there is, however, a common core: free speech, for example, or the right to travel, or freedom of religion. These rights trump all other acts of government. They are superior to acts of parliament, executive orders, regulations of administrative agencies—everything, in short. The state has a duty to protect these rights. And legislatures have no authority to tamper with them.

But these rights would mean little or nothing if they could not be enforced. Enforcement is all. Essentially, the government is supposed to respect these rights—voluntarily, without prodding. But if they do not, people can turn to the enforcement institution. Enforcement is the role of the courts, the role of judicial review. And this power is what gives legitimacy to these courts.

The justices of the United States Supreme Court have life tenure. The court has claimed the right to review acts of Congress since the great case of *Marbury v. Madison* in 1803.[21] The Supreme Court, however, exercised this right only rarely until the late nineteenth century, and only in the late twentieth century did protection of minority rights, and protection of fundamental freedoms, become a key factor in the work of the court. This is also the period—the late twentieth century—when other powerful courts emerged in other countries, like the European Court of Human Rights (on the national level), the German Constitutional Court, and the South African High Court, to mention a few salient examples.

Modern constitutions set out lists of fundamental rights and provide explicitly for judicial review. But constitutions are, after all, nothing but words, texts, pieces of paper. The United States Constitution is very old, and very short, as constitutions go. In theory, the Supreme Court simply interprets the language of this old constitution. The European Court of Human Rights also claims, no matter how bold the decision, to be doing nothing more than interpreting the words of the European Charter of Fundamental Rights. But no serious scholar, here or abroad, takes these claims at face value.

When a justice of the Supreme Court is appointed in the United States, the Senate must approve, and the Senate Judiciary Committee holds hearings. The senators, in recent times, have refused to rubber-stamp the president's appointments; they grill and question nominees quite thoroughly. The hearings have a curious, unrealistic quality; they are, in a way, nothing but a game of make-believe. To win senatorial votes, the nominee tells the panel that he or she intends simply to follow the law; to be faithful to the text of the Constitution; not to make new law; and, above all, never to act for political reasons. They pledge allegiance, in other words, to a theory of mechanical jurisprudence. They present themselves as political virgins, without beliefs or ideologies; and swear never never to make policy, or to let policy considerations influence their votes. As I said, no serious scholar believes this and neither, in all likelihood, do the senators. But any nominee whose testimony deviates from the ruling fairy tale is likely to be in trouble. Justice Sonia Sotomayor had some explaining to do, because, at one point, she had said that a "wise Latina" might have a better grasp of some judicial issues than a white male. Republicans in the Senate denounced this as some sort of foul heresy. Justice Sotomayor explained, disingenuously, that she was just trying to inspire Latino youth, and was not voicing a judicial philosophy.[22]

The question is: Is the charade really necessary? Does the legitimacy of the Supreme Court actually depend on this myth? James Gibson and Gregory Caldeira, in an interesting study,[23] claim that the answer is no. Most Americans, they find, "have a fairly realistic view of how Supreme Court justices make their decisions." They believe that "judges have discretion" and that they "make discretionary decisions on the basis of ideology and values." But, according to Gibson and Caldeira, this awareness does not impair the legitimacy of the court. People realize that the court makes policy, that it innovates. But they believe the justices act in a principled way. In other words, the justices are not politicians and do not behave like politicians. They do make policy decisions, but policy is not the same as politics. A more sophisticated observer would add: they make policy because they must. They are "interpreting" an old text, a short text, a text with many vague general clauses. A modern judge could hardly behave otherwise. Even high court judges in, say, India or Germany, despite more recent, long, and detailed constitutions, have enormous discretion with regard to the more general and inclusive aspects of the text.

The Other Side of the Coin: How Illegitimacy Works

Legitimacy may be an important factor in the decision to obey, or use, legal institutions. But even in open societies, democratic societies, there might be corners of the legal order where rules or institutions lack the glow of legitimate authority. In every society, there are dissenters, either from this or that law or institution, or from some aspect of it. Examples of civil disobedience range from sullen and begrudging behavior to more dramatic instances: young men who burn draft cards, ecological extremists who chain themselves to trees, Tibetan nationalists who set themselves on fire, prisoners on hunger strikes, and jihadists and revolutionaries of all sorts and stripes. In the course of history, dissenters have overthrown countless governments, and driven countless monarchs, despots, and panjandrums from their throne. Democratic regimes, too, have been overthrown. There have been countless military coups and innumerable cases in which faction A displaced faction B and took over some regime. On a humbler plane, whenever citizens go to court insisting that some law or regulation is unconstitutional, they are claiming that a legislature or executive agencies acted in an illegitimate way. Judicial review gives them this opening, gives them a legitimate way to attack (alleged) illegitimacy.

Tom Tyler's work on legitimacy could assume (correctly) that Americans are not revolutionaries and that the citizens consider their system, generally speaking, legitimate. He wanted to know how much influence on attitudes and behavior flowed from this sense of legitimacy. But in many countries, you cannot make any such assumption about legitimacy. Since world history is punctuated with bloody uprisings, revolutions, riots, and disorders, the sense of illegitimacy may be as common as the opposite, if not more so.

In contemporary society, the human rights culture has enormous tensile strength. Yet a good half of the countries in the world are not democracies at all, or are at best semi-democracies; this despite the presumed wishes of a large part of the population. Many contemporary societies flagrantly violate human rights; many are extremely corrupt. In many, the rule of law is weak to nonexistent. Before the modern period, all countries were authoritarian. Peasants in the Middle Ages did not vote. Riots came from hunger and despair, not from a demand for the ballot. But in today's world, democracy and the rule of law are deeply ingrained in the culture of millions or billions of people; so much so that even dictators give it lip service.[24] They sign on to human rights treaties and charters that they have no intention of taking seriously. Some of these regimes seem quite popular—Vladimir Putin's Russia, for example. In other cases, the population seems restless and disgruntled.

In societies where people largely consider the regime illegitimate, there is widespread violation of certain laws or, very often, people find ways to detour around them. Countries that peg currencies at artificial and unrealistic rates can be counted on to generate vibrant black markets. In Eastern Europe before 1990, people in Poland or East Germany tended to think that their governments were puppets of the Soviet Union. A wild efflorescence of "informal" law developed, underground law, whole systems of behavior that defied or evaded the formal rules. For example, in East Germany (the GDR), state ideology rejected capitalism; the government owned or controlled the major means of production. Individuals could own "personal" goods, like bicycles, dishes, and shoes, but not businesses or factories or farmland. Most citizens probably never accepted Marxist ideology; as the years went on, fewer and fewer people trusted or respected the government. A "shadow economy" grew up, "ruled by a private moral code."

This last phrase is a quote from an illuminating study by Inga Markovits describing legal life in a smallish city in East Germany between 1945 and 1990.[25] There was, for example, a vigorous underground market in used cars. The price of used cars was controlled, like all other prices. But only a fool would sell a car at the government price; this was much less than the value of even the worst jalopy. Instead, people bought and sold cars in a more or less free market, held once a month in a big, empty field. Sellers and buyers negotiated a price and manipulated the documents so that, if the deal went sour, the contract could be enforced in the regular courts. All of this was totally illegal. But everybody knew what was going on. The deals took place in the open. Judges and police, like the rest of the people in town, surely understood how the used car market actually worked. Nobody lifted a finger to get rid of it. The official rules, with regard to sales of used cars, had no moral salience. They were considered absurd or perverse.

Examples could be multiplied from all over the Soviet bloc. Maria Łoś studied criminality in Poland and the Soviet Union in the 1980s. Citizens, she felt, lacked faith in their governments. They considered these regimes corrupt and ineffective and tyrannical—in short, illegitimate. Ordinary workers, farmers, and civil servants consequently had no loyalty to the system. The whole atmosphere was, therefore, "conducive to the widespread criminal involvement of rank-and-file employees, industrial workers, and peasants."[26]

In an interesting study, Xin He interviewed rural migrants living in the Beijing area who worked in the garment industry or ran small businesses. Under Chinese law at the time, these workers and businesspeople had no legal right to live and work in Beijing. Shopkeepers needed business licenses and did not have them.[27] Local authorities, the migrants felt, cared only for money; they enforced rules in a random, arbitrary way and were open to corruption. Indeed, it was "prohibitively costly and inconvenient" to comply with the rules about licenses, even if you wanted to.[28] Pure illegality—going ahead without the licenses— had its costs, too; it was a precarious way to live your life and conduct your affairs.

Migrants found a sort of halfway solution, which Xin He calls "legal collusion." For example, migrants might make arrangements with legal residents, who acted as fronts for the migrants. Technically, this, too, was illegal; but less blatantly so. It lay in a kind of "gray area." The migrants paid rent to locals. Clearly, migrants felt no moral compunctions about breaking rules. They had to live, and they were contributing, they felt, to the city and to society in general. Local authorities, too, accepted the system. The migrants paid them off and also showed them "respect."[29] Everyone, including the public, benefitted from a vigorous and lively—if illegal—garment industry.

Xin He's work is a case study of one group coping with a situation of legal illegitimacy. Each situation, of course, is unique. In this case, it was China's system of residence permits and the complicated and expensive license rules that drove the garment industry into the gray area he described. The situation resembled, at least at one level, the situation in East Germany. Both studies remind us, too, that legitimacy and illegitimacy are not all-or-nothing concepts. Even in authoritarian societies, some aspects of the state, some aspects of law, are legitimate. Xin He's migrants had no faith in the local rules, but they were not revolutionaries. They were ordinary people trying to make a living in a tough environment. East Germans shopping for used cars in an open field were not manning barricades or risking their lives in the battle against state socialism. And in East Germany, the local courts functioned and were trusted in many minor matters of contract or family law. In many societies, perhaps most, particular rules and institutions may lack legitimacy. But the regime itself is in no danger of falling, and may even win a kind of grudging acceptance from the citizens. In these situations, people learn to find ways around the rules, or ways to work the rules. Low-level officials often support them, either because they take bribes or because they, too, have no great faith in official rules. And, of course, ordinary people in some of these societies simply assume that this is the way all systems work; that there is no realistic alternative.

Trust and Fairness

Trust is a concept closely related to legitimacy but analytically distinct. Faith in experts is a form of trust: you do what the doctor tells you because you trust the doctor, because you believe in her honesty and professional skill. A person might also trust the legislature, that is, assume that it knows what it is doing. A lot of the law has to be taken on faith. If the Food and Drug Administration approves a new drug for arthritis, people probably assume that the FDA has reviewed the clinical tests, and consequently, the drug works and is safe to use. This is not at all the same as following the FDA because it is a legitimate authority, with the right to oversee the market in drugs. There is also, of course, distrust. You can think, for example, that the FDA is legitimate, created by a valid law, and that it follows the rules laid down in the governing law; but you might still distrust its decision to approve this or that drug, for one reason or another; or the general attitude toward food dyes, or its position on folk remedies.

Fairness is another closely related concept. You might obey a rule not because the source was legitimate, and not because you trust the source, but because the rule applies to everybody, and why should you be any different? A student might think that it is unfair to other students to cheat on an exam, aside from any question of morality, especially if the course is graded on a curve. In New York City, home of the United Nations, thousands of men and women drive cars with diplomatic plates; for years, many of them ignored traffic rules. The drivers had diplomatic immunity. If they parked illegally, they might get a ticket, but they would not have to pay. Thousands of these tickets, in fact, went unpaid. But diplomats from many countries obeyed the rules; and if they violated a rule, they did, in fact, pay the fine. Surely a sense of fairness was one factor. If nobody else can park next to a fireplug, why should they be able to? Some countries—including the United Kingdom, Australia, Ecuador, Israel, and Jamaica—were scrupulous about paying for fines and tickets. Interestingly, there was a correlation—imperfect, to be sure—between a country's reputation for corruption and the refusal of their diplomats to pay. Kuwait, Egypt, Chad, and the Sudan were the worst offenders. Did cynicism about legal processes at home carry over into the streets of New York City?[30]

The scholarship on procedural justice is also relevant to issues of fairness and trust. If the research can be trusted, fair procedures are "central to the willingness to defer to decisions," and presumably help in insuring compliance with decisions.[31] This seems fairly plausible, but the question is: How far can you go with this idea? I doubt that an innocent man condemned to life in prison, or put on death row, would have a warm feeling about the trial verdict, even when (arguably) the state followed all the rules, dotted all the i's and crossed all the t's, and the proceedings were scrupulously fair. A good outcome—or, perhaps, an outcome better than expected—is what people, in general, want. Or one that is fair, in their opinion, because they were treated like everybody else.[32] But, of course, the treatment itself must be considered fair. Nobody thinks a situation is fair if it is uniformly unfair to all concerned.

Psychologists have wondered: What do people consider a just result, and why? Fair procedure is certainly one element. So is fairness: Is everybody, or everybody at least in your group, treated the same? Another aspect has to do with expectations: whether things turned out better or worse than expected.[33] In a study published in the 1970s, two German scholars studied winners and losers in lawsuits between landlords and tenants in three German cities. The winners were happy; the losers were not. No surprise. The interviewers asked litigants whether the experience had "strengthened or weakened their confidence" in the system of justice. None of the losers said their confidence had been strengthened; the experience soured more than two-thirds of them on the system to a lesser or greater degree. Winners did feel more confidence in the system, but they gained less in confidence than the losers lost.[34] Common sense (which is at least sometimes correct) suggests that this study gets it right. People want fair procedures, but, as we suggested, they like winning better than losing. They like fairness, too; but winning or losing might influence their judgment about fairness.

People who think a law is unfair might be more willing to break the law. This is surely true of people who engage in civil disobedience. But in some cases, it is tricky to tease out cause and effect. We can ask: Which comes first—the lawbreaking or the sense that the law is unfair? In an old study of rent control in Hawaii, by Harry Ball, landlords who thought rent control was unfair were the ones who broke the rules and overcharged tenants.[35] Did the sense of unfairness make these landlords willing to overcharge? Or was it the other way around: landlords who broke the rules rationalized what they did, telling themselves the rules were unfair, in this way justifying their actions to themselves.

Shiri Regev-Messalem studied Israeli women who cheated on the welfare laws; these women, she found, felt justified in cheating. They felt "morally entitled" to a level of support they could not (legally) get under the law. They also felt they simply had to cheat to survive. Again, we might ask which came first: the sense of unfairness or the feeling that they had to cheat to stay alive.[36] An interview study of shoplifters exposed a rich and varied menu of "neutralizations" ("excuses" might be a better word). Some of these "neutralizations" mix together cause and effect. Some shoplifters said that the stores "deserve it"; they were ripping people off. Or the stores could afford it: they "don't even miss the little bit I get." Or they "write if off their taxes . . . . So, nobody gets hurt." Or the shoplifter may refer to her personal situation; she has to have the money (like Regev-Messalem's welfare women): "I had to take care of three children," or "I got behind on all my bills." Or they might simply explain that the whole world shoplifts: "everybody does it."[37] A movie star, Winona Ryder, who seemed to have a passion for shoplifting, at one point claimed she was doing research for a role she would play as a kleptomaniac in a movie—a flimsy and unlikely excuse.[38] But no doubt each crime, each violation of a regulation, could produce its own menu of "neutralizations."

Morality

Another motive in this third cluster is something we might call morality. People obey rules because the rules are moral, or ethical, or even because they are God's will. Conversely, they disobey rules because they are immoral, or unethical, or against the will of God. Or we follow a rule because it is good policy, sound in principle, or necessary for society. Opposite feelings (the law does more harm than good) might conceivably influence the rate of noncompliance.

Religious beliefs, traditional customs, even superstitions play a big role in determining the impact of law, perhaps the most powerful role of all. Accident victims in Chiang Mai, Thailand, in the study by the Engels mentioned earlier, refused to go for compensation because of their brand of Buddhist beliefs (along with notions about ghosts and karma).[39] Devout Catholics who find themselves trapped in an unhappy marriage will avoid the divorce court, no matter what. We live in an age of suicide bombers, men (mostly young) who blow up themselves (and other people), presumably because of strong religious and political convictions. The rest of us find this detestable (and scary). We might feel differently about Tibetan monks who set themselves on fire in the cause of freedom for Tibet. All of these acts are, of course, illegal.

Religious doctrine is powerful among the strict believers; and it affects their attitudes toward law, and their use of law. But even among the faithful, there is considerable variation. The Catholic Church forbids contraception; but most Catholics, even those who are otherwise rather observant, pay no attention. There is no other way to explain the low birthrate in Poland, a firmly Catholic country, unless Polish couples do a lot of serious abstaining, which seems highly unlikely.

Yet moral notions, on the whole, can be extremely powerful. It is moral notions that flatten out the curve for crimes like rape and murder. We mentioned, earlier, a study (using vignettes) that tried to see whether male college students could imagine themselves committing sexual assault. For the most part, they could not; but not because of sanctions (formal and informal). The students' "moral beliefs were a more important source of social control." For students who thought it was just plain "morally wrong" to force sex on a woman, "concerns of cost/benefit" had no relevance. "Their moral condemnation of the action was so strong that they could not even consider the possibility of offending."[40] This "finding" is no surprise to anybody actually living on this planet. We all have moral red lines we absolutely will not cross. That some act or behavior is against the law is therefore irrelevant; we simply will not go there.

Patriotism is another powerful emotion, together with its cousin, civic duty. During times of crisis—wartime, for example—people rally around the flag. They donate time and money, volunteer for dangerous or disagreeable jobs, even put their lives on the line. Men rush to the recruiting office when war breaks out. There is also state, city, and local patriotism; people shout and holler and cheer for their city's team (even if nobody in a Dallas uniform actually comes from or lives in Dallas). Texans seems to indulge in an orgy of local patriotism that would baffle people from, say, Oregon or Ohio. Texas launched a campaign to cut down on highway littering. They appealed to general civic duty: no result. Then the state hit on a different scheme: invoking local pride. A new slogan, "Don't Mess with Texas," was wildly successful. Roadside litter declined dramatically.[41]

Patriotism, or, more accurately, love of country, is independent of the sense of legitimacy. Citizens can be intensely "patriotic" even when they despise their particular regime. The Soviet Union was a murderous dictatorship, but when German armies poured across the borders in 1941, people fought to save the fatherland, an emotion that trumped any reservations about the Soviet government. In Australia, voting is mandatory, but in the United States and most other countries, it is not. And, alas, although most people vote in crucial elections, millions of people can't be bothered either to register or to vote. In off-year elections in the United States, sometimes as few as a third of the eligible voters actually do so. Yet in South Africa, when finally, after the end of apartheid, blacks got the right to vote, they voted by the millions, standing in line long hours to exercise this new and precious right.

Civic duty is not a single, undivided thing. Much depends on the situation. California, as I mentioned, is subject to periodic bouts of drought (a recent cluster of dry years was particularly severe). Something has to be done. Rules are laid down, but often without any way to enforce them, or, at best, sporadic enforcement. A green, well-watered lawn is an obvious violation, but there are millions of lawns to patrol. There is no way to check whether people take shorter showers and flush their toilets less. In a crass, calculating sense, there is no incentive to cut down on use of water. It is easy to ignore the rules, easy to be a free rider on other people's efforts. Yet, during past droughts, millions of people did cut back on water use, even though enforcement was weak. People were willing, even eager, to do their part. Of course, there were violators, but no rule ever gets perfect obedience.

Culture and Consciousness

Two rather vexed concepts, legal culture and legal consciousness, have been used by scholars in a number of ways. Both refer to a kind of mental element that has an impact on the way people think about law, and use or misuse the law.

The term *legal culture* dates at least to 1969 (and probably earlier); in a 1969 article, I defined legal culture to mean people's ideas, expectations, and attitudes about law and the legal system.[42] Later scholars have criticized the term and its definition on a number of grounds, and this definition is not by any means fully accepted in the field. Other scholars use the term in other ways, not all consistent with each other, and possibly not even consistent with themselves.[43] Nevertheless, I think it is a useful concept. It might, I suppose, need a better name.

In any event, we need a term that refers to mental, emotional, and cognitive elements that are connected to, and perhaps determine, the use of legal tools and instruments. The legal system can be compared to a giant machine. The machine will not work unless you turn on the switch. The legal culture is the mental element—psychological, cultural, moral—that turns the switch on or off, other things being equal. The reason to hedge somewhat is that legal culture is not the only reason the switch gets turned on or off. After all, the machine might be out of order. It might be locked in a room to which only a few people have the key. Maybe it costs a big fat fee to use the machine. Similarly, the legal system can be too expensive for people, or paralyzed by corruption, or accessible only to the rich and powerful. These factors all bear on the question: Will the machine be turned on or off?

Nonetheless, legal culture (in the original sense) does make a difference. The Engels' accident victims in Chiang Mai refused to turn on the switch for religious reasons, and because of traditional habits and beliefs. People litigate, or not, not just for reasons of cost and convenience, but also because they might disapprove of litigation. A devout Catholic will stay away from divorce lawyers. This is third-cluster material: matters of morality and conscience. But these factors do not exist in a vacuum; they are culturally specific. Personality also makes a difference. People who are extremely rights-conscious, who "stick up for their rights," who "don't take things lying down," are more prone to turn on the switch. This, too, might be a matter of (general) culture. The Japanese are said to hate litigation and love mediation (unlike Americans). This, as we saw, may or may not be true, but the impact of general culture on legal culture, on the use of law, seems undeniable.

A concept closely related to legal culture is legal consciousness. Laura Beth Nielsen defines it to mean the "commonsense understanding" that people have about "the way law works." It is "how people think about the law."[44] So understood, legal consciousness is, in a way, a sub-category or aspect of legal culture. Patricia Ewick and Susan Silbey, in a widely cited and influential book, *The Common Place of Law*, explored the notion of legal consciousness.[45] Ewick and Silbey distinguished be-tween various types of people. Some, whose legal consciousness is "with the law," are ready and willing to use law, to turn on the switch. Some, whose consciousness is "against the law," see law as some kind of enemy or threat or obstacle. These are not inborn traits, of course, but products of the social context. Undocumented aliens in the United States are often paralyzed by fear that they might be caught and de-ported; they (quite rationally) do not dare take legal action of any sort, even when they have a perfect right to do so.[46] They are, then, "against the law" in the sense that they treat the (immigration) law as an enemy.

Many studies of legal consciousness are studies of litigation: what makes people go to court, or avoid it. Some studies look at the way or-dinary people react to rights and courts.[47] Obviously, though, to sue somebody or some company (or go to arbitration or mediation) is not the only way to use the legal system. You can decide to make out a will, or not. A family in financial trouble can decide to go through bank-ruptcy. If somebody backs into your car in a parking lot and puts a big dent in the side, you can try to collect compensation through an insurance company; you can also decide to forget the whole thing, like the Engels' people in Chiang Mai.

These concepts—legal culture and legal consciousness—can be useful in organizing and guiding research. "Culture," however, is a very iffy word, with a wide range of meanings. Sometimes people use it to mean some sort of deep-seated social tradition, aspects of society that, for whatever reason, have penetrated the collective soul and influenced thoughts and behaviors in society, and in a long-lasting way. This is what people sometimes seem to mean when they talk about Japanese culture, or Russian culture, or Chinese culture. In this sense, culture is something sticky, something tenacious, something that changes only slowly, if at all. In the legal world, some scholars use culture in a similar way. They think of common law as a culture, and civil law too—legal traditions, in an abiding, long-term, and influential sense. Litigiousness and rights-consciousness are also supposed to be cultural aspects of a system, in a deep and long-lasting sense.

But do societies really conform to their stereotypes? Some studies, like those of John Haley, for example,[48] have cast doubt on conventional ideas about Japanese legal culture. He has argued, as we saw, that the Japanese will litigate when it is cheap and convenient to do so. Eric Feldman studied the way legal institutions reacted to a specific crisis—blood tainted with the AIDS virus—in France, the United States, and Japan. The blood had been used for patients who needed transfusions, and for hemophiliacs. Victims went to court in all three countries, but the reaction of the courts—and the victims—did not conform to conventional stereotypes about legal culture. In Feldman's view, scholars should "reconsider" their conventional understandings—views about "Japanese group-based and harmony-rooted values" and "Western individualism and litigiousness." These simply did not fit the way societies responded to the problem of contaminated blood.[49] Incentive structures matter more than cultural traditions, customs, and deeply rooted moral systems. That was his argument.

There is no general rule. We can recall, once more, the Engels' study of accident victims in Chiang Mai. Here, they argued, culture in the sense of deep-seated traditions and religious beliefs did matter.[50] But perhaps the next generation in Chiang Mai, the children of the subjects the Engels studied, would have a different take on accident compensation. Culture is probably more changeable, more malleable, than many people think. Illiterate peasants emigrate to the United States and their grandchildren are totally American, culturally speaking. The culture of the old country vanishes like snow in summer. Family law, because it reflects an intensely personal, emotionally charged reality, is supposed be more sticky, less elastic than, say, commercial law or securities law. But in reality hardly anything has changed as dramatically in the past few generations as family law, both as cause and effect of a changing legal culture. Consider, for example, attitudes toward gay marriage in the United States. In less than one generation, this went from a crazy, fringe idea to a national norm.

Whatever their background, no powerful cultural or religious norm discourages rights-consciousness among Americans. People in the United States, according to Sally Merry, "see the law as a source of authority in a society organized by rules, not by violence." Law is taken as "symbolically powerful"; it "expresses a pervasive pattern of social ordering."[51] This inclines people to use law instrumentally, perhaps, in ways that a Russian or a Japanese citizen might not. If Americans go to court, however, they find (according to Merry) that "their legal consciousness differs in subtle ways from that of the clerks, prosecutors, and mediators they meet there."[52] Culture, including legal culture, varies by occupation, by situation, and by social stratum.

Consider, for example, the Shasta county ranchers studied by Ellickson.[53] From this study, and others, comes the general idea that close-knit groups, even though they seem quite different, do share some "cultural" traits. No two groups could resemble each other less than Orthodox Jewish city folks in the diamond business and cattle ranchers in northern California. But there are similarities of situation. Close-knit groups do not like to use formal law; they have an aversion to intervention by "outsiders"; and they rule themselves according to norms of trust and fairness and internal ideas of right and wrong.

For these groups, it is difficult to disentangle cluster three (the moral element) from cluster two (the peer group). Or cluster one, for that matter (rewards and punishments). If you disobey the rules in your close-knit group, you can be punished (by ostracism, for example), you will feel the pressure of the peer group, and very likely your own inner voice will add to the sense of discomfort; unless, of course, you have abandoned the values and goals of the group. In that case, for the most part, you are better off making your exit, though this is never (psychologically) easy to do.

All groups, whether small or large, have a legal culture in the sense of patterns of mental attitudes, beliefs, and expectations. We cannot assume that legal culture, unlike culture in the deep-seated sense, is fixed, relatively unchanging, and persists from generation to generation. It may do so, of course, among isolated groups like the Amish. But in the wilderness of modern urban life, the pace of cultural change can be quite fast, dizzyingly fast. Every large immigrant country is a melting pot. We are like passengers on a runaway train, which accelerates geometrically as it rushes along.

The Business World

Most of the discussion to this point has been about individuals, about people, why they do or don't comply, evade, disobey, or otherwise react to legal interventions. Perhaps more attention was paid to burglars than to businesses, though we did not ignore by any means styles and patterns of business regulation. In modern, developed societies, an immense body of rules, laws, and regulations are directed at businesses of various kinds, sometimes at businesses in general. The modern state is a regulatory state. Free markets, yes—in general. But laissez-faire, decidedly not. A perfect storm of directives, rules, statutes, regulations, and guiding principles swirls about, emanating from state and local governments, national governments, and transnational and international organizations like the EU, the WTO, and the IMF.

Big businesses are complex organisms. Of course, ultimately, people make the decisions. Corporations, legally speaking, are "artificial persons," but they are not run by robots (not yet). In a giant corporation, compliance with regulations, from the Securities and Exchange Commission or the Food and Drug Administration or the Equal Employment Opportunity Commission, can depend on the actions of a whole army of people, sometimes acting in groups. The main goal of a business, whatever its propaganda, is making money; otherwise, it will go into bankruptcy or get gobbled up by competitors. *Homo eco-*

nomicus may be something of a myth; *businessperson economicus* much less so. Presumably, cost-benefit analysis guides the behavior of corporations; if the benefits of compliance outweigh the costs, the business should comply. Otherwise not.

But this, it turns out, is much too simple a formulation. A corporation has no conscience and no peer group, but the people who run it do. "Normative factors" or the "moral evaluation of the act" weigh heavily on decisions to commit or not commit corporate crime.[54] Some of the studies already mentioned show in fact that "regulated enterprises" are sometimes "motivated to comply with regulations, and even to go beyond literal compliance, not only by fear of legal sanctions but also by social pressures and norms."[55] These norms and pressures work best in big business; less well in "small-firm, highly competitive markets," with "many low-visibility smaller firms." The quotes come from a study of the trucking industry. Size of firm was a factor; so was the "particular market niche—the kinds of goods hauled, how far, and what service and price package its customers wanted most."[56]

There are voluminous studies of business regulation: what works, what doesn't work. Mention or discussion of this subject has appeared at various points in this book. Deterrence theory—rewards and punishments—clearly plays a role. There is also input from peer influence (from businesspeople, for example). Perhaps each industry has its own story of compliance or, more generally, responses to laws, rules, and regulations: nuclear power plants have behaved differently from lobster fishermen. But the point can be made that businesses also can and do behave normatively. Principles and ideologies matter in the business world, just as they do in the world of John Doe and Mary Roe; the balance of ingredients, of course, may not be the same.

Goal Theory

The framework set out in previous chapters—the three clusters of motivations—can help, one hopes, in organizing discussion of issues of compliance and impact. A fair number of studies have also analyzed the three clusters, sometimes under different names.[57] Julien Etienne has focused attention on goals. To understand compliance and noncompliance for individuals and businesses, it helps to analyze their goals.[58] A goal, of course, is a purpose, an aim. Laws have goals, but so, too, do the people subject to law. Etienne mentions three types of goals. The first is "hedonic," that is, "to achieve pleasure and/or stimulation in the accomplishment of a task." We do things because they make us happy; we avoid what makes us sad. On the opposite side of the "hedonic" there are "guilt, anger, shame, and discomfort."[59] The second goal is "gain," or, in short, getting a reward or avoiding punishment. The third type of goal is "normative," the urge to do the right thing. Goals can also be mixed.

Gain maps quite obviously onto our first cluster (rewards and punishments); and the normative goal maps onto our third. The problem is the hedonic goal. In part, it maps onto the second cluster (the peer group), especially since Etienne mentions avoidance of shame as hedonic. The hedonic goal, however, seems to wobble about among all three clusters. *Homo hedonicus*, for example, is anxious to avoid fearful situations; but what is he anxious about? Punishment, for one thing. But that brings us back to rewards and punishments. Etienne also mentions "encouragements . . . from peers" and "appeals to self-esteem and pride."[60] Thus, the hedonic goal seems to jumble together all three clusters, though it gives fairly short shrift to peer group influence.

The Role of Duty

The formal law has a role in creating norms and influencing norms, but mostly it reflects preexisting norms. Other normative orders in society mediate impact. Religion is one of these, of course; it is connected significantly to a whole range of phenomena, from tort actions in Thailand to divorce in Chile to suicide bombers in Afghanistan. Lawyers, doctors, and other professionals have codes of ethics. Doctors internalize the rules of medical ethics; most doctors follow the rules out of a sense of duty. The code spells out the duties of a doctor. There is also, in professional codes, one overarching and implicit duty: the duty to do your job with professional standards. The Tarasoff case bothered psychiatrists partly because they felt it conflicted with therapeutic standards and practice and, therefore, with professional ethics.

The province of Ontario, Canada, required educators and social workers to report children who were neglected or abandoned, and any instances of child abuse. But in interviews, educators and social workers consistently admitted that "teachers often did not report abuse and neglect." They knew about the law. They approved of it. But reporting struck some of them as a breach of trust. Teachers needed to build trust with pupils and parents. A "report of abuse or neglect" jeopardized "the working relationship with parents." Reporting, according to one social worker, was "traumatic." Some teachers saw it "as a terrifying betrayal."[61] Professional ethics and the professional sense of duty overrode the duty to follow the law.

Putting Across the Message

Earlier in this book, I stressed the importance of communication. A law that nobody knows about has no impact. I discussed types of message, and what difference forms of message could make, and which ones work, and why. Communication is important in other regards. As we saw, what deters criminals (if anything does) is not the punishment itself, but the perception of punishment. Communication affects this perception. When the state makes an effort to crack down on some behavior and launches a publicity campaign, the point is to influence the shape and nature of the deterrence curve. It does this through various means of communication. An effective campaign, at the very least, has to reach its audience. Often the message is a message about toughness: more punishment, more enforcement, more certainty, and more severity. Not to mention celerity. Warnings not to drink and drive. The message, very often, also carries a moral appeal. Drunk driving is wrong behavior, not just illegal behavior. Depending on the campaign and the goal of the campaign, the moral message may be stronger than the punishment message. At times, it is also more effective.

In general, impact depends on all aspects of the message: about punishment, and possible incentives; but also about the moral, ethical, or policy meanings of the norm. Communication is a factor, too, in all three clusters of motives—rewards and punishments; peer group effects; and inner emotions. Telling people what their peers think makes a difference in many situations. And, of course, the moral message.

The moral norms may be, in general, preexisting; the conscience is there inside the person already. But communication still matters. A person might decide to act as a devout member of some religion and to follow its dictates. That is the primary decision. But the actual behavior may depend on many factors. Trust in authority, for example. An Orthodox Jew will only eat kosher food. But she will not know whether swordfish or venison is kosher unless somebody she trusts as an authority conveys to her the rabbinical rulings on these foods.

Is There a Fourth Cluster?

In this chapter so far, I listed a number of "third cluster" concepts and motives—legitimacy, morality, fairness, trust, and patriotism. A lot of what people do, day in and day out, including law-related behavior, does not fit neatly and easily into these categories. The three clusters do not include everything we need to explain behavior. There are models of behavior that "emphasize the choices we make without ever noticing,"[62] things we do out of habit or custom or tradition or just because that's what people do. Choices that are not conscious choices at all. Action that is the result of habit, laziness, inertia, or unthinking patterns of behavior. On a typical day, a person gets up, takes a shower, gets dressed, eats breakfast (or not), goes to work; a person drives cars, interacts with people, buys things, works, plays, makes love. Much of this is done without cost-benefit analysis, or conscious choice, or overt peer pressure, or even a sense of the moral meanings of what we do.[63] The legal system keeps this person company, however, every step of the way: rules of the road, for example. A driver obeys traffic signals (or maybe, at times, does not); but why? Yes, she doesn't want a ticket. Yes, she thinks it is the right thing to do. But also out of habit and training.

"Habit" or "inertia" can, of course, be analyzed in cost-benefit terms. When we say we do X out of habit, we are saying that changing to Y would not be worth the effort. But "habit" verges on "custom," and "custom" verges on culture, on patterns of behavior that have had staying power, and which, then, are presumably efficient, or at least not inefficient (or they would not have survived). Still, to talk about habit or inertia or custom or tradition in terms of cost-benefit analysis somehow seems wrong. Stop-sign behavior: it's not religion or patriotic fervor. Usually, no policeman is around. Maybe we think it is the right thing to do. Maybe it's analyzed in terms of avoiding accidents. Maybe it's just what we've always done since we first learned to drive. We can, if we try hard enough, shoehorn it into the clusters. We can also argue that, insofar as the behavior is unconscious, it does not belong in a discussion of impact because there is no impact at all; what the law is or is not is irrelevant. It is, as Mark Suchman puts it, "something of an epiphenomenon," and the correlation between legislation and behavior is "spurious, not causal."[64]

In a sense, habit, fashion, and the like defy analysis and are shrouded in mystery. Why hemlines go up and down; why men wear hats and ties or stop wearing hats and ties; why baggy trousers become the thing to wear; why baseball caps are worn backward; why people in Venezuela suddenly like sushi; why Mexicans drink Coca-Cola. Rule-following behavior is obviously not just fashion or habit. Much of it does lend itself to analysis in terms of our three clusters. But there is a residue that is all of them at once—or none of them—and that is best described as simply what people do, behavior that is almost but not quite instinctual.

To be sure, law is also "constitutive." It plays a role in the social construction of reality; it affects the way we think (and behave) by helping frame notions of basic facts and institutions: such institutions as marriage and divorce, employer and employee, what it means to "own" something, and whether "a slip of paper is legal tender."[65] It is a factor in making people accept the world as it is. In this way, but indirectly, law does have an "impact," but subtly and unconsciously. Unthinking behavior, then, would be part of the ripple effects of law.

9

FACTORS IN HARMONY; FACTORS IN BATTLE

U P   T O   T H I S   P O I N T, we have talked mainly about what makes people react as they do to a law, rule, doctrine, or regulation. People obey the law (if they do) out of one or more of the motives in the clusters of motives we discussed. In so doing, they advance or retard the goal or point of the law, rule, doctrine, or regulation.

All legal interventions have some sort of point or goal, and the goal, presumably, molds the techniques chosen to implement the rule. Or the very shape of the legal intervention. Take, for example, the goal of discouraging people from smoking. A country can impose a stiff tax on tobacco products. The state can try to persuade people that smoking is unhealthy. The state can appeal to the civic sense of smokers, warning, for example, about the dangers of secondhand smoke or the burden smokers put on the public health system. Smoking in public places can be restricted; smoking can be banned on airplanes. Societies can also try to stigmatize smokers, or to shame them. They can try to affect the communication process, as well, by insisting on warning labels and by outlawing ads for tobacco products. These techniques have been effective—especially in developed countries. The cumulative effect has been to "denormalize" smoking, to turn smoking itself into a kind of deviance, and to strip smoking of its glamour. To the extent that this works—and it has worked—people come to look down on smoking and smokers. This puts peer pressure on people to stop smoking, or at least not to smoke in other people's presence.[1] Smokers come to feel the force of disapproval, to feel "condemned, isolated, disenfranchised, alienated."[2]

The war on tobacco might be something of a special case, and a special success. The fight against obesity (another public health problem) seems to pose a more difficult problem. The law component is weak—a tax here and there, for example, and public health campaigns. After all, banning public smoking is one thing; forcing people to exercise or passing laws against potato chips would be close to impossible (and extremely unpopular).[3] Smoking is a single, discrete act; unhealthy behavior is much more diffuse. The goal—healthier people—is widely shared, but so far, policy has not succeeded in "denormalizing" cheeseburgers, and perhaps never will.

■ ■ ■

That all three of the clusters are important is generally conceded, and the results of research pretty much demonstrate that all three figure in determining legal impact. Economists love to explain things in terms of costs and benefits, and they love deterrence theory. You can, of course, even squeeze peer pressure and moral considerations into a "neoclassical rational choice model." You do this by recognizing disapproval as a cost, and a guilty conscience or shame as another kind of cost. But this makes the "neoclassical rational choice model" essentially meaningless. Or circular. More sensible to admit that "considerations of cost and benefit" do not work on behavior that is "already strongly inhibited by notions of morality."[4] The statement comes from a study that tried to look at corporate crime (or at least at the tendency to commit it); the study ended up with the (not surprising) conclusion that "decisions to commit corporate crime are primarily and directly influenced by the individual decision maker's assessment of the costs and benefits of the act, feelings of shame, and their moral sentiments."[5] All three clusters, in short.

Generally speaking, when the three factors work together, we can expect them to reinforce each other. Most people refrain from stealing,

robbing, and burglarizing for all three reasons. They know that burglary, say, is risky business, open to punishment. They also know that
acts of burglary would scandalize their family and friends. They also
surely think it is just plain wrong to steal other people's property or take
their hard-earned money. Norms that have triple support are, we assume, very strong. The deterrence curve soon flattens out. Double or
triple support of this type is common in society. Common, and even
essential. Force alone, as we said, cannot do the job by itself. And, alas,
neither can peer pressure and morality. There are, after all, people who
do commit burglary. Maybe their primary peers are other burglars.
And burglars do not seem to lose sleep over the morality of what they
are doing. Still, to keep burglary rates as low as possible, we need all
three clusters.

There is also the mirror image of the point just made; impact will be
minimal, or downright negative, where deterrence is weak, peer pressure is absent, and people have no qualms about the behavior in question. Jaywalking is a good example. Jaywalkers blithely cross the street
in the middle of the block. Nobody is going to catch them (or even try),
except during rare crackdowns. Social disapproval is low. Jaywalking
saves time; it isn't so bad. It doesn't harm anybody, everybody does it,
and what's so wrong with it? To get serious about jaywalking, then,
would require ramping up sanctions, and perhaps also mounting some
sort of campaign against it. Heavy enforcement and big fines might
make a difference; short of this, I would not put money on chances of a
major impact.

Recall the black market sale of used cars in Inga Markovits's description of legal life in East Germany. It was strictly illegal. But there was
no enforcement to speak of. Nobody in town seemed to disapprove; and
neither buyers nor sellers seemed to think they were doing anything
morally wrong. All three clusters worked together to create a thriving
node of illegality.

What happens, though, if the factors are in conflict? That is, what
happens when a person is subject to pressures from more than one
factor but the pressures move in opposite directions? A young gang
member, let us say, is under strong pressure from the gang, pressure to
go along with illegal acts; his mother, a pious woman, strongly disap-

proves, and begs him to leave the gang. No general rule can tell us whether the mother or the gang will win out.

A few studies have tried to measure the conflict between clusters, trying to figure out which has more bite: threat of punishment, for example, or appeals to the moral sense, or some other conflict along those lines. In one study, two researchers took a random sample of adults and asked them, first, whether they were likely to cheat a bit on their income tax, drive while drunk, or steal some small item (worth less than $20). Subjects who admitted they might commit such sins were asked whether they would "feel guilty" about this behavior; whether "people whose opinion you value" would lose respect for them; and whether the subject thought getting caught was likely. Notice that these three questions correspond to our three clusters. The subjects were also asked whether or not the possible guilt, peer disapproval, or risk of punishment would constitute a big problem for them. In this particular study, shame seemed to make more of a difference than peer pressure.[6]

In another study,[7] students in three sociology classes were peppered with quizzes. Students were allowed to mark their own quizzes, but the instructor (unknown to them) had a way of knowing if they cheated. Lots of them did. In midstream, the instructor told one class they had a moral duty not to cheat; cheating was unfair; the instructor expected them to follow the rules. Another class was told that there had been complaints about cheating; a spot check had turned up a case of cheating, and the cheater was going to be punished. (The third class, the control group, was told nothing.) The moral appeal had no impact whatsoever. The (implied) threat of punishment did.

In still another study, published in 1980,[8] a sample was drawn of adults in an American city in the southwest (probably in Oklahoma). The respondents were asked about "involvement in eight illegal activities," things like minor theft (goods worth less than $20—this seems to be a popular amount); illegal gambling; littering; use of forbidden fireworks; tax cheating; and drunk driving. Had they committed these offenses, or were they likely to do so? They were then asked to estimate the chance of getting arrested for these offenses. They were also asked to imagine they had been caught and found guilty; how big a problem would that create for their lives? Next, they were asked about social disapproval from "the five adults you know best." And, last, they were asked if they thought doing the offense was sometimes wrong, usually wrong, always wrong, or not wrong at all.

The results were hardly surprising. For example, the subjects thought they were more likely to be caught stealing than littering. They expected far more disapproval if they stole something than if they were litterbugs. Oddly enough, they themselves highly disapproved of littering—more so than of gambling or illegal fireworks.[9]

Clearly, the authors of these studies had an important goal: measuring and comparing the relative strength of the three clusters. But what did they prove? The Oklahoma study, for example, focused on one particular group of people in one particular city at one particular time in one particular country. This kind of limitation may be unavoidable. But there are more serious problems. The eight "crimes" were not crimes that make citizens tremble in their boots; some were downright trivial. Of course, one could hardly survey the good people of Oklahoma and ask men, say, how often they had raped a woman or blown up a building, and how likely they were to do so in the future, and whether other people would disapprove of such things. Necessarily, they had to be asked about minor offenses. These studies do not and cannot yield any sort of general rule. This is basically because the three clusters are, well, clusters, not single, fixed, stable things. There is no way to compare them in general. You have to ask: What moral appeal, which peer group, what kind of punishment or reward, and compared to what aspects of some other cluster? Moral appeals and peer groups, as we saw, come in all sorts of flavors and types and sizes; so, too, of rewards and punishment.

When a person says, "It's always wrong to litter, but I do it anyway," what are we to make of this? Clearly, this is not like saying, "It's always wrong to murder, but I do it anyway." Nobody will say that. The level of moral commitment is much deeper in the case of murder. Littering may be wrong, but in the same way that eating French fries is wrong for somebody on a diet. Moral commitments vary enormously. The same point can be made about fear of punishment. Littering might get you a small fine. It doesn't give you a criminal record. Theft or tax cheating can have more serious consequences. Murder, most of all. You simply cannot assume that something called "punishment" can be measured against something called "peer pressure" or "conscience." The disapproval of your peers is also different case by case; strong or weak, depending on how much disapproval and who it comes from. Imagine telling your mother, "I dropped a piece of paper on the street and was too lazy to put it in a garbage can," compared to telling her, "I'm thinking of robbing a bank."

This same sort of problem bedevils studies that try to figure out how to get people to comply with rules. A study consisting of a "large survey of the population age fifteen and over in New Jersey, Iowa, and Oregon"[10] was designed to measure and understand "rule breaking." The rules in question, though, included some moderately hefty offenses ("physically harming somebody on purpose" or "cheating on your income tax") and some that seem less so ("lying to your spouse or sweetheart") or downright silly ("remaining seated during the national anthem"). The subjects were asked whether they were likely to do such things or not (most subjects said they had never violated the particular rule in question, and there was no chance they were going to do so). Subjects were asked about their moral posture; their "social integration" (Were they married? Were they patriotic? Did they know a lot of people?); whether they suffered from "anomie" (Did they think they lived in a fair society? Would they welcome a revolution?); and, perhaps most important, did they think they would be caught and punished? The results were, not surprisingly, different for different sorts of offenses. And, also not surprisingly, threats of punishment made a difference (at least people said so); so did social disapproval. The "utility of the behavior for the person" was another "independent predictor of estimated future deviance,"[11] that is, whether doing the deed was worth the risk. Again, you simply cannot draw any general conclusions from this study. Research matching specific forms of, say, punishment, against specific forms of, say, moral appeal would be useful, for example, in deciding what kind of campaign against smoking or obesity is likely to work. But there is no way of flatly comparing the power of the clusters with each other.

In many situations, factors can be tested over time rather than simultaneously. Indeed, this is what we learn from various campaigns and crackdowns. Add or supplement a punishment and you get a certain result; relax enforcement and you get a different result. If you stop enforcing altogether, the compliance you do get (and, of course, you do get quite a bit) must be the result of some aspect of cluster three. Earlier, we mentioned the study of traffic tickets for diplomats in New York City. Many diplomats scrupulously followed the rules. Other diplomats, knowing they couldn't be fined, parked wherever they pleased—crosswalks, fire hydrants, whatever—and whenever they pleased. Finally, in 2002, New York City, fed up with the situation, got permission to punish persistent offenders by stripping them of their diplomatic plates. Parking violations immediately and dramatically declined—almost 98 percent. That really flattened out the curve. Cluster one (rewards and punishments) came to the rescue of a weak and inadequate cluster three.[12]

Crowding Out

As we noted, some laws try to encourage whistle-blowing by offering money to people who report illegal activities, fraud on the government, for example. People, of course, also have a moral obligation to tell the authorities about cheating and other misbehavior. Does it help to offer a reward? Offering rewards is, of course, a common tactic. The police offer rewards for information that might solve a crime. Rewards for whistle-blowing should work, too. Yet, apparently, a reward under some conditions will have the opposite effect: it will "crowd out" the moral motive. That is, it will suppress the moral element in whistle-blowing.[13] Where people might feel a duty to report, offering money can dilute "the moral dimension of the act."[14] And that might turn out to be counterproductive.

One study tried to test this idea. The researchers presented subjects with a vignette: imagine you're working for a large construction company. Your company has a big contract to build a highway at a fixed price. You come across evidence that the company is using cheaper materials than it promised, that it is failing to test the materials, and is violating the rules in other ways. As a result, the government is paying $10 million more than it should be paying for the project.[15] The subjects were divided into eight groups. In some groups, whistle-blowers were offered low rewards ($1,000); in other groups, very high rewards (a million dollars). Some groups were told about a legal duty, with or without the high or low reward; two groups were told about protections against retaliation; one group was told that failure to report could result in a stiff fine. The results were "clear" support for a crowding-out effect: "low rewards harm, rather than benefit, the willingness of individuals to engage in whistle-blowing when a duty is present."[16] In other words, people who felt a duty to report would, in fact, be less willing if offered some (but not much) money. If they were offered heaps of money, on the other hand, the crowding-out effect would disappear. But, as I read the study, the results were not very striking; differences seemed small and, when all is said and done, the subjects were reacting to vignettes—reacting to little stories. How this translates into real-life behavior is always open to doubt.

Uri Gneezy and an associate report on a real-world experience of "crowding out." In a number of day-care centers in Israel, parents were coming late to pick up their kids; this was making a problem for the centers. To fix this, why not charge a kind of fine if parents came late? In standard economic theory, coming late would be then be more costly for parents. Since the "price" of late-coming would go up, fewer parents would come late to pick up the kids. But the fines, in fact, had the opposite effect: more parents came late, rather than fewer. Why did this happen? Parents considered the fine the price for coming late; but simply a price, nothing more. Coming late had been commodified. No "guilt or shame . . . attached to the act of buying a commodity at will."[17] The moral duty to come on time disappeared.[18] Michael Sandel gives another example. Residents of a Swiss town were asked to approve of placing a nuclear waste site in the town. A bare majority said yes. But then the town was asked: suppose Parliament had added a money reward to this proposal—an annual payment of money to residents—if the site was approved. The rate of approval dropped by a stunning amount: now only 25 percent were willing. People refused to be "bribed."[19]

There is, in short, empirical evidence in support of "crowding out." But a lot depends on the circumstances. Moral principles can indeed be more powerful than incentives or punishments. If you put a price on behavior, you "shift a situation from a social to a monetary frame."[20] The quote is from a review of the literature by Uri Gneezy and associates. Money incentives can change the way people assess some particular behavior. Money might "crowd out" a moral motive by pinning a dollar label on behavior. They put the point in a striking way: you meet "an attractive person," and after a while, you say, "I like you very much and would like to have sex with you." Suppose that, instead, you say, "I like you very much and would like to have sex with you, and, to sweeten the deal, I'm also willing to pay you $20!" They add, ironically (Gneezy is an economist), that "[o]nly a certain kind of economist would expect your partner to be happier in the second scenario."[21] Most of us, not being economists, think neither approach is likely to work, but we get the point.

When does "crowding out" actually happen? As the evidence suggests, if the incentive (money, for example) is big enough, it crowds out crowding out. Moral considerations dominate when relationships are personal. Butting in with a money offer is likely to be counterproductive.[22] Some scholars (Bruno Frey, notably) have argued that "external interventions" (money payments, for example) can lead not only to a crowding-out effect, but also to a "spillover" effect.[23] That is, impact will be impaired in other ways and other situations. Consider what happened at the Israeli day-care centers. Suppose that commodifying latecoming not only made parents more likely to come late, it also made them less likely to volunteer to help out during the day. This would be a spillover effect. Commodifying would have had a general effect on behavior. However, this notion has not been tested empirically.

Unenforced or badly enforced laws are said to create another spillover effect. If the government fails to enforce Law A, compliance with Law A might suffer; but does this effect spill over to Laws B, C, and D? In a classic work, Herbert Packer argued that criminal laws that are "only sporadically enforced" can harm "respect for law." Arbitrary enforcement feeds a "sense of alienation."[24] Nonenforcement crowds out the general duty to obey the law. Better, in many cases, to simply get rid of these poorly enforced laws. The classic example has always been national Prohibition, the "noble experiment" of the 1920s. Full enforcement was politically impossible and socially unacceptable. Enforcement was sporadic and chaotic. As we mentioned before, during Prohibition there was an orgy of municipal corruption. Liquor poured over the border from Canada, or from boats in international waters. Speakeasies were common in the cities; homemade liquor (moonshine) was available everywhere. Large sections of the country were awash with drink.[25] The drys struggled valiantly to make Prohibition palatable; they failed. After a decade or so, the Prohibition amendment was revoked by another amendment, and the "noble experiment" was consigned to the ash heap of history.

Did the failure of Prohibition have a spillover effect? Did it breed more general disrespect for law and lead to more violations of law? Certainly, Prohibition opened the door to certain kinds of organized crime. This was the period of Al Capone and other mobsters, who got fat and rich on the proceeds of the illegal liquor business. Organized crime thrives, in general, on illegal but popular commodities, like the drug trade today. Still, there is reason to be skeptical about the spillover effect. After all, nonenforcement, arbitrary enforcement, and sporadic enforcement are not rare in any society. The question is: with what result? At least one study suggests, on the basis of psychological experiments, that "perceived legal injustice" can lower "respect for the law generally."[26] But how far would this go? Take the white-collar worker who went to a speakeasy during Prohibition to have his beer. He might detest Prohibition. He might consider it a ghastly and corrupt mistake. He might suspect that the police, city officials, even Prohibition agents, were corrupt. Was he more likely to embezzle money from his boss or beat his wife or cheat on his income tax? I doubt it.

Suppose a community fails to enforce the laws against speeding; drivers may think less of the traffic police, but they do not start robbing banks. Nonenforcement might tempt them to drink and drive. They might make more illegal U-turns, or park overtime more often; but in each instance, the spillover effect, if any, is only in related areas, if it occurs at all. Prohibition's liquor fiasco could have possibly spilled over into related areas: drug use, let us say, or vice laws in general. In a study of Australian taxpayers who faced huge bills for back taxes and penalties and considered all this grossly unfair, at least one interviewed taxpayer showed "signs of more extreme defiance toward the tax system." He said he would pay cash to every "carpenter or plumber or electrician" that he used. "They don't have to declare it," and this would be a victory for him, because it would make the tax authorities "lose a little bit more."[27] But how often this occurs, and to what extent, is unclear. On the other hand, if laws in general are not enforced, or badly enforced, or corruptly enforced, corruption and cynicism could become a way of life. The diplomats from corrupt countries were, generally speaking, the ones who were the most cavalier about New York City's traffic rules.[28]

Does the spillover effect work in the other direction? Does strict, efficient enforcement of Law A improve compliance with Law B? This is, in part, the idea behind the well-known "broken windows" theory. This was a crime-fighting technique notably used in New York City. The authorities crack down heavily on petty crime: people who jump turnstiles to ride the subway free, kids who commit petty acts of vandalism, or the infamous "squeegee men," who pester drivers by wiping their windshields and nag them for money. Zero tolerance for small infractions (according to the theory) will have a big payoff; it makes life in the city more livable, and big crime declines, as a result of the war on small crime. Does the technique work? The jury is still out. Crime has, indeed, declined in New York and other cities that tried this approach. But crime has also gone down in other cities where the technique was never used.[29]

Paying Taxes

In a classic study of tax compliance (1967), Richard Schwartz and Sonya Orleans tried to pit a moral appeal and the threat of punishment against each other.[30] Taxpayers in one group were asked questions designed to bolster willingness to comply on ethical grounds; the questions were meant to arouse motives ranging from feelings of guilt to a "patriotic desire to support the government in its most valued activities." This group was told, for example, that "hundreds of millions of dollars" are "not available for programs of great importance" because some people fail to pay their taxes. Another group was told about punishments for tax violators; the idea was to scare this group with threats. (There was also a placebo group.) Schwartz and Orleans measured the attitudes of their subjects and, for purposes of the study, they were also able to find out whether their tax returns showed any differences. Apparently this happened. Both the threat group and the ethics group complied more than the placebo group. And appeals to conscience were more effective than the threat of sanctions.

The effects, however, were hardly gigantic. And a later study (1991) of taxpaying behavior came out quite differently.[31] The subjects here were taxpayers in Long Island, New York, mostly men (76 percent) who agreed to participate in the experiment. One group was shown a videotape that emphasized the "normative principles" underlying the tax law, with talk about fairness, social responsibility, and patriotism. A second group saw a tax planning tape, about tax strategies, ways to minimize taxes, and tax shelters; the tape stressed "aggressive" tax planning. The study found "no evidence that the normative and self-interested treatments had an impact on taxpaying behavior, either as reported by the taxpayer or as evident in officially documented records."[32] A review of the studies since Schwartz and Orleans came to a similar conclusion. Studies that tried to contrast threats and moral talk found either small results or no results or conflicting results. The reviewer, Barak Ariel, did his own study, this time on corporations (in Israel) rather than individuals.[33] One group got letters warning that noncompliance with tax laws could result in severe punishment. It spoke darkly about new methods of auditing. The other letter said that noncompliance hurts society; tax money goes for good, public purposes. Ariel was able to get data on behavior before and after the letters—data on gross sales, on tax payments (of value-added tax), and on tax deductions. There was also a large control group.

The results were basically: nothing. Neither letter seemed to produce much in the way of results. Ariel himself pointed out one major problem in the study: the companies had been picked at random. There was nothing to suggest that any of them were tax cheaters. But if most of them were honest taxpayers, then the taxpayers did not need to do anything different—they were already paying what they owed in taxes. Letters could only influence a subgroup of corporations that could have been induced by these letters to change their tax returns.[34] In short, the curve had already flattened out. And these studies all suffer from a problem already noted: you can only test one particular sort of threat against one particular kind of appeal to conscience or morality. Beyond that, you cannot come to any general conclusions.

Modern governments have enormous appetites for taxes, so it is hardly surprising that scholars (and governments) should be interested in tax compliance. Policy can be tough or lenient. Which style works best? Toughness might be counterproductive; it might more or less "crowd out" the moral compulsion to pay up on time and in full. Leniency toward taxpayers, or at least a nonthreatening attitude, and a stress on the legitimacy and social value of taxation might produce a better result. One study, apparently carried out in Vienna, used vignettes describing a mythical country (Tovland). This was a study of attitudes, with predictions about behavior rather than behavior itself.[35] Common sense—not always a good guide—suggests, as this study does, that both techniques do work: trust, fairness, and patriotic duty, and, on the other hand, an occasional iron fist.

The tax studies are, on the whole, quite parochial. They have to be. Taxpayers on Long Island, New York, might have a different chemistry from taxpayers in Arizona or Australia, let alone taxpayers in Sicily (or Vienna). And the levels of enforcement are never the same. And whether experiments with taxpayers carry over to drunk drivers, burglars, or embezzlers is extremely doubtful. Replications in other cultures might produce general rules—for taxpaying behavior in developed countries, for example, and for the influence of the various clusters on this (or some other) specific form of legal behavior. That is the most we could hope for, at the present time.

■ ■ ■

The reader has probably noticed that many studies pitting factors against each other or trying to measure their relative strength have been studies of what people say—studies of attitudes, not behavior. Behavior is inferred from attitudes. Only a few studies actually try to tap into behavior. Schwartz and Orleans, and some of the follow-up studies on tax compliance, did manage to get information about actual taxes paid. In an older study, a Polish sociologist asked people whether they crossed

the street when the light was red and no cars were around. About
40 percent said never; and another third, only occasionally. This turned
out to be, more or less, what people actually did. Why so much obedience? About 16 percent were afraid of a fine; a little over a third said they
liked "order"; about a fifth just said it was a habit.[36] This reminds us of
the study of the campaign in hotels to induce guests to reuse their towels
and sheets. There, somewhat oddly, appeals to conscience (please save
the environment) did not work as well as information about peers, including an odd set of "peers," people who had stayed in that very room
before. Apparently, "sharing commonalities" with people, even such
irrelevancies as birthdays, fingerprint type, or "physical space," does "induce surprisingly powerful feelings of affiliation."[37] In the Texas campaign against littering, also mentioned earlier, appeals to local patriotism
worked better at producing results than other kinds of moral appeals.[38]
Again, we have to be cautious about assuming that what works on Texas
highways, or in nice American hotels, would work in other situations of
conflict or cooperation among norms.

Defiance

We can look at crowding out as an important limit on deterrence theory.
Money incentives under some conditions do not improve compliance.
This is because of the way they affect motives in our third cluster:
conscience, psychological motives. When crowding out occurs, it may
distort the shape of the deterrence curve.

A parallel phenomenon is one that Lawrence Sherman has called
"defiance." Punishment, sometimes, actually increases deviance, because
it induces a negative reaction in people, which leads them to defy the
law.[39] When would this actually happen? Sherman suggests some
specific conditions: when offenders "experience sanctioning conduct as
illegitimate," or when they have "weak bonds to the sanctioning agent
and community." Under these circumstances, an offender is likely to
"deny" his "shame"; that is, he will fail to feel any guilt.[40] A young man,
say, is arrested for reckless driving. He is treated badly, cursed, humili-
ated. He feels alienated from the police and from "the system." He might
be, so the argument goes, more rather than less apt to commit his crime

again, or perhaps some other crime. Discrimination, hopelessness, maltreatment by the police, we are told, are the soil out of which terrorism grows. In the United States, minority communities often feel (with much justice) that the police are racially biased; perhaps this also produces defiance.

Sherman distinguishes between "specific or individual defiance" and "general defiance." Specific defiance is "the reaction of one person to that person's own punishment." Sherman refers, for example, to a study of men in a Chicago bar. Some of these men had jobs; some of them were unemployed. The men with jobs were anxious "to avoid trouble with police at all costs." If they were arrested, they might lose their jobs. The others, the "hoodlums," positively relished encounters with the police. They bragged about these battles; they invited "trouble with the law to prove their toughness."[41] General defiance is the "reaction of a group or collectivity to the punishment of one or more of its members."[42] A man brutalized by the police, who becomes a repeat criminal, would show specific defiance. General defiance might explain the outbreak of urban riots in some cases. In Los Angeles, a video showed the police brutally beating a black man, Rodney King. When a jury acquitted the police officers in 1992, riots broke out.[43] The trial of Dan White in 1979 also led to an urban riot in San Francisco. White had killed the mayor of San Francisco, George Moscone, and Harvey Milk, the first openly gay supervisor. White was charged with first-degree murder, but was convicted only of manslaughter. The verdict touched off the so-called "White Night" riots in San Francisco.[44]

There are many less grandiose instances of defiance. In Australia in the 1990s, thousands of taxpayers used tax schemes that had been touted as big money-savers, and (they were told) perfectly legal. After a number of years of shilly-shallying, the tax authorities decided the schemes were illegal; they told investors they were liable for back taxes, together with interest and penalties. This was a big shock to the taxpayers. No warning had been given; investors felt the proceedings were grossly unfair. They were "overwhelmed, confused, and angry."[45] Many simply refused to pay. Ultimately, of course, they could be forced to pay up. But the recalcitrance stemmed, in large part, from what they saw as a violation of procedural justice. Presumably, better ways of handling the issue would have produced less defiance and more cooperation. Still, as the old saw has it, you can't cheat an honest man. These taxpayers were aggressively looking for ways to cut taxes. They may have been "disgruntled" to begin with; perhaps the experience raised the level of defiance but, conceivably, it was already rather high.

Defiance theory sounds plausible as a kind of parallel to crowding out. Some people, under some circumstances, react to sanctions with defiance.[46] The amount of sanction makes a difference. Consider the case of "nonviolence." An oppressed group—people of color under apartheid in South Africa, African Americans in the American South in the late 1950s and 1960s—defy the regime, using mostly nonviolent methods: sit-ins, demonstrations, Gandhian techniques of protest. More sanctions—arrests, especially—do not end the protests. They may even have the opposite effect. They make the protesters bolder and increase their ranks. These rebels take pride in their defiance. They are suffering for a noble cause.

Techniques of defiance can be, at times, extremely effective, but only against certain types of regime and under certain circumstances. There was violence against civil rights leaders in the south—and even murder. The apartheid regime in South Africa did not hesitate to use harsh, violent methods against men like Nelson Mandela and other leaders of the resistance. But in the end, defiance proved to be effective, both in the American South and in South Africa. This, however, was partly because the regimes in question, as awful as they were, showed at least some minimal constraint. In Nazi Germany, on the other hand, defiance did not and could not work. Anybody who moved against the regime, or spoke against it, was simply asking for a quick and merciless death.

Exactly what constitutes defiance? The extremes are clear; the less extreme forms unclear. Modern democratic states tolerate dissatisfaction, criticism, and even, at times, principled acts of civil disobedience. Modern societies are pluralistic. Democracy, indeed, is pluralism; it is a commitment to letting a thousand flowers bloom. Minorities have rights. Dissent is not suppressed. All voices are supposed to be heard. All religions are supposed to be tolerated. Political parties can be formed, expressing different ideologies and policies, and representing different groups.

But, of course, only up to a point. Dissent is accepted, but not revolution. Religions have to play by certain rules. In Muslim countries, men can have four wives. France or Germany will only recognize one. The United States government reacted to Mormon polygamy with fury and horror, even though leaders of the church claimed plural marriage was their religious duty. Congress enacted a succession of laws, each one harsher than the last, to stamp out polygamy in Utah Territory. In the late 1870s, in *Reynolds v. United States*,[47] the Supreme Court faced the church–state issue of Mormon polygamy. George Reynolds, secretary to the president of the church, had taken a second wife; he was tried and convicted of violating the law. The Supreme Court upheld his conviction; it refused to recognize polygamy as a religious duty. The church eventually renounced polygamy. A century later, in *Wisconsin v. Yoder* (1972), mentioned earlier,[48] the Supreme Court showed a more tolerant attitude; the Conservative Amish Mennonite Church in Wisconsin successfully resisted a requirement to let kids get a high school education. Eight grades of school were enough for Amish children; further learning threatened the Amish way of life. The old, conservative ways of the Amish, drenched in quaintness and poverty, cast a romantic glow that seemed to dazzle the court.

■   ■   ■

To sum up: Studies on the clash of clusters, on the whole, are disappointing. Some rely on experiments, or vignettes, or surveys of small or unrepresentative groups, rather than real-world experience. Some studies contradict other studies. Some findings are not robust. The research, on the whole, is a fairly thin, watery soup. The fundamental problem has already been mentioned: the three clusters are not hard, brittle, unified. Each cluster is itself a cluster. Each is made up of different motives and emotions; each comes in different sizes and shapes. People will do things for a million dollars that they would not do for a handful of coins.[49] Crowding out is real, but if you offer enough money, you can crowd out crowding out. The threat of a $5 fine for overtime parking has less impact than the threat of death by lethal injection.

What is true of sanctions is true of peer pressure, or the nagging inner voice of morality. According to one survey, young people who "anticipate shame in committing illegal acts" are somewhat less likely to give in to "deviant peer influence." And if they face shame, disapproval, and threats of punishment, the factors, working together, act as a kind of vaccine, protecting them against involvement in crime.[50] Fair enough, but there is no such thing as "peer pressure"; there are particular peers and particular pressures. In some gangs, or in some closed societies like the Amish, or on the old island of Tristan da Cunha, peer pressure can be positively crushing. In some societies, and in some periods, parents are absolute monarchs; disobeying or displeasing a parent is unthinkable. In other societies, this is simply not the case. And when the peers are just other people (strangers, say, who stayed in the same hotel room you did), the pressure must be fairly light.

Nor is there any such thing as a "moral claim." Moral claims, too, are infinitely various. A martyr is willing to defy state law and die for the cause; nothing could be more powerful than his beliefs. Offering him $10 or even $1,000 or possibly even a million would not get him to throw off his belt of explosives. But to get people to recycle paper, is it better to tell them it's their duty or to threaten them with a fine? Hard to say. How much is the fine? How likely is it to get caught? Or does threatening people make them resentful and resistant?

The world is full of moral campaigns. Some are successful; some are not. Moral claims also change over time. More people recycle newspapers now than at the start of the campaign. People have a greater sense of urgency; they are more likely to feel that our poor planet is in trouble: this message has been drummed into their heads. The moral claim here has gotten stronger. Same, too, as to smoking cigarettes in public, or drunk driving. Then habit takes over. Fastening the seat belt becomes almost automatic. Convenience matters. If there are recycling bins on every corner, more people will recycle. If more and more places forbid smoking and mean it, fewer people will smoke in those places, or perhaps smoke at all.

Culture and Personality

The clusters vary from society to society, from community to community. Many examples have been given already. Most of the studies cited were American. They leave behind a nagging doubt: Are they only valid for Americans? And which Americans? And only for Americans today, as opposed to yesterday or tomorrow? In principle, culture makes a difference. But how much of a difference? We pointed out, earlier, that the concept of culture is itself difficult and ambiguous. In the modern world, in my opinion, cultures are converging rapidly and powerfully, at least among developed countries. To be sure, the cultures of Japan, Chile, and Finland are far from identical; there is no guarantee that people in these countries will react the same way. Take traffic rules, for example. Italian drivers are notoriously reckless (it is said). American drivers are much more law-abiding. Accident rates are different in different countries. But to focus on these differences is to ignore the bigger picture, which is one of convergence, of sameness. Medieval Japan and medieval Sweden diverged much more dramatically than modern Sweden and Japan. All modern countries are automobile cultures. The rules governing traffic are much the same everywhere: red lights and green lights, speed limits, highway lanes, and so on. The similarities, not just in the rules, but in observance of the rules, far outweigh the differences. At least, that is a plausible conjecture.

Harold Grasmick and Emiko Kobayashi tried to test the three clusters, this time in Japan.[51] The subjects worked for a university hospital in Japan (doctors were excluded from the study). They were asked what might happen if they committed various work sins—too long lunches or breaks, coming to work late or leaving early, or abusing rules about sick leave. Would they suffer shame, or embarrassment? Did they think they would be "caught by people in authority" and be subject to punishment? The authors expected embarrassment to loom larger in Japan than among Americans, because Japanese culture was "more collectivistic." But in fact, shame trumped embarrassment, as it had in the United States.

The usual skepticism, of course, is in order. The study may tell us something about the culture of Japanese hospital workers. It may tell us something about attitudes toward long lunch breaks, or leaving work early. The study does not and cannot show us that shame is stronger than embarrassment, or that any factor (in isolation) carries more weight than any other factor, for the reasons already given. On the other hand, this sort of study does go to demonstrate convergence in world cultures. Grasmick and Kobayashi felt they would find a cultural differ-ence between Japan and the United States. They did not find it. This is not a trivial result. Note, however, the tremendous similarity between the contexts in the two (modern) nations—hospitals, medical science, use of medical techniques, the institutional structure of medical prac-tice. This convergence is what made the study possible in the first place.

■ ■ ■

Studies of such things as claims consciousness, willingness to sue people, and the like presuppose both "culture" and "personality"; it is hard to disentangle these two. Personality, of course, is intensely individual. But there are modal personality types, personality patterns; height and weight, too, are intensely individual, but there are taller societies, on average, and heavier and lighter ones.

The three clusters of motives obviously affect different people in dif-ferent ways. Some people are risk-takers; some people are risk-averse; some are risk-neutral. Risk-averse people are presumably more sensitive to the threat of punishment than risk-takers. Most people grow up ac-cepting most social norms. Some grow up with violent, aggressive, anti-social personalities.

Michael Gottfredson and Travis Hirschi, whose work I discussed ear-lier,[52] argued that low self-control and short-term, rather than long-term, thinking were the source of criminal behavior, and the source of deviant behavior in general. A potential burglar who took Economics 101 and absorbed its lessons would give up burglary immediately. What he might gain from breaking into the usual house has got to be less than the risk of ten years in prison, though, as we have seen, burglars are pretty bad at estimating risks. A young gang member who, in a flash of anger, kills someone from a rival gang because the man dissed him or invaded his turf might gain a transient sense of satisfaction, or the glow of revenge, or approval from other gang members, but at high risk of rotting in prison, perhaps for life, or getting killed by the rival gang. Bernard Madoff ran a Ponzi scheme. He now sits in prison for life.

Personality structures, like cultures, may also be converging. There might well still be a modal or typical American, or Brazilian, or

Italian—or an upper level Nigerian—and this modal personality would be distinctive; but the differences are diminishing everywhere. Societies with clocks are strikingly different from societies that had no clocks. Time sense, and the very meaning of time: these have converged; and this is only one example of the many aspects of contemporary life that are truly global. To be sure, there were and are huge variations in psychology and in demographic traits within societies. The typical burglar is not like the typical CPA or hospital nurse. For this reason, ethnography often seems to illuminate legal behavior much more than analysis of masses of data. A good ethnographer has more of a chance to get inside the heads of real people who do real crimes in real circumstances, or who bring real lawsuits (or not) within real societies.

What makes our burglar tick? Why does he do it? The job is risky; the payoff hardly seems worthwhile. Gottfredson and Hirschi would say the burglar has trouble with impulse control. This might be true. The burglar, like the armed robber, might have a drug habit to support. Practically speaking, burglars usually have no other way to get the money they need. But the money is not just for living expenses; it is also for flash, for prestige, for show. To some burglars, the job is a thrill, a kind of high. Shoplifters may steal for excitement, plain and simple. Shoplifting, one student said, "was almost orgasmic for me." A thief called stealing "thrilling"; it evoked "a feeling much like the anticipation of sex."[53] One burglar said, "I used to get a kick . . . a buzz" out of outwitting the authorities.[54] "Mark," a Texas burglar, was "high" every time he broke into a house. "Because when I'm not high . . . I'm too scared." He never "really planned a burglary," but sometimes, "I'd just be cruising and see a house that looked empty." Mark has been in and out of prison. His brother had this to say: "Mark will never make it in the free world. He never learned how."[55] Rarely if ever, though, do these men talk about the moral aspects of the things they do. That stealing might be wrong never seems to form part of their calculus.[56]

Most men in a study of armed robbers in St. Louis felt they had no real choice. Drudge jobs at low pay were the only honest work they could get. As one robber put it, "I'm broke and need money."[57] Do they worry about getting caught? They know it's possible, but as one robber said, "I try not to think about that because if I dwell on it too much I may talk myself or scare myself out of doing [the robbery]."[58] And, like the burglars, armed robbers have no moral compunctions. "I don't feel sorry . . . because I ain't got no money and [the victims] . . . do."[59] Like burglars, some holdup men found the life and the action exciting. These men pursue "fast living," and this pursuit, the researchers thought, "is more than symbolic or dramaturgical." Rather, it went to the heart of the way offenders perceived their identity. The goal was to be cool, hip, to be "in"; their aim was hedonic. They liked the high life, liked to display, but that called for money, cash. It called for "street-corner capitalism."[60] Similarly, gamblers in an illegal casino in Israel experienced a kind of high when they won (it never lasted); winning made the gambler felt like a "king! I can do whatever I want." Needless to say, this feeling soon evaporated, but the addicted gambler would keep right on gambling and end up destitute, sometimes suicidal.[61]

A study of English street robbers struck similar notes: desperation, drug use, the "buzz" and excitement of crime, and a street culture in which stealing was a normal way of life. The street robbers responded to a "desire for fast cash to purchase drugs, alcohol, or various status-enhancing items." They were committed "not to sustain the offenders' lives, but rather to maintain a particular sort of hedonistic lifestyle."[62] One cannot dismiss out of hand the idea of rational choice; after all, these people had an economic motive: it was money they were stealing, after all. They were also trying to stay out of prison, and they structured their activities accordingly. But the social and cultural context was also critical, and cost-benefit analysis simply does not do the job of accounting for their behavior. Street robberies, after all, "often appear . . . irrational in the sense that they net little cash relative to the lengthy prison sentences that can follow."[63] Interviews with car thieves in Tennessee revealed familiar motives: thrills, easy money, living life in the fast lane, a sense of no alternative, living for the moment, even a feeling of accomplishment (one said, "To be able to get away with it, I mean, it would just give me goose pimples"). All in all, auto theft was a "product of the hedonistic culture of the street."[64] Interviews with identity thieves—a noxious modern crime—sounded similar themes: the lure of easy money, the urge to live the high life; also the sheer thrill of it all.[65]

These rich accounts of life on the streets and other crime sites do not, of course, give us material for a general theory of crime, even about crime in a particular society at a particular time, or about anything but specific crimes in specific societies. They do give us insights otherwise hard to get, but they are, of course, limited to offenders. We do not get inside the heads of non-burglars and non-shoplifters, the millions and millions who never shoved a gun in somebody's face and demanded their cash and their wallets. Presumably these include the readers of this book. And myself.

The subjects of these studies are members of a small group, a small minority in most of our societies. The curve has flattened out, and they are the few who are left at the top of the deterrence curve. They are also the survivors of a peer group curve and a conscience curve. The studies tell us who survives the flattened curve, and why, at least in modern societies; this is valuable information. In holdup men and burglars and car thieves, whatever else we can say about them, the inner voice that acts as a moral shield is missing or defective, the shield that makes most people immune from criminal urges. The peer group is absent or feeble or, more to the point, works perversely; their friends and colleagues are also criminals or men and women who, at least, tolerate a life of crime. Sanctions do work, but obviously not effectively enough to keep the burglar from burgling. It would be good to have rich ethnographic studies of other kinds of offenders—insider traders, embezzlers, air polluters, rapists—and to expand the research into more societies and cultures.

■ ■ ■

One lesson we learn from the studies of clusters in conflict is a fairly negative lesson. When clusters conflict, it is hard to predict the results. Moreover, the clusters interact with each other. Michael Wenzel, building on earlier work, talks about "three general processes through which legal sanctions can inhibit crime."[66] First, there is deterrence, legal sanctions and their power "in and of themselves." Second, there is "normative validation," where "legal sanctions increase the perception that the criminal act is morally wrong." Illegality and threats of punishment, in other words, act as signals or signs that tell people some kind of behavior is wrong, and validate or reinforce moral objections to that behavior. And then, third, there is "a socially mediated process of deterrence." People react to and stigmatize offenders who are arrested and punished. This is a kind of peer group effect. A person may avoid actions that will get him a prison sentence if he thinks nobody will hire him when he gets out.

Mixed motives are common, even normal. Motives and perceptions influence each other. Taxpayers might feel a duty to pay taxes; they might also be afraid of getting caught. And they might worry about what other people might think. And, as we pointed out, it complicates matters that taxpayers, like burglars and everybody else, have no way of knowing whether they will be caught or not; nor do they know what the consequences might be. According to one study, taxpayers who had a strong sense of duty overestimated the risks of getting caught. If so, moral obligations influence and strengthen the deterrent effect of threats of punishment.[67] The converse might be true for burglars. A burglar with no compunction against stealing might underestimate his chances of getting caught. This would, then, weaken the deterrent effect of the possible punishment.

Use, Nonuse, and the Real World of Impact

We have asked the question: Under what conditions do people obey or disobey law, or adjust their behavior in response to law? Many of the examples were drawn from criminal justice. But, as we said, impact matters also in the rest of the law: in contract law, torts, intellectual property, business regulation. Here we can ask about use, nonuse, misuse, and adjustment. When and why does a patient bring a lawsuit against a surgeon who bungled an operation? Who sues for divorce? Who makes out a will? Who applies for a patent? Who complains against a landlord?

In theory, the analysis is pretty much the same as in criminal law. There are incentives or disincentives. Peer groups exert pressure one way or another. People react to feelings of fairness, trust, morality, legitimacy, patriotic and religious fervor. There is a kind of curve, analogous to the deterrence curve, for each type of civil action. This idea lies

at the base of the pyramid notion in the Wisconsin study of legal behavior. There is definitely a malpractice pyramid; out of the thousands
of bad outcomes in medicine, only a few produce claims, and very few
generate lawsuits.

Culture makes an obvious difference with regard to use and nonuse.
So does personality. And reactions change over time. In some societies,
cheating on taxes is positively epidemic; in others, less so. What accounts
for this? Some factors are cultural; some seem to be structural. Enforcement techniques matter. How rigorous is it? Also, do the tax authorities
open the door to compromise? Culture and structure heavily influence
rates of litigation. Is it hard or easy to sue? Are courts accessible? Are they
cheap or expensive? Does it take ten years to decide a case, or are the
courts quick and efficient? But, in addition, is this a rights-conscious
society or not? Someone backs into your car in a parking lot; do you
bring a lawsuit or do you "lump it"? In the Engels' study, injury victims in
Chiang Mai, Thailand, failed to pursue compensation because of culture
and religion (beliefs in karma, and the influence of forms of Buddhism).[68]
A Swiss friend, living and working in the United States, lost his job. I suggested unemployment compensation; he refused to apply because, he
said, in Swiss culture that would be shameful, humiliating. It might have
been just his own personality speaking; or then again, it might be true of
the Swiss in general. Whether the process of claiming any benefit is
pleasant or unpleasant, bureaucratic or efficient, would also make a big
difference to potential claimants.

Many people who should have a will never execute such a document.
Why? Ignorance, perhaps; reluctance to go to a lawyer, maybe. Or simple
procrastination. Making a will can cost time and money. It means
thinking about death, which people hate to do. Default rules matter,
as we have seen. On which side of the scale do laziness and inertia fall?
As we know, people who think divorce is a sin, along with happy couples,
do not care whether divorce is easy and cheap. No-fault divorce encourages divorce, but only among unhappy couples. Higher punishment for
burglars makes a difference only to burglars. The famous abortion decision, *Roe v. Wade*,[69] held that women had a constitutional right to an
abortion, at least in the early months of pregnancy. But, of course, most
women prefer to carry their babies to full term. Each field of law, each

legal institution, has its own deterrence curve, just as murder and bur-glary does.

Doing something about a car accident has a different dynamic from deciding to sue your boss for sex discrimination, or deciding to make out a will or file for divorce, or deciding to file for bankruptcy. Reporting a burglary in your apartment has a different dynamic from reporting a sexual assault. The actual law or rule in question might be the starting point of analysis, but the behavior depends on the factors discussed in this book: communication, and the clusters of motives.

Benefits and costs massively influence use and nonuse. A legal aid program can subsidize tenants who want to complain about their land-lords, or help someone wrestle with the immigration service. The con-tingent fee makes it possible for a tort victim in the United States to find a lawyer to handle his case. If the tort victim had to pay a lawyer by the hour, win or lose, she would be much less likely to sue. The welfare state, social insurance, the social safety net: these also have an enormous im-pact on impact. Bankruptcy laws blunt the effect of failure. A couple opens a new restaurant; it fails, like most new restaurants do, and they go into bankruptcy court. But there is no debtors' prison, as there was in Dickens's London. The couple can start over again. Bankruptcy laws are a kind of social safety net. And like the net in a circus, they en-courage risk-taking; they blunt the effect of failure. Falling from the trapeze does not mean losing your life.

Insurance is a pervasive feature of modern society. Life insurance, accident insurance, auto insurance. Deposit insurance. Insurance surely has an impact on compliance and on use of elements of the legal system. Insurance is a kind of social safety net. Would we drive differently without liability insurance? The insurance industry, in the 1990s, introduced a new product: Employment Practices Liability insurance. It covers liability for claims of race and sex discrimination, wrongful termination, and sexual harassment. The insurance companies do more than insure: they also offer services—hotlines, forms, policies, checklists—that help customers cope with the laws and regulations. Thus they act as "a legal intermediary between what civil rights laws say in cases and statutes and how civil rights are implemented and enforced by employers."[70] But the main function, the overarching function, is insurance against liability and loss. In our society, the insurance function colors the way we behave; it must be added to the equation, along with structure and culture.

Moral Passages and Enemy Deviants

Impact, of course, is a dynamic process. The legal system changes as society changes. Impact also changes; it can rise and fall. A rule has one impact in Time A, another in Time B. Communication systems change. Levels of enforcement change. Public attitudes change. Consider, for example, the impact of *Roe v. Wade*.[71] The court struck down virtually all existing state laws on abortion. The decision had a direct effect on women who wanted to end their pregnancy; it had an impact, too, on doctors and on family planning clinics. It made abortion safer and easier to get. The decision, of course, also had side effects. Millions of people believed, and continued to believe, that abortion is actually murder. This belief has had political consequences. It led to a certain amount of backlash, as we have seen. The school segregation case, bitterly resisted in the 1950s and 1960s, is now untouchable; and its indirect impact, at least, has grown over time. This has not happened to *Roe v. Wade*. Its acceptance has been politically frozen for years.

Of course, long-term impact or acceptance is not predictable. It can only be explained with the benefit of hindsight. The astonishing changes in the acceptance of gay rights—and even gay marriage—owe a lot to the media, to the gay rights movement, to the sheer visibility of gay people, people coming out of the closet, college students seeing gay people in their dorms, acceptance in some churches, and so on. But still, the pace of change has been surprising. As a result of the civil rights movement and civil rights laws, race relations also changed—though somewhat more slowly, and, of course, in an incomplete way. Here, too, the media have played a role. Abortion is a different story. There is an abortion rights movement, but abortion itself remains intensely private. Very few women come out of the abortion closet. Religious opposition remains powerful; the two sides are still, after all these years, more or less in a state of stalemate.

In most developed countries, fewer and fewer people smoke cigarettes. The law has had a role: restrictions on sale, on use, on advertising. Moral and health campaigns probably had a bigger role. At one time, most people smoked. Movie stars lit up. Smoking was cool. Today, smoking has been denormalized. In many circles, it is not socially acceptable.[72] In the battle against drunk driving, campaigns, crackdowns, fines, even jail sentences have been used. The crackdowns produce results, but these tend to decay over time.[73] Organizations like Mothers Against Drunk Driving make a huge effort to demonize and denormalize drunk driving. Police departments join in. Moral campaigns like this do not promise quick payoffs, but they sometimes have a slow, long-run impact. Seat belts at first met with a good deal of resistance. Enforcement, education, and propaganda worked to normalize buckling up. Something seemed to work; seat belts for most people are now a habit; putting on your seat belt has become almost automatic. "Moral passages" are common, in short: changes in the moral status of certain behaviors. These moral passages can radically alter impact. Joseph Gusfield, in an interesting (and relevant) essay, described four types of "deviant."[74] Repentant deviants are people who break the rules, even though they consider the rules legitimate. Sick deviants are what the name implies; they simply cannot help themselves. The cynical deviant is self-serving; he or she breaks the rules for personal gain. Most burglars would fall into this category. The most dangerous type, in Gusfield's view, is the enemy deviant. These deviants are defiant, rebellious. They attack the norms themselves, in a way that, say, the typical burglar does not. Other things being equal, enemy deviants threaten the social order, or the regime; shoplifters, embezzlers, even murderers do not. Antiwar activists during the Vietnam crisis who burned draft cards, refused to register, and raised hell were trying to change foreign policy, end a war, perhaps even change the political structure. Jihadists, unlike pickpockets and burglars, aim to disrupt, dismember, and destroy. Suicide bombers, revolutionaries, fanatics who murder infidels are enemy deviants; but so, too, were Mahatma Gandhi and Nelson Mandela.

Societies create codes of law; they hope for impact and take steps accordingly. Perfect compliance is something that never happens. Society has to tolerate a certain amount of slippage. Police, tax auditors, and regulators work to keep slippage under control. Social norms and moral codes are their most powerful allies. A country can put up with burglars so long as enough of them get caught, and so long as there is no epidemic of burglary, just as a healthy bush or tree can survive its aphids and mealybugs, so long as birds eat enough of these bugs to keep the bush or tree alive. Terrorist attacks are another story. There are probably more burglars than terrorists, but the level of tolerance is lower for terrorists. Potential hijackers of planes are even rarer, and billions are spent to keep them away from the planes.

I Did It Because I Could

As we have seen, impact is a complicated social process. It depends on communication. Once a law is communicated, the decision to respond will be shaped by the three clusters we discussed: rewards and punishments, peer group influence, and internal motivation. And each of these, in turn, is complex.

Opportunity—the actual situation—is also enormously important for impact. Drivers who have the bad habit of leaving car keys inside the car make car theft easier—and more likely. To be sure, most of us are not about to steal cars, no matter what. But those who are ready, willing, and able to steal cars will take advantage of the careless driver who leaves his doors unlocked and the keys in position. The way people live, where they live, how they come and go, and how society is structured: these and many other factors can increase or decrease crime opportunity. People who get paid in cash (moonlighting plumbers, for example) have a "structural opportunity" to cheat on their taxes,[75] compared to employees subject to withholding, a prominent cloverleaf. A branch of the small-claims court opens up around the corner from an apartment building. Most tenants will not care, but one or two may bring their claim against a department store—a claim they might have ignored if the court was fifty miles away and had inconvenient hours.

Lawrence Cohen and Marcus Felson have stressed the importance of what they call "routine activity" in any analysis of crime rate. These rates, they argued, depend on three "minimal elements": people who are inclined to commit crimes ("motivated offenders"); available victims ("suitable targets"); and the "absence of capable guardians." Even if the number of motivated offenders stays constant, along with the number of capable guardians, the crime rate might increase because of more or easier targets.[76] People who work the night shift, for example, and go home in the dark are more exposed to crime than workers on the day shift. Families where both parents work and nobody is home during the day are more exposed to burglaries than houses full of people all day.

Burglars, in fact, look for empty homes, those with few guardians (in this case, watchful neighbors).[77] This is true the world over.[78] Also, detached houses with lots of good shrubbery, homes without dogs and burglar alarms. None of this, of course, explains why burglars choose their way of life, but opportunity and the "routine activity" of potential victims help explain how burglars work and how they choose their targets.[79]

Most of us are as unlikely to pick pockets as to break and enter, for all the usual reasons: deterrence, peer pressure, and individual conscience. Pickpockets, however, need pockets to pick. The more crowds and crowded places, the better for them; not to mention clothing styles, the ways pockets are designed, whether people carry a lot of cash as a rule, and so on. In our day, the Internet revolution has opened the door to a gaudy array of scams. People love to shop on the web, but the more they do this, the higher the risk they run of falling victim to Internet fraud.[80]

Victims and potential victims, of course, are not helpless. "Opportunity" is something we can do something about. We lock our cars and our houses. Buttons and zippers help us against pickpockets. A store can foil shoplifters with cameras and devices that set off alarms. These do more deterring than the police.[81] We buy bolts and locks, and avoid dark streets in bad neighborhoods. Stores hire security guards. "Routine activities" can be criminogenic, or the opposite. Dogs and burglar alarms can foil burglars.[82] Even signs that claim a house is equipped with a burglar alarm probably cuts down on burglary. Similarly, "Lojacks," hidden radio transmitters, reduce auto theft. They make it possible to locate stolen cars; a thief has no way of knowing whether or not a car has installed a Lojack.[83] A city can put more police on the beat, can keep streets well lit, and so on, with more or less effect. The Mexican government began putting radio frequency stickers on the inside windshield of cars. The aim was to create a centralized database of all the cars in Mexico; the stickers could be read by scanners. This would be, it was hoped, "a critical tool in the state's fight against organized crime, allowing it to more quickly respond to car thefts, kidnappings, and drugs and weapons trafficking."[84] And, of course, "incapacitation"—locking criminals up—takes away any opportunity to commit most crimes.

On the civil side, an ounce of prevention is also worth a pound of liability. You can avoid tort suits if you drive carefully. You can buy cars with good safety features. Society has prescribed airbags and seat belts; smart cars and driverless cars are on the way. Car insurance is mandatory. The Food and Drug Administration has required, since 1938, clinical tests for new drugs before they go on the market.[85] Food safety rules are meant to head off the need for tort suits. OSHA rules are meant to make workplaces safe. Vaccination against diseases is mostly compulsory. Tax withholding maximizes revenue—and makes tax evasion tougher; this is the cloverleaf effect, mentioned earlier. In general, prevention is integral to the modern legal order, both at the level of the individual and of society. It is mentioned here in the briefest of ways, but it deserves a book-length treatment of its own.

10

A CONCLUDING WORD

THIS BRINGS US to the end of our trip through the world of impact. What have we learned? A great many studies have been cited. Sometimes, it was possible to draw general conclusions. But at other times, this goal has been elusive. Much more research is needed. More replications. More attempts at pulling the strands together. Otherwise, everything depends. On time. On place. On situation.

In a way, this is paradoxical. Time and time again, I reported that the cup of research has been filled to overflowing. Hundreds of studies of deterrence. Hundreds of studies of regulation of business. And yet the results are often inconclusive. There are big gaps and holes in the research; but, more disturbingly, no consistency. The reader faces a volcanic eruption of research, but it hardly seems to be cumulative; it rarely adds up. Because of, or despite, the volume, the results leave the reader dizzy and bewildered, unsure of what she has learned.

Was the trip worthwhile? Despite some doubts, my answer is yes. I set out to build a framework, a skeleton. Some of this had been done before, but perhaps in less detail. Above all, I wanted to help make impact itself a field of study. Most impact studies fail to position themselves as impact studies. Yet there is a case to be made that "impact" deserves to be looked at as a whole. There are commonalities. All impact studies have to confront the issue of communication; that is, how the legal message is delivered. To measure or assess results, they have to analyze, implicitly or explicitly, behavior in terms of the three clusters of motives in one form or another. It is useful, I believe, to fit the various studies into the relevant boxes, as far as this can be done. General rules—laws about laws—are not within our grasp. But the framework is. I think the concept of the deterrence curve, for example, has value. It may make the pilgrimage worthwhile. Each crime, each legal act, has its own deterrence curve, and it may be helpful to think in terms of this curve.

It is easy to feel overwhelmed by the sheer volume of relevant work. But if you stand back and look at the landscape from a distance, as it were, some of the peaks and valleys look much clearer. Impact studies taken as a whole are like an impressionist painting. If your nose is inches from the canvas, all you see is a blur; walk several paces to the rear and you see flowers, a garden, a seascape.

I tried to provide a framework, a standpoint, a dose of clarity. At some points in this account, I expressed skepticism—sometimes about the results of this or that study, more often about the chance of making general sense out of the findings of particular studies. Impact, after all, is about human behavior. And human behavior is incredibly and incurably complex. Perhaps scientists will some day understand it well enough to make predictions of the sort they can make about the orbits of planets. I am not sure this will ever happen; not sure, besides, whether this would be Utopia or dystopia. At any rate, that state of the world has not yet arrived.

Impact, the subject of this book, is about the effect of law (in the broadest sense) on human behavior. In modern societies, law is ubiquitous. The rules and regulations of a modern society—statutes, ordinances, regulations, court decisions—run to thousands and thousands of pages. And this is only the formal outerwear of a vast, pulsating, and vital system, which has an impact on the public, in many ways, and every day. Moreover, we distinguished, at the very beginning, between two meta-questions in the sociology of law: the forces that determine where it comes from in the first place, and the forces that determine what its impact might be. This book was about the second of these questions, and only that. But the two are, of course, intimately connected, as I pointed out. The dynamics of, say, the passage of a major statute through a legislature has a lot to do with what impact it will ultimately have on society.

One generalization can be made fairly safely. No law, no decision, no rule is totally effective, totally obeyed, without dissent or noncompliance or nonuse. There is always some sort of shortfall. Why should this be? Some reasons are obvious. People differ: in personality, in their position in society, in their powers and strengths, in their ideologies. Impact is never total. By the same token, there is rarely total noncompliance or nonuse. After all, laws come out of a social context. They reflect social norms. On the whole, they depend on cooperation, on voluntary action, more than force. Erhard Blankenburg has pointed out an apparent paradox: the more that laws ask us to do something remote from what we want to do anyway, the more ineffective the laws are likely to be.[1] By the same token, the more law asks us to do what we want to do and are willing to do, the more effective it is likely to be. The law asks—no, demands—that we refrain from burglary. For almost all of us, that is not a problem. We have no intention of becoming burglars. The burglary curve has mostly flattened out. Laws tell us not to smoke, and to wear seat belts. If we come to believe that smoking is dangerous and that seat belts save lives, the law becomes, to that extent, more effective. It is telling us to obey something we want to obey—or have learned to want to obey.

Much legal scholarship—most of it, perhaps—is formalistic, stuck in the dreary task of analyzing texts; much of it is highly normative. Normative is fine, but not if the norms are unexamined. And especially not when jurists reach normative conclusions based on what they imagine to be fact, but without the slightest evidence to back up their assertions. This is also true of judgments about the impact of legal acts. Learned essays on what the law does in society, without looking to see what the impact actually is, are like essays on the sex life of the unicorn. What matters is the lived experience of law. This book has tried to look at law from the outside, from the standpoint of the social sciences, and not from the "inside," the standpoint of the jurists.

The standpoint of the social sciences: but which ones? All of them. I have to confess a bias toward sociology (including criminology) and the closely related work of political scientists, psychologists, and anthropologists. I should say a word about the reigning king of the social sciences, economics. Economics has, of course, made a huge contribution to the science of human behavior, including legal behavior. It has made great progress, but at a price. Generally speaking, economists make certain assumptions about human behavior, and these assumptions are often far too narrow, if not downright wrong. The science is not, perhaps, fatally flawed when it analyzes business behavior (though at least somewhat flawed), but for the understanding of armed robbers, carjackers, and drug dealers, its contribution, though not without merit, has less to say, and provides us with fewer insights than the work of the men and women who actually go out and talk to these people and watch them at work and try to understand what makes them tick. The newer economics, behavioral economics, is trying valiantly to make up for past sins.

There are, obviously, big differences between people: ordinary people on the one hand and businesses, organizations, and bureaucracies on the other. Differences, too, between small and large businesses. Between democratic bureaucracies and autocratic ones. Between honest people and burglars. And, of course, within each of these categories, differences in time and place and culture. Between the Middle Ages and now. Between a small group in the Amazon jungle and the residents of Stockholm or Tokyo. Is there any hope for something larger, more sweeping, more like a "law" of legal behavior? A lot can be said, in quite general terms, about modern, developed, democratic societies. A lot, I suspect, can also be said about preliterate societies, wherever they were or are. Or ancient kingdoms. Or modern dictatorships. But stitching all of these together, if it can be done at all, has to be left to future generations.

NOTES

ACKNOWLEDGMENTS

INDEX

NOTES

1. Introduction

1. I dealt with this issue in *The Legal System* (1975), pp. 45–136, in some detail. There are a few other attempts to deal with the subject in general, notably in German socio-legal scholarship, for example, Andreas Diekmann, *Die Befolgung von Gesetzen: Empirische Untersuchungen zu einer Rechtssoziologischen Theorie* (1980); Michelle Cottier, Josef Estermann, and Michael Wrase, eds., *Wie Wirkt Recht?* (2010). A recent and quite comprehensive book on one important aspect of impact is Christopher Hodges, *Law and Corporate Behaviour: Integrating Theories of Regulation, Enforcement, Compliance, and Ethics* (2015). And see the material in Stewart Macaulay, Lawrence M. Friedman, and Elizabeth Mertz, eds., *Law in Action: A Socio-Legal Reader* (2007), pp. 367–650.

2. To get something of an idea about the scope of scholarship on the subject, I asked a reference librarian to list for me every article in the most recent ten years in the *Index to Legal Periodicals* if it contained the word *impact* in the title. To my surprise, the result was a printout 195 pages long. The vast majority of the articles, however, dealt with the "impact" of a decision on later decisions, or on such matters as environmental impact statements. Very few were "impact" studies in the sense I am using the term here.

3. One exception is Stephen L. Wasby, *The Impact of the United States Supreme Court: Some Perspectives* (1970). The first hundred pages or so of this book are a general discussion of concepts relating to impact. See also

Bradley C. Canon and Charles A. Johnson, *Judicial Policies: Implementation and Impact*, 2d ed. (1999). Both of these, of course, confine themselves to the impact of court decisions. See also Theodore L. Becker and Malcolm M. Feeley, *The Impact of Supreme Court Decisions: Empirical Studies*, 2d ed. (1973).

4. See, notably, Gerald N. Rosenberg's book, *The Hollow Hope: Can Courts Bring About Social Change?* (1991).

5. Many examples appear in David Larcker and Brian Tayan's book, *Corporate Governance Matters: A Closer Look at Organizational Choices and their Consequences* (2011).

6. Shauhin A. Talesh, "The Privatization of Public Legal Rights: How Manufacturers Construct the Meaning of Consumer Law," *Law & Society Review* 43:527 (2009).

2. Getting Out the Message

1. Stewart Macaulay, "Images of Law in Everyday Life: The Lessons of School, Entertainment, and Spectator Sports," *Law & Society Review* 21:185 (1987). Audiences—spectators at a football game, people watching baseball on television—also learn and know the rules.

2. Stefan Machura and Annette Kammertöns, "Recht im Schulunterricht, Medieneinflüsse und die Attraktivität von Rechtsberufen," *Zeitschrift für Rechtssoziologie* 30:235, 236 (2009).

3. 2014 General Social Survey: Gallup Poll, www.gallup.com/poll/10474/public-justice-system-fair-still-too-soft.aspx.

4. James Q. Whitman, *Harsh Justice: Criminal Punishment and the Widening Divide between America and Europe* (2005), p. 70.

5. Elayne Rapping, *Law and Justice As Seen on TV* (2003), p. 263.

6. Ibid., p. 262.

7. Klaus Merten, "Die Rolle der Medien bei der Vermittlung zwischen Recht und Gesellschaft," *Z. für Rechtssoziologie* 18:16, 27–29 (1997). The study in question was Werner Glogauer, *Kriminalisierung von Kinder und Jugendlichen durch Medien* (1991).

8. Donald E. Shelton, Young S. Kim, and Gregg Barak, "A Study of Juror Expectations and Demands Concerning Scientific Evidence: Does the 'CSI Effect' Exist?" *Vanderbilt J. Entertainment & Tech. Law* 9:331 (2006).

9. See Kimberlianne Podlas, "Testing Television: Studying and Understanding the Impact of Television's Depictions of Law and Justice," in Peter Robson and Jessica Silbey, eds., *Law and Justice on the Small Screen* (2012), pp. 87, 105–106; Lawrence M. Friedman, "Judge Judy's Justice," *Berkeley J. of Entertainment and Sports Law* 1:124 (2012). Such programs exist also in other countries and are widely watched; see Stefan Machura and Annette Kammertöns, "Recht im

Schulunterricht, Medieneinflüsse und die Attraktivität von Rechtsberufen," *Z. für Rechtssoziologie* 30:234, 244 (2009).

10. William Haltom and Michael McCann, *Distorting the Law: Politics, Media, and the Litigation Crisis* (2004), p. 186. On the McDonald's case in general, see pp. 183–226.

11. The radio host was Mike Rosen. For this quote, see Haltom and McCann, *Distorting the Law*, p. 209.

12. Ibid., pp. 208, 215–216.

13. Laura Beth Nielsen and Aaron Beim, "Media Misrepresentation: Title VII, Print Media, and Public Perceptions of Discrimination Litigation," *Stanford Law and Policy Review* 15:237, 252 (2004).

14. Ibid., p. 253.

15. Alexander Kose, "Wie Wirkt Antidiskriminierungsrecht?" in Michelle Cottier, Joseph Estermann, Michael Wrase, eds., *Wie Wirkt Recht?* (2010), pp. 347, 357.

16. This was a study by the California Assembly Committee on Criminal Procedure and is discussed in Kirk R. Williams, Jack P. Gibbs, and Maynard L. Erickson, "Public Knowledge of Statutory Penalties: The Extent and Basis of Accurate Perception," *Pacific Sociological Review* 23:105, 107–108 (1980).

17. Ibid., p. 117.

18. Robert MacCoun et al., "Do Citizens Know Whether their State Has Decriminalized Marijuana? Assessing the Perceptual Component of Deterrence Theory," *Review of Law and Economics* 5:347 (2009).

19. 354 U.S. 476 (1957).

20. James P. Levine, "Constitutional Law and Obscene Literature: An Investigation of Bookseller Censorship Practices," in Theodore L. Becker and Malcolm M. Feeley, *The Impact of Supreme Court Decisions*, 2d ed. (1973), pp. 119, 131.

21. Martha Williams and Jay Hall, "Knowledge of the Law in Texas: Socioeconomic and Ethnic Differences," *Law & Society Review* 7:29 (1972).

22. Stan L. Albrecht and Miles Green, "Cognitive Barriers to Equal Justice before the Law," *J. Research in Crime and Delinquency* 14:206 (1977). The questions asked revealed a good deal of downright ignorance. Most people thought the loser in a civil case must pay the attorney fees for the winner (only one out of four knew this was not so), and more than half agreed with the proposition that, in a trial, "an accused person must prove the charges are false." See pp. 213–214.

23. Vilhelm Aubert, "Some Social Functions of Legislation," *Acta Sociologica* 10:98 (1967).

24. Israel Doron and Perla Werner, "Facts on Law and Ageing Quiz: Older People's Knowledge of their Legal Rights," *Ageing and Society* 28:1159, 1170 (2008).

25. Mary Nell Trautner, Erin Hutton, and Kelly E. Smith, "What Workers Want Depends: Legal Knowledge and the Desire for Workplace Change among Day Laborers," *Law and Policy* 35:319 (2013).

26. Compare the findings of Aubert with regard to Norwegian housewives, in Aubert, "Some Social Functions of Legislation," supra, n. 23.

27. Erin L. Kelly, "Failure to Update: An Institutional Perspective on Noncompliance with the Family and Medical Leave Act," *Law & Society Review* 44:33 (2010).

28. Sally Engle Merry, *Human Rights and Gender Violence: Translating International Law into Local Justice* (2005).

29. Hazel Genn, "Business Responses to the Regulation of Health and Safety in England," *Law & Policy* 15:219 (1993).

30. 355 U.S. 225 (1957).

31. In *United States v. International Minerals & Chemical Corp.*, 402 U.S. 558 (1971), a federal rule required shipments of sulfuric and hydrofluosilicic acids to be shown on the shipping papers. The company failed to do so. The Supreme Court remarked that with "dangerous or deleterious devices or products . . . the probability of regulation is so great that anyone who is aware that he is in possession of them . . . must be presumed to be aware of the regulation." No reason, then, to assume that "knowledge of both the fact and the pertinent law" had been intended. See Michael Cottone, "Rethinking Presumed Knowledge of the Law in the Regulatory Age," *Tennessee Law Review* 82:137 (2014).

32. *Bush v. Gore*, 531 U.S. 98 (2000); *Brown v. Board of Education*, 347 U.S. 483 (1954).

33. 410 U.S. 113 (1973).

34. 17 Cal. 3rd 425, 551 P. 2d 334 (1976). This was the result of a rehearing. The earlier version was *Tarasoff v. Regents of the University of California*, 13 Cal. 3rd 177, 529 P. 2d 553 (1974); the study is Daniel J. Givelber, William J. Bowers, and Carolyn L. Blitch, "Tarasoff: Myth and Reality: An Empirical Study of Private Law in Action," *Wisconsin L. Rev.* 1984:443.

35. Pascoe Pleasence and Nigel J. Balmer, "Ignorance in Bliss: Modeling Knowledge of Rights in Marriage and Cohabitation," *Law & Society Review* 46:297 (2012).

36. In a few American states, the "common law marriage" does survive, but length of time even in these states has nothing to do with the situation. A couple in a common law marriage state, who agree to be married, are married, even if they have been together for half an hour or less.

37. Pauline T. Kim, "Norms, Learning, and Law: Exploring the Influences on Workers' Legal Knowledge," *U. of Ill. L. Rev.* 1999:447. The text of the survey is on p. 508. Workers were wrong about other issues, too: whether the employer had a right to get rid of an employee simply because the boss disliked

the worker. This is perfectly lawful, but a staggering 89 percent of the workers in Missouri thought this was against the law.

38. Ibid., p. 459.

39. John M. Darley, Paul H. Robinson, and Kevin M. Carlsmith, "The Ex Ante Function of the Criminal Law," *Law & Society Review* 35:165 (2001).

40. Katherine V. W. Stone, "Revisiting the At-Will Employment Doctrine: Imposed Terms, Implied Terms, and the Normative World of the Workplace," *Industrial Law Journal* 36:84 (2007).

41. 557 P. 2d 106 (1976).

42. A court awarded her a mere $104,000, so that she could "rehabilitate" her skill, and even that was overturned by an appellate court; *Marvin v. Marvin*, 5 Fam. L. Rep. (BNA) 3077 (Cal. Super. Ct. 1979). The appellate case was *Marvin v. Marvin*, 122 Cal. App. 3d 871 (1981). See Joanna L. Grossman and Lawrence M. Friedman, *Inside the Castle: Law and the Family in Twentieth-Century America* (2011), pp. 128–136.

43. There is a website devoted to palimony cartoons, in which this cartoon appears.

44. "Ex-Liberace Employee Sues for $113 Million," *New York Times,* Oct. 15, 1982. The "employee" was Scott Thorson, who had been Liberace's chauffeur and, he claimed, his lover.

45. For a rich description of the legal culture of an autocratic society, see Inga Markovitz, *Justice in Lüritz: Experiencing Social Law in East Germany* (2010).

46. *Gideon v. Wainwright*, 372 U.S. 335 (1963); Anthony Lewis, *Gideon's Trumpet* (1964).

47. This information comes from Maeve P. Carey, *Counting Regulations: An Overview of Rulemaking, Types of Federal Regulations, and Pages in the Federal Register* (Congressional Research Service, November 26, 2014).

48. See, for example, Louis Kaplow, "Rules versus Standards: An Economic Analysis," *Duke Law Journal* 42:557 (1992).

49. The study is Kelly Galagher-Mackay, "Teachers' Duty to Report Child Abuse and Neglect and the Paradox of Non-Compliance: Relational Theory and 'Compliance' in the Human Services," *Law and Policy* 36:256 (2014).

50. This material is from Jerry Wiley, "The Impact of Judicial Decisions on Professional Conduct: An Empirical Study," *So. Cal. L. Rev.* 55:345 (1981).

51. The case is *Helling v. Carey*, 83 Wash. 2d 514, 519 P. 2d 981 (1974). The case meant that specialists had to change their practice and test routinely for glaucoma. Actually, despite what the doctors had argued, many eye doctors already did this.

52. Wiley, "The Impact of Judicial Decisions on Professional Conduct," p. 381. The statute is RCW 7.70.040.

53. James F. Spriggs II, "The Supreme Court and Federal Administrative Agencies: A Resource-Based Theory and Analysis of Judicial Impact," *Am. J. Political Science* 40:1122, 1138 (1996).

54. H. Laurence Ross, *Settled Out of Court: The Social Process of Insurance Claim Adjustments* (1970).

55. Lauren B. Edelman, Christopher Uggen, and Howard S. Erlanger, "The Endogeneity of Legal Regulation: Grievance Procedures as Rational Myth," *American J. Sociology* 105:406 (1999).

56. Stephen Wasby, *The Impact of the United States Supreme Court: Some Perspectives* (1970), p. 44.

57. 358 U.S. 1 (1958).

58. Kazumasu Aoki and John W. Cioffi, "Poles Apart: Industrial Waste Management Regulation and Enforcement in the United States and Japan," *Law & Policy* 23:213 (1999).

59. Ibid., p. 215.

60. Brian K. Chen and Chun-Yuh Yang, "Increased Perception of Malpractice Liability and the Practice of Defensive Medicine," *J. Empirical Legal Studies* 11:446, 452 (2014).

61. Zahn Bozanic, Mark W. Dirsmith, and Steven Huddart, "The Social Constitution of Regulation: The Endogenization of Insider Trading Laws," *Accounting, Organizations, and Society* 37:461, 471 (2012).

62. Mark C. Suchman and Mia L. Cahill, "The Hired Gun as Facilitator: Lawyers and the Suppression of Business Disputes in Silicon Valley," *Law & Social Inquiry* 21:679, 681 (1996).

63. The official website is Healthcare.gov.

64. Daniel E. Ho, "Fudging the Nudge: Information Disclosure and Restaurant Grading," *Yale L. Journal* 122:574, 577 (2012).

65. Michelle M. Mello and Troyen A. Brennan, "Deterrence of Medical Errors: Theory and Evidence for Malpractice Reform," *Texas L. Rev.* 80:1595, 1597 (2002).

66. Justine E. Tinkler, "'People Are Too Quick to Take Offense': The Effects of Legal Information and Beliefs on Definitions of Sexual Harassment," *Law & Social Inquiry* 33:417 (2008).

67. Justine E. Tinkler, "Resisting the Enforcement of Sexual Harassment Law," *Law & Social Inquiry* 37:1 (2012).

68. A violator of minor traffic laws who chooses "traffic school" thereby avoids "adverse" effects on a driver's record—and a possible hike in insurance costs.

69. Scott Wortley, Benedikt Fischer, and Cheryl Webster, "Vice Lessons: A Survey of Prostitution Offenders Enrolled in the Toronto John School Diversion Program," *Canadian J. of Criminology* 44:369, 373 (2002).

70. Benjamin van Rooij, "The People's Regulation: Citizens and Implementation of Law in China," *Columbia J. of Asian Law* 25:116, 158 (2012).

71. Mary E. Gallagher, "Mobilizing the Law in China: 'Informed Disenchantment' and the Development of Legal Consciousness," *Law & Society Review* 40:783 (2006).

72. Thomas Gawron and Ralph Rogowski, "Effecktivität, Implementation und Evaluation: Wirkungsanalyse am Beispiel von Entscheidungen des Bundesverfassungsgerichts," *Z. für Rechtssoziologie* 17:177 (1996).

73. Rose Corrigan, "The New Trial by Ordeal: Rape Kits, Police Practices, and the Unintended Effects of Policy Innovation," *Law & Society Review* 38:920, 930–931 (2013).

74. Harry Kalven Jr. and Hans Zeisel, *The American Jury* (1966), pp. 249–254.

75. Ulrike Lembke, "'Vergeblich Gesetzgebung': Die Reform des Sexualstrafrechts 1997/1998 als Jahrhundertprojekt und ihr Scheitern in und an der sogenannten Rechtswirklichkeit," *Z. für Rechtssoziologie* 34:252 (2014).

76. Timothy J. Gilfoyle, *City of Eros: New York City, Prostitution, and the Commercialization of Sex, 1790–1920* (1992), p. 131.

3. An Anatomy of Compliance

1. See, on this point, Malcolm M. Feeley, "Power, Impact, and the Supreme Court," in Theodore L. Becker and Malcolm M. Feeley, eds., *The Impact of Supreme Court Decisions*, 2d ed. (1973), pp. 218, 225.

2. Discussed in Hubert Rottleuthner and Margret Rottleuthner-Lutter, "Recht und Kausalität," in Michelle Cottier, Josef Estermann, and Michael Wrase, eds., *Wie Wirkt Recht?* (2010), pp. 17, 33–36.

3. The other two are compliance by countries with demands coming from international courts, or international law, and fourth, "compliance with high court decisions by subnational public authorities," for example, by lower courts. See Diana Kapiczewski and Matthew M. Taylor, "Compliance: Conceptualizing, Measuring, and Explaining Adherence to Judicial Rulings," *Law and Social Inquiry* 38:803, 805 (2013).

4. See Neil Donnelly, Wayne Hall, and Paul Christie, "The Effects of Partial Decriminalisation on Cannabis Use in South Australia, 1985 to 1993," *Australian J. Public Health* 19:281 (1995).

5. Griffin Edwards, "Doing Their Duty: An Empirical Analysis of the Unintended Effect of *Tarasoff v. Regents* on Homicidal Activity," http://ssm.com/abstract=1544574.

6. Eric A. Feldman and Ronald Bayer, "The Triumph and Tragedy of Tobacco Control: A Tale of Nine Nations," *Ann. Rev. Law Soc. Sci.* 7:79, 87–88 (2011). See also Michael McCann, William Haltom, and Shauna Fisher, "Criminalizing Big Tobacco: Legal Mobilization and the Politics of Responsibility for Health Risks in the United States," *Law & Social Inquiry* 38:288 (2013).

7. In a survey of economists published in 1992, the "greatest degree of consensus" on any proposition was the proposition that rent control "reduces the quantity and quality of housing." This was the view of 93.5 percent of the surveyed economists. The study is cited in Richard Arnott, "Time for Revisionism on Rent Control?" *J. Economic Perspectives* 9:99 (1995). As the title suggests, Arnott is one of the rare dissenters.

8. Philip J. Cook, "Criminal Incapacitation Effects Considered in an Adaptive Choice Framework," in Derek B. Cornish and Ronald V. Clarke, eds., *The Reasoning Criminal: Rational Choice Perspectives on Offending* (1986), pp. 202, 207–208. The leading article, which expresses this point of view, is Sam Peltzman, "The Effects of Automobile Safety Regulation," *J. Political Economy* 25:677 (1975). Peltzman's conclusion was that drivers "offset" any safety advantages by riskier driving, shifting the "burden" of accidents to pedestrians, who became more likely to be killed. Drunk driving also apparently increased (according to Peltzman), p. 717.

9. John J. Donohue III, "Using Market Incentives to Promote Auto Occupant Safety," *Yale Law & Policy Rev.* 7:449, 458 (1989).

10. N. J. Ch.'s 128, Public Laws of 1994. The current law is N. J. S. A. 2C:7-1 through 7-11. Each state has its own version; for example, the California "Sex Offender Registration Act," California Penal Code §290. A federal law, 110 Stat. 1345 (May 17, 1996), which "may be cited as 'Megan's Law,'" provides that information "collected under a State registration program" can be released if "necessary to protect the public," and identifying a "specific person required to register," but the "identity of a victim" was not to be released.

11. Richard Tewsbury and Westley G. Jennings, "Assessing the Impact of Sex Offender Registration and Community Notification on Sex-Offending Trajectories," *Criminal Justice and Behavior* 37:570 (2010).

12. Jill Levenson and Richard Tewksbury, "Collateral Damage: Family Members of Registered Sex Offenders," *Am. J. Crim. Justice* 54:54 (2009).

13. Joseph R. Gusfield, "Moral Passage: The Symbolic Process in Public Designations of Deviance," *Social Problems* 15:175 (1967).

14. Ibid., p. 174.

15. Erhard Blankenburg, "Über die Unwirksamkeit von Gesetzen," in *Archiv für Rechts-und Sozialphilosophie* 1977:31, 43.

16. In *Texas v. Johnson*, 491 U.S. 397 (1989), the Supreme Court reversed a conviction for burning the flag, on free speech grounds, where the act of desecration had been a deliberate attack on the flag as a symbol.

17. Michael W. McCann, *Rights at Work: Pay Equity Reform and the Politics of Legal Mobilization* (1994).

18. Jens Newig, "Symbolische Gesetzgebung zwischen Machtausübung und gesellschaftlicher Selbsttäuschung," in Michelle Cottier, Josef Estermann, and Michael Wrase, eds., *Wie Wirkt Recht?* (2010), pp. 301, 310–312.

19. Thomas M. Keck, "Beyond Backlash: Assessing the Impact of Judicial Decisions on LGBT Rights," *Law & Society Review* 43:151, 152 (2009).

20. Michael J. Klarman, "*Brown*, Racial Change, and the Civil Rights Movement," *Virginia Law Review* 80:7, 85 (1994).

21. Michael J. Klarman, *From the Closet to the Altar: Courts, Backlash, and the Struggle for Same-Sex Marriage* (2013).

22. Michael J. Klarman, "*Brown*, Racial Change, and the Civil Rights Movement," p. 85.

23. Keck, "Beyond Backlash," p. 163.

24. *U.S. v. Windsor*, 133 S. Ct. 2675 (2013).

25. This was *Obergefell v. Hodges*, 135 S. Ct. 2584 (2015).

26. 539 U.S. 558 (2003).

27. 332 U.S. 325 (1963).

28. Klarman, *From the Closet to the Altar*, p. 172.

29. John J. Donohue III and Steven D. Levitt, "The Impact of Legalized Abortion on Crime," *Quarterly Journal of Economics* 116:379, 381 (2001).

30. Jessica Wolpaw Reyes, "Lead Exposure and Behavior: Effects on Antisocial and Risky Behavior among Children and Adolescents," *Economic Inquiry* 53:1580, 1582, 1601–1602 (2015).

31. Mark J. Mills, Greer Sullivan, and Spencer Eth, "Protecting Third Parties: A Decade after *Tarasoff*," *Am. J. Psychiatry* 144:1 (1987).

32. And the difference between the two legal families is even less with regard to the way in which the bureaucracy reacts to and interprets statutes.

33. For example, Christine Parker and Vibeke Lehmann Nielsen, *Explaining Compliance: Business Responses to Regulation* (2011).

34. John L. McMullan and David C. Perrier, "Lobster Poaching and the Ironies of Law Enforcement," *Law & Society Review* 36:679 (2002).

35. Paul D. Cromwell, James N. Olson, and D'Aunn Wester Avary, *Breaking and Entering: An Ethnographic Analysis of Burglary* (1991), pp. 14–16.

36. Ibid., p. 14.

37. *Gideon v. Wainwright*, 372 U.S. 335 (1963); *Miranda v. Arizona*, 384 U.S. 436 (1966).

38. William J. Stuntz, *The Collapse of American Justice* (2011).

39. Hung-en Liu, "Custody Decisions in Social and Cultural Contexts: In-Depth and Focus Group Interviews with Nineteen Judges in Taiwan," *Columbia J. Asian Law* 17:250 (2004).

40. Donald T. Campbell and H. Laurence Ross, "The Connecticut Crackdown on Speeding: Times Series Data in Quasi-Experimental Analysis," *Law & Society Review* 3:33 (1968).

41. Julie Horney and Cassia Spohn, "Rape Law Reform and Instrumental Change in Six Urban Jurisdictions," *Law & Society Review* 25:117 (1991). On the failure of German reform of the law in the 1990s, see C. Lembke, "Changing the

Rules of the Game: The Role of Law and the Effects of Party Reform on Gender Parity in Germany," in Jyette Clausen and Charles S. Maier, eds., *Has Liberalism Failed Women? Assuring Equal Representation in Europe and the United States* (2001).

42. *Helling v. Carey*, 83 Wash. 2d 514, 519 P. 2d 981 (1974).

43. Jerry Wiley, "The Impact of Judicial Decisions on Professional Conduct: An Empirical Study," *So. Cal. L. Rev.* 55:345 (1981).

44. See Lawrence W. Sherman, "Police Crackdowns," *Crime & Justice* 12:35 (1990). "Displacement" does not occur in citywide crackdowns on drunk driving.

45. John J. Donohue, Daniel E. Ho, and Patrick Leahy, "Do Police Reduce Crime? A Reexamination of a Natural Experiment," in Yun-Chien Chang, ed., *Empirical Legal Analysis: Assessing the Performance of Legal Institutions* (2014).

46. See Lawrence M. Friedman, *Crime and Punishment in American History* (1993), pp. 328–332; Peter C. Hennigan, "Property War: Prostitution, Red-Light Districts, and the Transformation of Public Nuisance Law in the Progressive Era," *Yale J. Law and Humanities* 16:1 (2004); Thomas C. Mackey, *Red Lights Out: A Legal History of Prostitution, Disorderly Houses, and Vice Districts, 1870–1917* (1987).

47. Minzee Kim et al., "When Do Laws Matter? National Minimum-Age-of-Marriage Laws, Child Rights, and Adolescent Fertility, 1989–2007," *Law & Society Review* 47:589 (2013).

48. Ibid., p. 611.

49. The whole subject is very well dealt with in Franklin E. Zimring, *The City that Became Safe: New York's Lessons for Urban Crime and Its Control* (2012).

50. Gerald N. Rosenberg, *The Hollow Hope: Can Courts Bring About Social Change?*, 2d ed. (2008).

51. Michele Maroto and David Pettinicchio, "The Limitations of Disability Anti-discrimination Legislation: Policymaking and the Economic Well-Being of People with Disabilities," *Law and Policy* 36:370 (2014).

52. The exact figure is 25,369. It is worth pointing out that most of these were found to be groundless. On the other hand, the EEOC did pursue a number of these cases and money damages for the year came to almost $100 million. Figures are from www.eeoc.gov/eeoc/statistics.

53. David M. Engel and Frank W. Munger, *Rights of Inclusion: Law and Identity in the Life Stories of Americans with Disabilities* (2003).

54. Ibid., p. 241.

55. Katherine Gelber and Luke McNamara, "The Effects of Civil Hate Speech Laws: Lessons from Australia," *Law & Society Review* 49:631, 658 (2015).

56. Bettina Shell-Duncan et al., "Legislating Change? Responses to Criminalizing Female Genital Cutting in Senegal," *Law & Society Review* 47:803 (2013).

57. Elisabeth Noelle-Neumann, "Rechtsbewusstsein im wiedervereinigten Deutschland," *Z. für Rechtssoziologie* 16:121, 137–138 (1995).

58. Ibid., p. 139.

4. A Typology of Responses

1. Michael Cherbonneau and Heith Copes, "'Drive It Like You Stole It': Auto Theft and the Illusion of Normalcy," *British J. of Criminology* 46:193 (2005).

2. Thomas J. Holt, Kristie R. Blevins, and Joseph B. Kuhns, "Examining Diffusion and Arrest Avoidance Practices among Johns," *Crime and Delinquency* 60:261, 269 (2014).

3. Ibid., p. 276.

4. John C. Cross, "Passing the Buck: Risk Avoidance and Risk Management in the Illegal/Informal Drug Trade," *International J. of Sociology and Social Policy* 20:68, 84–85 (2000).

5. Bruce A. Jacobs, "Crack Dealers and Restrictive Deterrence: Identifying Narcs," *Criminology* 34:409, 417 (1996).

6. On Taiwanese practice, see, for example, Brian K. Chen and Chun-Yuh Yang, "Increased Perception of Malpractice Liability and the Practice of Defensive Medicine," *J. Empirical Legal Studies* 11:446 (2014).

7. *Engel v. Vitale,* 370 U.S. 432 (1962); *Abington School District v. Schempp,* 374 U.S. 203 (1963).

8. Kenneth M. Dolbeare and Phillip E. Hammond, *The School Prayer Decisions: From Court Policy to Local Practice* (1971), pp. 30, 32; Robert H. Birkby, "The Supreme Court and the Bible Belt: Tennessee Reaction to the 'Schempp Decision,'" *Midwest J. Political Science* 10:304 (1966).

9. Dolbeare and Hammond, *The School Prayer Decisions: From Court Policy to Local Practice,* p. 138.

10. Jon B. Gould, "The Precedent that Wasn't: College Hate Speech Codes and the Two Faces of Legal Compliance," *Law & Society Review* 35:345 (2001).

11. Ibid., p. 388.

12. See Andrew Sinclair, *Prohibition: The Era of Excess* (1962); Daniel Okrent, *Last Call: The Rise and Fall of Prohibition* (2010).

13. Neil Miller, *Banned in Boston: The Watch and Ward Society's Crusade against Books, Burlesque, and the Social Evil* (2010).

14. See the report website, www.drugsense.org/tfy/stillcraz.htm.

15. See Jeffrey A. Schafer, "Prosecution for Selective Service Offenses: A Field Study," *Stanford L. Rev.* 22:356 (1970).

16. The study is Seksan Khruakham and Brian A. Lawton, "Assessing the Impact of the 1996 Thai Prostitution Law: A Study of Police Arrest Data," *Asian Criminology* 7:23 (2012).

17. Joanna L. Grossman and Lawrence M. Friedman, *Inside the Castle: Law and the Family in Twentieth Century America* (2011); Glenda Riley, *Divorce: An American Tradition* (1991); J. Herbie DiFonzo, *Beneath the Fault Line: The Popular and Legal Culture of Divorce in Twentieth-Century America* (1997).

18. See "Collusive and Consensual Divorce and the New York Anomaly," *Columbia L. Rev.* 36:1121 (1936).

19. See Colin S. Gibson, *Dissolving Wedlock* (1994), pp. 96–97.

20. Under Chilean law, a marriage had to be celebrated in a place where at least one of the parties lived. When a couple wanted to split up, they would simply claim that this had never been true, that they got married in the wrong place, and hence that the marriage was never valid. In this way, there was introduced into the Chilean system "divorce by consent," even though it was "not authorized by the text of the law," but was the product of "fraudulent conduct" by the parties. Hernán Corral Talciani, "Indisolubilidad Matrimonial y Divorcio Ante el Derecho Civil," *Revista Chilena de Derecho*, 35:35, 36 (1992). I am indebted to Claudio Fuentes for this reference.

21. A few states have tried to reverse the tide of history. In Louisiana, a couple can choose either an ordinary marriage or a "covenant marriage," La. Rev. Stats. 2011, Title 9, §237. Couples who enter into a covenant marriage promise, in effect, to stay married for life. They can divorce, but only for cause. So far, it seems covenant marriage has not been particularly popular.

22. Hazel Genn, *Paths to Justice: What People Do and Think about Going to Law* (1999), p. 23. The results were roughly similar in the later study of Scotland, Hazel Genn and Alan Paterson, *Paths to Justice: Scotland: What People in Scotland Do and Think about Going to Law* (2001).

23. William L. F. Felstiner, Richard L. Abel, and Austin Sarat, "The Emergence and Transformation of Disputes: Naming, Blaming, Claiming . . ." *Law & Society Review* 15:631 (1980).

24. Genn, *Paths to Justice: What People Do and Think about Going to Law*, p. 39. Thirteen percent did nothing.

25. See Marlynn L. May and Daniel B. Stengel, "Who Sues Their Doctors? How Patients Handle Medical Grievances," *Law & Society Review* 24:105, 106 (1990).

26. Only a small percentage of negligent actions by doctors result in actual claims; see Michelle M. Mello and Troyen A. Brennan, "Deterrence of Medical Errors: Theory and Evidence for Malpractice Reform," *Texas Law Review* 80:1595, 1609 (2002).

27. Robyn Fairman and Charlotte Yapp, "Enforced Self-Regulation, Prescription, and Conceptions of Compliance within Small Businesses: The Impact of Enforcement," *Law and Policy* 27:491, 499 (2005).

28. See Stewart Macaulay, "Lawyers and Consumer Protection Laws: An Empirical Study," *Law & Society Review* 14:115 (1979).

29. See Deborah R. Hensler et al., *Class Action Dilemmas: Pursuing Public Goals for Private Gain* (2000).

30. See, for example, Herbert M. Kritzer, "Propensity to Sue in England and the United States of America: Blaming and Claiming in Tort Cases," *J. of Law and Society* 18:400 (1991). See also J. Fitzgerald, "Grievances, Disputes and Outcomes: A Comparison of Australia and the United States," *Law in Context* 1:31 (1983).

31. David M. Engel and Jaruwan S. Engel, *Tort, Custom, and Karma: Globalization and Legal Consciousness in Thailand* (2010), p. 89.

32. Mark Fathi Massoud, *Law's Fragile State: Colonial, Authoritarian, and Humanitarian Legacies in Sudan* (2013), pp. 177–178.

33. Felstiner et al., "The Emergence and Transformation of Disputes," p. 641.

34. Catherine R. Albiston, Lauren B. Edelman, and Joy Milligan, "The Dispute Tree and the Legal Forest," *Ann. Rev. Law. Soc. Sci.* 10:105, 109 (2014).

35. Under the Fourteenth Amendment, "All persons born . . . in the United States . . . are citizens of the United States." *U.S. v. Wong Kim Ark*, 169 U.S. 649 (1898) held that a person of Chinese descent born in the United States was a citizen, even though the Chinese could not (in general) legally enter the country or become naturalized citizens.

36. Tamar Lewin, "California Apartments Raided in Federal Investigation of Chinese 'Birth Tourism,'" *New York Times*, March 3, 2015. The businesses charged up to $60,000 for this service.

37. Estelle T. Lau, *Paper Families: Identity, Immigration Administration, and Chinese Exclusion* (2006), p. 36.

38. Virginia G. Cartoof and Lorraine V. Klerman, "Parental Consent for Abortion: Impact of the Massachusetts Law," *American J. of Public Health* 76:397, 399 (1986).

39. Sarah Morando Lakhani, "Producing Immigrant Victims' 'Right' to Legal Status and the Management of Legal Uncertainty," *Law and Social Inquiry* 38:442 (2013).

40. Lauren B. Edelman and Shauhin A. Talesh, "To Comply or Not to Comply—That Isn't the Question: How Organizations Construct the Meaning of Compliance," in Christine Parker and Vibeke Lehmann Nielsen, eds., *Explaining Compliance: Business Responses to Regulation* (2011), p. 103.

41. See, for example, Zahn Bozanic, Mark W. Dirsmith, and Steven Huddart, "The Social Constitution of Regulation: The Endogenization of Inside Trading Laws," *Accounting, Organizations, and Society* 37:461 (2012), on this process in the development of insider trading rules; Catherine R. Albiston, "Bargaining in the Shadow of Social Institutions: Competing Discourses and

Social Change in Workplace Mobilization of Civil Rights," *Law & Society Review* 39:11 (2005).

42. Edelman and Talesh, "To Comply or Not to Comply—That Isn't the Question: How Organizations Construct the Meaning of Compliance," pp. 103, 108.

43. The study is Sharon Gilad, "Beyond Endogeneity: How Firms and Regulators Co-Construct the Meaning of Regulation," *Law and Policy* 36:134 (2014).

44. Fairman and Yapp, "Enforced Self-Regulation, Prescription, and Conceptions of Compliance within Small Businesses," pp. 491, 514.

45. 467 Fed. 2d 1000 (C.A. 9, 1972).

46. 564 U.S., 131 S. Ct. 2541 (2011).

47. Bradley C. Canon and Charles A. Johnson, *Judicial Policies: Implementation and Impact*, 2d ed. (1999), pp. 24–25. See also Bradley C. Canon, "Courts and Policy: Compliance, Implementation, and Impact," in John B. Gates and Charles A. Johnson, *The American Courts: A Critical Assessment* (1991), pp. 435, 438.

48. Herb M. Simpson, "The Evolution and Effectiveness of Graduated Licensing," *J. Safety Research* 34:25 (2003); but see Michelle M. Mello and Kathryn Zeiler, "Empirical Health Law Scholarship: The State of the Field," *Georgetown L. Rev.* 96:649, 667–670 (2008).

5. Rewards and Punishments: The Punishment Side

1. See, for example, Franklin E. Zimring and Gordon J. Hawkins, *Deterrence: The Legal Threat in Crime Control* (1973). A useful summary of the history of the concept is in Raymond Paternoster, "How Much Do We Really Know about Criminal Deterrence?" *J. Criminal Law & Criminology* 100:765 (2010). For an overview of the research in the field of criminal justice, see Daniel S. Nagin, "Criminal Deterrence Research at the Outset of the Twenty-First Century," *Crime and Justice* 23:1 (1998).

2. Daphne W. Yiu, Yue Hua Xu, and William P. Wan, "The Deterrence Effects of Vicarious Punishments on Corporate Financial Fraud," *Organization Science* 25:1549 (2014). The authors carried out a study of "vicarious punishment" effects in China. They argue that the concept is particularly valuable in China because China is in "transition" to a market economy and firms in China "learn by observing the corporate behaviors and consequences of their industry peers."

3. See, on this point, Dorothy Thornton, Neil A. Gunningham, and Robert A. Kagan, "General Deterrence and Corporate Environmental Behavior," *Law and Policy* 27:262 (2005). There is a large body of work on deterrence in the business environment. See, for example, Christopher Hodges, *Law and Corporate Behaviour* (2015), pp. 139–157; Sally S. Simpson et al., "An Empirical

Assessment of Corporate Environmental Crime-Control Strategies," *J. of Crim. Law & Criminology* 103:231 (2013).

4. Mark C. Stafford and Mark Warr, "A Reconceptualization of General and Specific Deterrence," *J. Research in Crime and Delinquency* 30:123, 127 (1993). See also Raymond Paternoster and Alex Piquero, "Reconceptualizing Deterrence: An Empirical Test of Personal and Vicarious Experiences," *J. Research in Crime and Delinquency* 33:251 (1995).

5. For a comprehensive discussion, and a review of the literature (at least up to the mid-1990s), see Franklin E. Zimring and Gordon Hawkins, *Incapacitation: Penal Confinement and the Restraint of Crime* (1995).

6. Whether capital punishment, which surely is an "incapacitator," also acts as a significant general deterrent is a vexed question I deal with later in this chapter.

7. See, for example, Jacqueline Cohen, "Selective Incapacitation: An Assessment," *University of Illinois Law Review* 253 (1984); Don Weatherburn, Jiuzhao Hua, and Steve Moffatt, "How Much Crime Does Prison Stop? The Incapacitation Effect of Prison on Burglary," *Int'l J. of Punishment and Sentencing* 2:8 (2006).

8. Stephan Van Dine, Simon Dinitz, and John Conrad, "The Incapacitation of the Dangerous Offender: A Statistical Experiment," *J. Research in Crime and Delinquency* 14:22, 32 (1977).

9. Steven D. Levitt, "Understanding Why Crime Fell in the 1990s: Four Factors that Explain the Decline and Six that Do Not," *J. of Economic Perspectives* 18:163, 177–179 (2004).

10. Gina Stoduto et al., "Impact of Ontario's Remedial Program for Drivers Convicted of Drinking and Driving on Substance Use and Problems," *Canadian J. of Criminology and Criminal Justice* 56:201 (2014).

11. John C. Cross, "Passing the Buck: Risk Avoidance and Risk Management in the Illegal/Informal Drug Trade," *International Journal of Sociology and Social Policy* 20:68, 87–88 (2000).

12. Neil Shover, *Great Pretenders: Pursuits and Careers of Persistent Thieves* (1996), p. 178.

13. See Greg Pogarsky and Alex R. Piquero, "Can Punishment Encourage Offending? Investigating the 'Resetting' Effect," *Journal of Research in Crime and Delinquency* 40:95 (2003).

14. Robert E. Kraut, "Deterrent and Definitional Influences on Shoplifting," *Social Problems* 23:358, 362 (1976).

15. Shover, *Great Pretenders*, pp. 122–123.

16. There are hints of this in Alex Piquero and George F. Rengert, "Studying Deterrence with Active Residential Burglars," *Justice Quarterly* 16:451 (1999).

17. Peter J. Van Koppen and Robert W. J. Jansen, "The Time to Rob: Variations in Time of Number of Commercial Robberies," *Journal of Research in Crime and Delinquency* 36:7, 25 (1999).

18. Lawrence M. Friedman, *Crime and Punishment in American History* (1993), pp. 37–41.

19. Malcolm Feeley, *The Process Is the Punishment: Handling Cases in a Lower Criminal Court* (1992).

20. Daniel S. Nagin and Raymond Paternoster, "The Preventive Effects of the Perceived Risk of Arrest: Testing an Expanded Conception of Deterrence," *Criminology* 29:561, 563 (1991).

21. Joan Petersilia, *When Prisoners Come Home: Parole and Prisoner Reentry* (2003), p. 105; see also Devah Pager and Bruce Western, *Race at Work: Realities of Race and Criminal Record in the NYC Job Market*, Report of the NYC Commission on Human Rights (December 2005).

22. Anthony M. Pate and Edwin E. Hamilton, "Formal and Informal Deterrents to Domestic Violence: The Dade County Spouse Assault Experiment," *American Sociological Review* 57:691 (1992).

23. Trevor Bennett and Richard Wright, *Burglars on Burglary: Prevention and the Offender* (1984), p. 37.

24. See Neil Miller, *Banned in Boston* (2010).

25. Lawrence M. Friedman, *The Legal System: A Social Science Perspective* (1975), p. 76.

26. Kenneth D. Tunnell, "Choosing Crime: Close Your Eyes and Take Your Chances," in Barry W. Hancock and Paul M. Sharp, *Criminal Justice in America: Theory, Practice, and Policy*, 2d ed. (2000), p. 38.

27. Ibid., pp. 43, 48.

28. Rüdiger Lautman, "Körperzwang im Konzentrationslager," *Z. für Rechtssoziologie* 28:3 (2007).

29. Gresham Sykes, *The Society of Captives: A Study of a Maximum Security Prison* (1958), pp. 42, 51.

30. Diana B. Henriques, "Madoff Is Sentenced to 150 Years for Ponzi Scheme," *New York Times*, June 29, 2009.

31. William J. Chambliss, "Types of Deviance and the Effectiveness of Legal Sanctions," 1967, *Wisconsin Law Review* 703.

32. Jonathan Klick and Thomas Stratmann, "Abortion Access and Risky Sex among Teens: Parental Involvement Laws and Sexually Transmitted Diseases," *J. Law & Economic Organization* 24:2 (2007). The effect seemed to be greatest among Hispanics and whites, less or nonexistent for African Americans. After passage of a law in Texas that made doctors notify the parents of a minor child who wanted an abortion at least forty-eight hours before carrying out the abortion, the abortion rate fell—for example, 11 percent among fifteen-year-olds. Theodore Joyce, Robert Kaestner, and Silvie Colman, "Changes in Abortions and Births and the Texas Parental Notification Law," *New England J. of Medicine* 354:1031 (2006).

33. John N. Gallo, "Effective Law-Enforcement Techniques for Reducing Crime," *J. Criminal Law & Criminology* 88:1475 (1998).

34. Ibid., p. 1483. Gallo feels that some "mules" think—wrongly—that "if they are not physically in possession of the cocaine, or if they do not receive the money at the same time they deliver the cocaine, they cannot be prosecuted."

35. Ibid., pp. 1475–1476.

36. John Carroll and Frances Weaver, "Shoplifters' Perceptions of Crime Opportunities: A Process-Tracing Study," in Derek B. Cornish and Ronald V. Clarke, eds., *The Reasoning Criminal: Rational Choice Perspectives on Offending* (1986), pp. 19, 22–23.

37. Iris Yen, "Of Vice and Men: A New Approach to Eradicating Sex Trafficking by Reducing Male Demand through Educational Programs and Abolitionist Legislation," *J. Criminal Law & Criminology* 98:653, 678–679 (2008).

38. A. Nicholas Groth, *Men Who Rape: The Psychology of the Offender* (1979), p. 6.

39. See, for example, Kate B. Carey et al., "Incapacitated and Forcible Rape of College Women: Prevalence across the First Year," *J. Adolescent Health* 16:678 (2015).

40. Ronet Bachman, Raymond Paternoster, and Sally Ward, "The Rationality of Sexual Offending: Treating a Deterrence/Rational Choice Conception of Sexual Assault," *Law & Society Review* 26:343 (1992).

41. Ibid., p. 365.

42. Eric A. Feldman and Ronald Bayer, "The Triumph and Tragedy of Tobacco Control: A Tale of Nine Nations," *Ann. Rev. Law Soc. Sci.* 7:79, 88 (2011).

43. For a discussion, see Silvia M. Mendes, "Certainty, Severity, and Their Relative Deterrent Effects: Questioning the Implications of the Role of Risk in Criminal Deterrence Policy," *Policy Studies Journal* 32:59 (2004).

44. See, for example, the discussion in Harold G. Grasmick and George J. Bryjak, "The Deterrent Effect of Perceived Severity of Punishment," *Social Forces* 59:471 (1980).

45. Greg Pogarsky, "Identifying 'Deterrable' Offenders: Implications for Research on Deterrence," *Justice Quarterly* 19:431 (2002).

46. See Raymond Paternoster, "How Much Do We Really Know about Criminal Deterrence?" *J. Crim. Law & Criminology* 100:765, 811 (2010).

47. Jiang Yu, "Punishment Celerity and Severity: Testing a Specific Deterrence Model on Drunk Driving Recidivism," *J. of Criminal Justice* 22:355 (1994).

48. Ibid., p. 361.

49. Antonio F. Tavares, Silvia M. Mendes, and Claudia S. Costa, "The Impact of Deterrence Policies on Reckless Driving: The Case of Portugal," *European J. of Criminal Policy* 14:417 (2008).

50. See Daniel S. Nagin and Greg Pogarsky, "Integrating Celerity, Impulsivity, and Extralegal Sanction Threats into a Model of General Deterrence: Theory and Evidence," *Criminology* 29:865 (2001).

51. Jo Thomas, "McVeigh Ends Appeal of His Death Sentence," *New York Times*, Dec. 13, 2000. See, on the trial and its aftermath, Jody L. Madeira, *Killing McVeigh: The Death Penalty and the Myth of Closure* (2012).

52. Death Penalty Information Center, www.deathpenaltyinfo.org.

53. *New York Times*, February 26, 1933; March 21, 1933.

54. 408 U.S. 238 (1972).

55. *Gregg v. Georgia*, 428 U.S. 1953 (1976).

56. In a few states, notably Alabama, the judge can override the jury's decision— either by imposing the death penalty when the jury said no or by refusing it when the jury said yes. Ala. Code §13A-5-47(e).

57. On the death penalty cases, see Evan J. Mandery, *A Wild Justice: The Death and Resurrection of Capital Punishment in America* (2013); Robert Weisberg, "Deregulating Death," *Supreme Court Review* 1983:305.

58. Stuart Banner, *The Death Penalty in American History* (2002), pp. 169–207.

59. On the Innocence Project, see www.innocenceproject.org/causes.wrongful -conviction.

60. Figures from the Death Penalty Information Center, www.deathpenaltyinfo .org/execution-list-2014, visited on March 19, 2015. Only one of those executed that year, Lisa Coleman, had been on death row less than ten years (in her case, eight). She was also one of only two women to be executed in 2014 (thirty-three men were put to death).

61. Michael Tonry, "The Mostly Unintended Effects of Mandatory Penalties: Two Centuries of Consistent Findings," in Michael Tonry, ed., *Crime and Justice: A Review of Research* 38:65, 91 (2009).

62. Ian Kershaw, *The End: The Defiance and Destruction of Hitler's Germany, 1944–1945* (2011), p. 220.

63. For example, Scott W. Decker and Carol W. Kohfeld, "The Deterrent Effect of Capital Punishment in the Five Most Active Execution States: A Time Se-ries Analysis," *Criminal Justice Review* 15:173 (1990).

64. Ideology is at work, too, in the controversy over concealed gun laws. Do they deter crime by scaring criminals, create more gun crime, or do nothing at all? This and other issues are discussed in Steven Levitt and Thomas J. Miles, "Economic Contributions to the Understanding of Crime," *Ann. Rev. Law Soc. Sci.* 2:147 (2006).

65. Isaac Ehrlich, "The Deterrent Effect of Criminal Law Enforcement," *J. Legal Studies* 1:259 (1972).

66. On this, see John J. Donohue III, "Empirical Evaluation of Law: The Dream and the Nightmare," *American Law Econ. Rev.* 17, issue 2 (Fall 2015), first pub-

lished online May 25, 2015, doi:10.1093/aler/ahv007. Ehrlich is definitely part of the nightmare.

67. John J. Donohue and Justin Wolfers, "Uses and Abuses of Empirical Evidence in the Death Penalty Debate," *Stanford Law Review* 58:791, 794 (2005).

68. On the concept and its application to a specific situation, see Madeira, *Killing McVeigh,* especially pp. 38–60; Franklin E. Zimring, *The Contradictions of American Capital Punishment* (2003), p. 61.

69. William J. Bowers and Glenn L. Pierce, "Deterrence or Brutalization: What Is the Effect of Executions?" *Crime and Delinquency* 20:453 (1980).

70. John K. Cochran, Mitchell B. Chamlin, and Mark Seth, "Deterrence or Brutalization? An Impact Assessment of Oklahoma's Return to Capital Punishment," *Criminology* 32:107 (1994).

71. Ibid., pp. 129–130.

72. Donohue, "Empirical Evaluation of Law: The Dream and the Nightmare."

73. See Maynard L. Erickson and Jack P. Gibbs, "Objective and Perception Properties of Legal Punishment and the Deterrence Doctrine," *Social Problems* 25:253 (1978).

74. Lonn Lanza-Kaduce, "Perceptual Deterrence and Drinking and Driving among College Students," *Criminology* 26:321 (1988).

75. H. Laurence Ross, *Deterring the Drinking Driver: Legal Policy and Social Control* (1982), p. 111.

76. Lawrence W. Sherman, "Police Crackdowns: Initial and Residual Deterrence," *Crime and Justice* 12:1 (1990).

77. For an overview, see Robert Apel, "Sanctions, Perceptions, and Crime: Implications for Criminal Deterrence," *J. Quant. Criminology* 29:67 (2013).

78. Raymond Paternoster, "How Much Do We Really Know about Criminal Deterrence?" *J. Criminal Law & Criminology* 100:765, 805 (2010). See, for an example of an attempt to measure this, Lanza-Kaduce, "Perceptual Deterrence and Drinking and Driving Among College Students."

79. Gordon P. Waldo and Theodore G. Chiricos, "Perceived Penal Sanction and Self-Reported Criminality: A Neglected Approach to Deterrence Research," *Social Problems* 19:522 (1972).

80. David A. Anderson, "The Deterrence Hypothesis and Picking Pockets at the Pickpocket's Hanging," *American Law and Economics Review* 4:295, 304 (2002).

81. Tunnell, "Choosing Crime: Close Your Eyes and Take Your Chances," in Hancock and Sharp, *Criminal Justice in America: Theory, Practice, and Policy,* 2d ed., pp. 38, 44, 45.

82. Gary Kleck et al., "The Missing Link in General Deterrence Research," *Criminology* 43:623 (2005).

83. Shover, *Great Pretenders*, pp. 164–165.

84. Kimberly N. Varma and Anthony N. Doob, "Deterring Economic Crimes: The Case of Tax Evasion," *Canadian J. of Criminology* 40:165 (1998).

85. Kraut, "Deterrent and Definitional Influences," p. 360. But if a shoplifter does get caught, he or she tends to "reset" the perception of risk. See ibid., p. 362.

86. Richard T. Wright and Scott H. Decker, *Armed Robbers in Action: Stickups and Street Culture* (1997), pp. 120–125.

87. Bruce A. Jacobs and Richard Wright, "Stick-Up, Street Culture, and Offender Motivation," *Criminology* 37:149, 155 (1999).

88. Anderson, "The Deterrence Hypothesis and Picking Pockets at the Pickpocket's Hanging," p. 305.

89. The evidence for any of this is not that robust. For a review of the literature, see Michelle M. Mello, "Medical Malpractice: Impact of the Crisis and Effect of State Tort Reforms," Robert Wood Johnson Foundation, Research Synthesis Report No. 10 (May 2006). On the distorted view of malpractice claims, see Mello and Brennan, "Deterrence of Medical Errors: Theory and Evidence for Malpractice Reform," at p. 1609. For an empirical study of "defensive medicine" in Taiwan, finding some evidence of increased laboratory tests and so on, see Brian K. Chen and Chun-Yuh Yang, "Increased Perception of Malpractice Liability and the Practice of Defensive Medicine," *Journal of Empirical Legal Studies* 11:446 (2014).

90. The actual impact of the reforms, however, has been spotty. See Joan T. Schmit, Mark J. Browne, and Han Duck Lee, "The Effect of State Tort Reforms on Claim Filings," *Risk Management & Insurance Rev.* 1:1 (1997).

91. See Kraut, "Deterrent and Definitional Influences," p. 362.

92. Apel, "Sanctions, Perceptions, and Crime," p. 85.

93. Jan M. Chaiken, Michael W. Lawless, and Keith A. Stevenson, *The Impact of Police Activity on Crime: Robberies on the New York City Subway System* (1974), p. 23.

94. Bettina Shell-Duncan et al., "Legislating Change? Responses to Criminalizing Female Genital Cutting in Senegal," *Law & Society Review* 47:823 (2013).

95. Keith Hawkins, "Bargain and Bluff: Compliance Strategy and Deterrence in the Enforcement of Regulation," *Law & Policy Quarterly* 5:35 (1983).

96. See Nigel McCrery, *Silent Witness: The Often Gruesome and Always Fascinating History of Forensic Science* (2013).

97. The Transportation Security Agency was also created in the aftermath of the attack on the World Trade Center in 2001. Its budget for 2013 was over $80 billion.

98. Franklin E. Zimring, *The City that Became Safe: New York's Lessons for Urban Crime and Its Control* (2012).

99. James Q. Whitman, *Harsh Justice: The Widening Divide between America and Europe* (2003).

100. William J. Stuntz, *The Collapse of American Criminal Justice* (2011).

101. See the essays collected in Richard A. Leo and George C. Thomas III, *The Miranda Debate: Law, Justice, and Policing* (1998). For an early example of an attempt to measure the impact of this case, see Richard H. Seeburger and R. Stanton Wettick Jr., "*Miranda* in Pittsburgh—A Statistical Study," *Univ. Pittsburgh L. Rev.* 29:1 (1967).

102. Ryan Devereaux, "Scrutiny Mounts as NYPD 'Stop-and-Frisk Searches' Hit Record High," *Guardian*, February 12, 2012. According to Devereaux, in 2011, the police stopped and questioned 684,330 people in the city; 92 percent of these were male, 87 percent were African American or Latino. See also Tracy Meares, "The Law and Social Science of Stop and Frisk," *Ann. Rev. Law Soc. Sci.* 10:335 (2014).

103. Alex R. Piquero et al., "Elaborating the Individual Difference Component in Deterrence Theory," *Ann. Rev. Law Soc. Sci.* 2011:335, 346.

104. Gary Becker, "Crime and Punishment: An Economic Approach," *J. Political Economy* 76:169, 179 (1968). But Becker's basic assumption is that "a person commits an offense if the expected utility to him exceeds the utility he could get by using his time and other resources at other activities." This means that some people become criminals "not because their basic motivation differs from that of other persons, but because their benefits and costs differ," p. 176.

105. Michael R. Gottfredson and Travis Hirschi, *A General Theory of Crime* (1990).

106. Ibid., p. 89.

107. Per-Olof H. Wikström and Kye Treiber, "The Role of Self-Control in Crime Causation: Beyond Gottfredson and Hirschi's *General Theory of Crime*," *European J. of Criminology* 4:237, 238 (2007).

108. See, for example, Ann Marie Sorenson and David Brownfield, "Adolescent Drug Use and a General Theory of Crime: An Analysis of a Theoretical Integration," *Canadian J. of Criminology* 37:19 (1995).

109. Michael L. Benson and Elizabeth Moore, "Are White-Collar and Common Offenders the Same? An Empirical and Theoretical Critique of a Recently Proposed General Theory of Crime," *J. Research in Crime and Delinquency* 29:251, 267 (1992). Middle-class white-collar offenders, they claim, "have sufficient self-control to hold back from crime and deviance most of the time." But then "something happens"—a financial crisis in their lives, for example. They violate out of a "desire to avoid failure" and to protect their "relative position in life."

110. Sally S. Simpson and Nicole Leeper Piquero, "Low Self-Control, Organizational Theory, and Corporate Crime," *Law & Society Review* 36:509, 537 (2002).

111. John O. Haley, "The Myth of the Reluctant Litigant," *J. Japanese Studies* 4:359 (1978). In a later article, Haley wrote that the "current consensus . . . challenges the view that Japan is exceptional." The litigation rate is low, but "universally applicable factors" probably explain this litigation rate, rather

than the notion of some sort of unique Japanese culture; John O. Haley, "Litigation in Japan: A New Look at Old Problems," *Willamette J. Int'l L. & Dispute Resolution* 10:121, 140 (2002).

112. Kathryn Hendley, "Resolving Problems among Neighbors in Post-Soviet Russia: Uncovering the Norms of the *Pod"ezd*," *Law and Social Inquiry* 36:388 (2011).

113. Floyd Feeney, "Robbers as Decision-Makers," in Derek B. Cornish and Ronald V. Clarke, eds., *The Reasoning Criminal: Rational Choice Perspectives on Offending* (1986), pp. 53, 59–60.

114. Neil Vidmar and Regina A. Schuller, "Individual Differences and the Pursuit of Legal Rights: A Preliminary Inquiry," *Law and Human Behavior* 11:299 (1987).

115. Greg Pogarsky, "Identifying 'Deterrable' Offenders: Implications for Research on Deterrence," *Justice Quarterly* 19:431 (2002).

116. See Ted R. Gurr, Peter N. Grabosky, and Richard C. Hula, *The Politics of Crime and Conflict: A Comparative History of Four Cities* (1977). The American development is probably roughly the same, but quite complex. On the United States, see Randolph Roth, *American Homicide* (2009).

117. Neil Shover, "The Later Stages of Ordinary Property Offense Careers," *Social Problems* 31:208, 210 (1983).

118. Maurice Cusson and Pierre Pinsonneault, "The Decision to Give Up Crime," in Derek B. Cornish and Ronald V. Clarke, eds. *The Reasoning Criminal: Rational Choice Perspectives on Offending* (1986), pp. 72–73, 76.

119. Mark S. Fleisher, *Beggars and Thieves: Lives of Urban Street Criminals* (1995), p. 218.

120. Teresa C. LaGrange and Robert A. Silverman, "Low Self-Control and Opportunity: Testing the General Theory of Crime as an Explanation for Gender Differences in Delinquency," *Criminology* 37:41, 62 (1999).

121. There has been, however, research on the Gottfredson and Hirschi theory (low self-control, basically) that claims to find a good deal of cross-cultural support. See, for example, Cesar J. Rebellon, Murray A. Strauss, and Rose Medeiros, "Self-Control in Global Perspective: An Empirical Assessment of Gottfredson and Hirschi's General Theory within and across 32 National Settings," *European J. of Criminology* 5:331 (2008).

122. Daniel S. Nagin, "Deterrence in the Twenty-First Century," *Crime and Justice* 42:199, 262–263 (2013).

123. There are, however, situations where rape is either allowed or is distressingly common. Conquering armies may consider rape one of the perquisites of victory; prisons may be another example of a locus where rape is epidemic.

124. Per-Olof H. Wikström, Andromachi Tseloni, and Dimitris Karlis, "Do People Comply with the Law Because They Fear Getting Caught?" *European J. of Criminology* 8:401, 402, 404 (2011).

6. Rewards and Punishments: Incentives and the Civil Side

1. General Stats. Colo. 1883, §3652, p. 1063.

2. See Michelle M. Mello and Troyen A. Brennan, "Deterrence of Medical Errors: Theory and Evidence for Malpractice Reform," *Texas L. Rev.* 80:1595 (2002); Brian K. Chen and Chun-Yuh Yang, "Increased Perception of Malpractice Liability and the Practice of Defensive Medicine," *J. Empirical Legal Studies* 11:446 (2014).

3. The scholarship is reviewed in Uri Gneezy, Stephan Meier, and Pedro Rey-Biel, "When and Why Incentives (Don't) Work to Modify Behavior," *Journal of Economic Perspectives* 25:191, 195–199 (2010).

4. See David Freeman Engstrom, "Whither Whistleblowing? Bounty Regimes, Regulatory Context, and the Challenge of Optimal Design," *Theoretical Inquiries in Law* 15:605 (2014).

5. Yuval Feldman and Orly Lobel, "The Incentives Matrix: The Comparative Effectiveness of Rewards, Liabilities, Duties, and Protections for Reporting Illegality," *Texas L. Rev.* 88:1151 (2010).

6. Yuval Feldman and Orly Lobel, "Individuals as Enforcers: The Design of Employee Reporting Systems," in Christine Parker and Vibeke Nielsen, eds., *Explaining Compliance: Business Responses to Regulation* (2011), pp. 263, 273; Feldman and Lobel, "The Incentives Matrix," p. 1196.

7. Selena Roberts, "When Peer Pressure, Not a Conscience, Is Your Guide," *New York Times*, March 31, 2006, p. D1.

8. Peter Baker and Ellen Barry, "U.S. Traces Path as N.S.A. Leaker Flees Hong Kong," *New York Times*, June 24, 2013, p. A1.

9. See below, in Chapter 9.

10. Alexandra Natapoff, *Snitching: Criminal Informants and the Erosion of American Justice* (2009), p. 3.

11. See Ethan Brown, *Snitch: Informants, Cooperators, and the Corruption of Justice* (2007).

12. Benjamin van Rooij, "The People's Regulation: Citizens and Implementation of Law in China," *Columbia J. of Asian Law* 25:116, 145–146 (2012).

13. Suzanne Daley and Raphael Minder, "In Slovakia, Real Lottery Prize Goes to Tax Man," *New York Times*, April 20, 2014, p. 1.

14. Richard H. Thaler and Cass R. Sunstein, *Nudge: Improving Decisions about Health, Wealth, and Happiness* (2008), p. 33.

15. Ibid., p. 85.

16. Lorenz Kähler, "Zur Durchsetzungskraft abdingbaren Rechts," in Michelle Cottier, Josef Estermann, and Michael Wrase, eds., *Wie Wirkt Recht?* (2008), pp. 431, 433.

17. Jacob Golden, "Sales Tax Not Included: Designing Commodity Taxes for Inattentive Consumers," *Yale L. Journal* 122:1 (2012).

18. Ben M. Crouch, "Is Incarceration Really Worse? Analyses of Offenders' Prefer-ence for Prison over Probation," *Justice Quarterly* 10:67, 79, 84 (1993). An even more surprising 25 percent said they would prefer a three-year term over ten years on probation. Preference for prison was "more likely among offenders who are African American, older, unmarried . . . and who share beliefs that probation has grown stricter." See also Joan Petersilia, "When Probation Be-comes More Dreaded Than Prison," *Federal Probation* 54:23 (1990). Petersilia argues that short prison stays, for the prison-prone population, are sometimes preferred to intensive supervision programs.

19. On the penitentiary system, see Lawrence M. Friedman, *Crime and Punish-ment in American History* (1993), pp. 77–82; Adam J. Hirsch, *The Rise of the Penitentiary: Prisons and Punishment in Early America* (1992).

20. Professor Marc Galanter attributes this concept to Llewellyn; Galanter was a student of Llewellyn at the University of Chicago Law School when Llewellyn was on the law school faculty.

21. Stewart Macaulay, Lawrence M. Friedman, and John Stookey, eds., *Law and Society: Readings on the Social Study of Law* (1995), p. 444.

22. Thaler and Sunstein, *Nudge: Improving Decisions about Health, Wealth, and Happiness*.

23. See also the section on "crowding out" in Chapter 9.

24. W. Jonathan Cardi, Randall D. Penfield, and Albert H. Yoon, "Does Tort Law Deter Individuals? A Behavioral Science Study," *J. Empirical Legal Studies* 3:567, 593 (2012).

25. Michelle M. Mello, Jennifer Pomeranz, and Patricia Moran, "The Interplay of Public Health Law and Industry Self-Regulation: The Case of Sugar-Sweetened Beverage Sales in Schools," *American J. Public Health* 98:595 (2008).

26. John Braithwaite, "Enforced Self-Regulation: A New Strategy for Corporate Crime Control," *Michigan L. Rev.* 80:1466 (1982).

27. Robyn Fairman and Charlotte Yapp, "Enforced Self-Regulation, Prescription, and Conceptions of Compliance within Small Businesses: The Impact of En-forcement," *Law & Policy* 27:491 (2005).

28. Mello, Pomeranz, and Moran, "The Interplay of Public Health Law," p. 601.

29. Christopher Hodges, *Law and Corporate Behaviour* (2015), pp. 479–480.

30. Joseph V. Rees, *Hostages of Each Other: The Transformation of Nuclear Safety since Three Mile Island* (1994).

31. See, for example, Lee Grieveson, *Policing Cinema: Movies and Censorship in Early Twentieth-Century America* (2004).

7. The Pressure of Peers

1. Johannes Feest, "Compliance with Legal Regulation," *Law & Society Review* 2:447 (1968).

2. Lionel I. Danick, "Influence of an Anonymous Stranger on a Routine Decision to Act or Not to Act: An Experiment in Conformity," *Sociological Q.* 14:127 (1973).

3. Deborah M. Capaldi, Hyoun K. Kim, and Lee D. Owen, "Romantic Partners' Influence on Men's Likelihood of Arrest in Early Adulthood," *Criminology* 46:267 (2008).

4. Ibid.

5. See Stacey Nofziger and Don Kurtz, "Violent Lives: A Lifestyle Model Linking Exposure to Violence to Juvenile Violent Offending," *Journal of Research in Crime and Delinquency* 42:1 (2005).

6. Margo Gardner and Laurence Steinberg, "Peer Influence on Risk Taking, Risk Preference, and Risky Decision Making in Adolescence and Adulthood: An Experimental Study," *Developmental Psychology* 41:625, 629 (2005).

7. See, for example, Ross L. Matsueda and Kathleen Anderson, "The Dynamics of Delinquent Peers and Delinquent Behavior," *Criminology* 36:269 (1998).

8. Mark S. Fleisher, *Beggars and Thieves: Lives of Urban Street Criminals* (1995), pp. 117–118.

9. Robert H. Aseltine Jr., "A Reconsideration of Parental and Peer Influences on Adolescent Deviance," *J. Health and Social Behavior* 36:103, 116 (1995).

10. Paul B. Stretesky and Mark R. Pogrebin, "Gang-Related Gun Violence: Socialization, Identity, and Self," in Paul Cromwell and Michael L. Birzer, eds., *In Their Own Words: Criminals on Crime*, 6th ed. (2014), pp. 301–302.

11. For example, the attack at Garissa University College in Kenya, in early April 2015, with horrendous loss of life. See Robyn Dixon, "At Kenya College, Christian Students Foretold Massacre," *Los Angeles Times*, April 5, 2015.

12. Christopher W. Mullins and Michael G. Cherbonneau, "Establishing Connections: Gender, Motor Vehicle Theft, and Disposal Networks," in Cromwell and Birzer, eds., *In Their Own Words: Criminals on Crime*, 6th ed., pp. 93, 95, 97–98.

13. Frederick Milton Thrasher, *The Gang: A Study of 1,313 Gangs in Chicago* (1927).

14. Lawrence M. Friedman, *The Horizontal Society* (1999).

15. Stanley Milgram, *Obedience to Authority: An Experimental View* (1974). The Milgram experiment was controversial on ethical grounds at the time and would certainly not be permitted today under rules pertaining to human subjects.

16. Milgram, *Obedience to Authority*, pp. 116–122.

17. Laws of New Hampshire, Vol. 1, Province Period, 1679–1702 (1904), p. 676.

18. Susie M. Ames, ed., *County Court Records of Accomack–Northampton, Virginia, 1632–1640* (1954), p. 111.

19. Charles T. Libby, ed., *Province and Court Records of Maine* (Vol. 2, 1931), p. 224.

20. *Laws and Liberties of Massachusetts* (1648), p. 3.

21. Daniel A. Cohen, *Pillars of Salt, Monuments of Grace: New England Crime Literature and the Origins of American Popular Culture, 1674–1860* (2006).

22. Military commanders can use these as punishments, under Art. 15(b), Uniform Code of Military Justice, in addition to other forms of punishment, at their discretion.

23. Mentioned in Lauren C. Porter, "Trying Something Old: The Impact of Shame Sanctioning on Drunk Driving and Alcohol-Related Traffic Safety," *Law and Social Inquiry* 38:863 (2013).

24. Ricardo Perez-Truglia and Ugo Troianer, "Shaming Those Who Skip Out on Taxes," *New York Times*, April 15, 2015, p. A19.

25. Porter, "Trying Something Old," p. 888.

26. James Q. Whitman, "What Is Wrong with Inflicting Shame Sanctions?" *Yale Law Journal* 107:1055 (1998).

27. Richard D. Schwartz and Jerome H. Skolnick, "Two Studies of Legal Stigma," *Social Problems* 10:133 (1962).

28. Whitman, "What Is Wrong with Inflicting Shame Sanctions?" p. 1090.

29. Ibid., p. 1091.

30. Discussed in Daniel J. Solove, *The Future of Reputation* (2007), pp. 2–3.

31. This is one of the themes of Jon Ronson's book, *So You've Been Publicly Shamed* (2015). Ronson feels we now have "the power to determine the severity of some punishments," and vowed that he, personally, would "no longer take part in the ecstatic public condemnation of people unless they've committed a transaction that has an actual victim" (p. 275), and perhaps not even then.

32. Joanna L. Grossman and Lawrence M. Friedman, "The Power and Peril of the Internet: How Should 'Revenge Porn' Be Handled?" *Justia's Verdict*, February 4, 2015.

33. Larry Bumpass and Hsien-Hen Lu, "Trends in Cohabitation and Implication for Children's Family Contexts in the United States," *Population Studies* 54:29 (2000).

34. Indeed, in some countries in northern Europe, many or even most couples never bother to get married, and thousands and thousands of children are technically illegitimate, not that anybody seems to care. In the United States, in *Levy v. Louisiana*, 391 U.S. 68 (1968), the Supreme Court struck down a statute that prevented illegitimate children from collecting damages in tort after their mother had been killed. Illegitimacy is no longer, even legally, much of a blemish. In Washington State, to take one example out of many, the law provides that, for purposes of inheritance, a "parent–child relationship shall not depend on whether or not the parents have been married," Wash. Rev. Code sec. 11.04.081.

35. See Judith van Erp, "Naming and Shaming in Regulatory Enforcement," in Christine Parker and Vibeke Lehmann Nielsen, eds., *Explaining Compliance: Business Responses to Regulation* (2011), p. 322.

36. Ibid., pp. 327–328.

37. James Q. Whitman, *Harsh Justice: Criminal Punishment and the Widening Divide between America and Europe* (2003).

38. Mari Sakiyama, Hong Lu, and Bin Liang, "Reintegrative Shaming and Juvenile Delinquency in Japan," *Asian Criminology* 6:161 (2011).

39. On incapacitation, see Franklin E. Zimring and Gordon Hawkins, *Incapacitation: Penal Confinement and Restraint of Crime* (1995).

40. Especially John Braithwaite, *Crime, Shame, and Reintegration* (1989).

41. See Carter Hay, "An Exploratory Test of Braithwaite's Reintegrative Shaming Theory," *J. Research in Crime and Delinquency* 38:132 (2001); Sheldon X. Zhang, "Measuring Shaming in an Ethnic Context," *British J. Criminology* 35:248 (1995).

42. Jon Vagg, "Delinquency and Shame: Data from Hong Kong," *Brit. J. Criminology* 38:247 (1998).

43. Toni Makkai and John Braithwaite, "Reintegrative Shaming and Compliance with Regulatory Standards," *Criminology* 32:361 (1994). But integrative shaming did not work with inspectors who met managers for the first time, p. 379.

44. Braithwaite, *Crime, Shame, and Reintregration*, p. 157.

45. See, for example, Emilio Crenzel, "Argentina's National Commission on the Disappearance of Persons: Contributions to Transitional Justice," *International Journal of Transitional Justice* 2:173 (2008); Carlos Santiago Nin, *Radical Evil on Trial* (1996).

46. Julie Stubbs, "Beyond Apology? Domestic Violence and Critical Questions for Restorative Justice," *Criminology and Criminal Justice* 7:169, 181 (2007).

47. Frank Bleckmann and Stefanie Tränkle, "Täter-Opfer-Ausgleich: Strafrechtliche Sanktion oder Alternative zum Strafrecht?" *Z. für Rechtssoziologie* 25:79, 91 (2004).

48. Kristina Murphy and Irene Helmer, "Testing the Importance of Forgiveness for Reducing Repeat Offending," *Australian and New Zealand Journal of Criminology* 46:138 (2013).

49. After some vacillation, the Supreme Court, in *Payne v. Tennessee*, 501 U.S. 808 (1991), a death penalty case, held that a jury, considering whether or not to impose the death penalty, can consider impact statements.

50. Apparently, victim statements in the United States have little or no effect on the sentence, but they are effective at parole hearings, where they lead to a higher percentage of parole denials. Kathryn Morgan and Brent L. Smith, "Victims, Punishment, and Parole: The Effect of Victim Participation on Parole Hearings," *Criminology and Public Policy* 4:330 (2005).

51. On this issue, see Julian V. Roberts, "Listening to the Crime Victim: Evaluating Victim Input at Sentencing and Parole," in Michael Tomry, ed., *Crime and Justice: A Review of Research*, 38:347, 354–356 (2009); Lynne Henderson,

"The Wrongs of Victims' Rights," *Stanford L. Rev.* 37:937 (1985); Edna Erez, "Victim Voice, Impact Statements and Sentencing: Integrating Restorative Justice and Therapeutic Jurisprudence Principles in Adversarial Proceedings," *Criminal Law Bulletin* 40:483 (2004).

52. A classic work is Max Gluckman, *The Judicial Process among the Barotse of Northern Rhodesia* (1955); see also Laura Nader, ed., *Law in Culture and Society* (1997).

53. Aseltine, "A Reconsideration of Parental and Peer Influences on Adolescent Deviance."

54. Roger H. Peters and Mary R. Murrin, "Effectiveness of Treatment-Based Drug Courts in Reducing Criminal Recidivism," *Criminal Justice and Behavior* 27:72 (2000).

55. Joseph V. Rees, *Hostages of Each Other: The Transformation of Nuclear Safety since Three Mile Island* (1994).

56. Peter J. May, "Compliance Motivations: Affirmative and Negative Bases," *Law & Society Rev.* 38:41, 55 (2004).

57. Christopher Hodges, *Law and Corporate Behaviour* (2015), pp. 144–145.

58. Marco Verweij, "Why Is the River Rhine Cleaner than the Great Lakes (Despite Looser Regulation)?" *Law & Society Review* 34:1007 (2000).

59. Ibid., p. 1047.

60. Ibid., p. 1048.

61. Robert A. Kagan, *Adversarial Legalism: The American Way of Law* (2001).

62. Robert A. Kagan, Neil Gunningham, and Dorothy Thornton, "Fear, Duty, and Regulatory Compliance: Lessons from Three Research Projects," in Christine Parker and Vibeke Lehmann Nielsen, eds., *Explaining Compliance: Business Responses to Regulation* (2011), p. 37.

63. Ibid., p. 46.

64. Peter J. May and Soren C. Winter, "Regulatory Enforcement Styles and Compliance," in Parker and Nielsen, eds., *Explaining Compliance*, pp. 222, 229.

65. Jonas Talberg, "Paths to Compliance: Enforcement, Management, and the European Union," *International Organization* 56:609 (2002).

66. Robert A. Kagan and Lee Axelrad, "Adversarial Legalism: An International Perspective," in Pietro S. Nivola, ed., *Comparative Disadvantages? Social Regulations and the Global Economy* (1997), pp. 146, 150.

67. Kazumasu Aoki and John W. Cioffi, "Poles Apart: Industrial Waste Management Regulation and Enforcement in the United States and Japan," *Law & Policy* 21:213 (1999).

68. Ibid., p. 215.

69. Ibid., pp. 234, 238.

70. Robert A. Kagan and John T. Scholz, "The 'Criminology of the Corporation' and Regulatory Enforcement Strategies," in Keith Hawkins and John M. Thomas, eds., *Enforcing Regulation* (1984), p. 67.

71. Ian Ayres and John Braithwaite, *Responsive Regulation: Transcending the De-regulation Debate* (1992), p. 26.

72. John Braithwaite, "Enforced Self-Regulation: A New Strategy for Corporate Crime Control," *Michigan Law Review* 80:1466, 1471 (1982).

73. Robyn Fairman and Charlotte Yapp, "Enforced Self-Regulation, Prescription, and Conceptions of Compliance within Small Businesses: The Impact of Enforcement," *Law & Policy* 27:491, 493 (2005).

74. See Stephen D. Sugarman, "Enticing Business to Create a Healthier American Diet: Performance Based Regulation of Food and Beverage Retailers," *Law & Policy* 36:91 (2014).

75. Cary Coglianese, Jennifer Nash, and Todd Olmstead, "Performance-Based Regulation: Prospects and Limitations in Health, Safety, and Environmental Protection," *Administrative Law Review* 55:705 (2003). The authors stress that "the advantages and disadvantages . . . need to be assessed concretely, within the context of specific regulatory problems and possible alternative standards," p. 711.

76. Fairman and Yapp, "Enforced Self-Regulation, Prescription, and Conceptions of Compliance within Small Businesses," p. 515.

77. Hazel Genn, "Business Responses to the Regulation of Health and Safety in England," *Law & Policy* 15:223 (1993), p. 224.

78. Ayako Hirata, "Regulatory Enforcement of Environmental Law in Japan: An Analysis of the Implementation of the Water Pollution Control Act," in Dimitri Vanoverbeke et al., eds., *The Changing Role of Law in Japan: Empirical Studies in Culture, Society, and Policy Making* (2014), pp. 133, 136.

79. Robert Baldwin and Julia Black, "Really Responsive Regulation," *Modern Law Review* 71:59 (2008).

80. Ibid., p. 76.

81. Ibid., p. 77.

82. For a general discussion, see Michael E. Levine and Jennifer L. Forrence, "Regulatory Capture, Public Interest, and the Public Agenda: Toward a Synthesis," *J. of Law, Economics, and Organization* 6:167 (1990).

83. "Capture" can be used in a broader sense. Levine and Forrence use the word to "refer to the entire family of regulatory theories based on private motivation and private-interest domination," p. 169, but I use it in the narrower sense to refer to what they call "private-interest domination."

84. In the 1970s, it was revealed that Lockheed, the aircraft company, had been bribing governments in various countries, including Japan, where $3 million was paid to the prime minister's office. The prime minister, Kakuei Tanaka, was forced out of office and had to face criminal charges. See Sam Jameson, "Ex-Japanese Prime Minister Retires," *Los Angeles Times*, October 5, 1989.

85. Matthew Day, "Bulgarian Corruption at 15-Year High," *The Telegraph*, December 12, 2014.

86. See "EFCC Hails Buhari over Anti-Corruption Pledge," *Premium Times* (Nigeria), August 10, 2015.

87. Benjamin van Rooij, "The People's Regulation: Citizens and Implementation of Law in China," *Columbia Journal of Asian Law* 25:117, 145 (2012).

88. Ibid., 145.

89. Edward Banfield, *The Moral Basis of a Backward Society* (1958), p. 10.

90. See James C. Scott, *Comparative Political Corruption* (1972).

91. On lynching, see Leon F. Litwak, *Trouble in Mind: Black Southerners in the Age of Jim Crow* (1998), pp. 280–312. On the death squads in Guatemala, see Larry Rohter, "Death Squads in Guatemala: Even the Elite Are Not Safe," *New York Times*, August 23, 1995, p. A1.

92. Leonard Berkowitz and Nigel Walker, "Laws and Moral Judgments," *Sociometry* 30:410 (1967).

93. The study is Noah J. Goldstein, Robert B. Cialdini, and Vladas Griskevicius, "A Room with a Viewpoint: Using Social Norms to Motivate Environmental Conservation in Hotels," *J. Consumer Research* 35:472 (2008).

94. On this point, see Marc C. Stafford and Mark Warr, "A Reconceptualization of General and Specific Deterrence," *J. Research on Crime and Delinquency* 30:123, 127 (1993); also Raymond Paternoster and Alex Piquero, "Reconceptualizing Deterrence: An Empirical Test of Personal and Vicarious Experiences," *J. Research on Crime and Delinquency* 33:257 (1995).

95. John L. McMullan and David C. Perrier, "Lobster Poaching and the Ironies of Law Enforcement," *Law & Society Review* 36:699 (2002).

96. On this, see Jiarui Liu, "The Tough Reality of Copyright Piracy: A Case Study of the Music Industry in China" (JSM dissertation, Stanford Law School, 2009).

97. See Rachel Aviv, "The Outcast," *New Yorker,* November 10, 2014.

98. The phrase appears in Carmen Alguíndigue and Rogelio Pérez-Perdomo, "The Inquisitor Strikes Back: Obstacles to the Reform of Criminal Procedure in Revolutionary Venezuela," *Southwestern J. of Law and Trade in the Americas* 15:101 (2008).

99. Lisa Bernstein, "Opting Out of the Legal System: Extralegal Contractual Relations in the Diamond Industry," *Journal of Legal Studies* 21:115 (1992); Barak D. Richman, "How Community Institutions Create Economic Advantage: Jewish Diamond Merchants in New York," *Law & Social Inquiry* 31:383 (2006). See also, on Chinese rubber traders, Janet T. Landa, "A Theory of the Ethnically Homogeneous Middleman Group: An Institutional Alternative to Contract Law," *J. Legal Studies* 10:349 (1981).

100. Robert C. Ellickson, *Order without Law: How Neighbors Settle Disputes* (1991).

101. *Wisconsin v. Yoder*, 406 U.S. 205 (1972).

102. Eric A. Feldman, "The Tuna Court: Law and Norms in the World's Premier Fish Market," *California L. Rev.* 94:313 (2006).

103. Stewart Macaulay, "Non-Contractual Relations in Business: A Preliminary Study," *Am. Sociological Review* 28:55 (1963).

104. Peter A. Munch, "Sociology of Tristan da Cunha," in Erling Christopher, ed., *Results of the Norwegian Scientific Expedition to Tristan da Cunha, 1937–1938*, vol. 1 (Oslo, 1946), p. 305. Of course, today the island is much less isolated. On the later history of the island, see Conrad Glass, *Rockhopper Copper* (2005). The subtitle is "The Life and Times of the People of the Most Remote Inhabited Island on Earth." I am indebted to Grant Hayden for this reference (and for a copy of the book itself).

105. Richard D. Schwartz, "Social Factors in the Development of Legal Control: A Case Study of Two Israeli Settlements," *Yale L. Journal* 63:471 (1954). The second type of settlement Schwartz studied, the moshav, was far less extreme; families lived in individual bungalows, and each family was responsible for raising its own children. In this community, there was a formal legal institution that handled disputes.

106. Kathy Marks, *Lost Paradise* (2009). The subtitle of the book is "From Mutiny on the Bounty to a Modern-Day Legacy of Sexual Mayhem, the Dark Secrets of Pitcairn Island Revealed." The atmosphere on the island, according to Marks, was "one of general promiscuity." Girls were routinely "abused by older men." The island was tiny, "sealed, and cut off from the outside world," a situation that produced "the kind of crude power dynamics that favor dominant males." Sexual abuse "thrives in secluded places" and in "isolated areas," pp. 264, 265, 272. Compare the fictional society of boys on an island in William Golding's famous novel, *Lord of the Flies* (1954).

107. See Goldstein et al., "A Room with a Viewpoint: Using Social Norms to Motivate Environmental Conservation in Hotels," p. 475. The guests were also told that almost 75 percent of hotel guests "do help by using their towels more than once." Noah J. Goldstein, Vladas Griskevicius, and Robert B. Cialdini, "Invoking Social Norms: A Social Psychology Perspective on Improving Hotels' Linen-Reuse Programs," *Cornell Hotel and Restaurant Administration Quarterly* 48:145 (2007).

108. Described in Richard H. Thaler and Cass. R. Sunstein, *Nudge: Improving Decisions about Health, Wealth, and Happiness* (2008), p. 66.

8. The Inner Voice

1. Lars P. Feld and Bruno S. Frey, "Tax Compliance as the Result of a Psychological Tax Contract: The Role of Incentives and Responsive Regulation," *Law and Policy* 29:102 (2007).

2. Ibid., p. 113.

3. Max Rheinstein, ed., *Max Weber on Law in Economy and Society* (1954), p. 4.

4. Niklas Luhmann, *Legitimation durch Verfahren* (1969), p. 28.

5. See the discussion in Erik de Bakker, "Der (beinahe) weisse Fleck in der Legitimitäts-Forschung: Über Akzeptanz, Verborgenes Unbehagen und Zynismus," *Zeitschrift für Rechtssoziologie* 24:219 (2003).

6. Stig S. Gezelius and Maria Hauck, "Toward a Theory of Compliance in State-Regulated Livelihoods: A Comparative Study of Compliance Motivations in Developed and Developing World Fisheries," *Law & Society Review* 45:435, 444 (2011).

7. Ibid., p. 461.

8. These studies are Wolfgang Kaupen, "Public Opinion of the Law in a Democratic Society," and Adam Podgorecki, "Public Opinion on Law," in Adam Podgorecki et al., eds., *Knowledge and Opinion about Law* (1973), pp. 43, 46, 67, 83.

9. Tom R. Tyler, *Why People Obey the Law* (2006 edition; with a new afterword by the author), p. 45. Seventy-nine percent agreed that "Disobeying the law is seldom justified." A second wave of respondents basically had the same attitude; 85 percent either agreed or agreed strongly that people should obey the law even if it goes against their sense of what is right.

10. Ibid., p. 65. See also Stanley Milgram, *Obedience to Authority* (1974).

11. Tyler, *Why People Obey the Law.*

12. Ibid., p. 271.

13. There is also a certain amount of confusion as to what we mean exactly by the fuzzy term *legitimacy.* See the discussion, for example, in Devon Johnson, Edward R. Maguire, and Joseph B. Kuhns, "Public Perceptions of the Legitimacy of the Law and Legal Authorities: Evidence from the Caribbean," *Law & Society Review* 48:947 (2014), making the point that a "felt obligation to obey" is arguably not "legitimacy" itself, but something that comes about as a result of the sense of legitimacy.

14. Lauren B. Edelman, "Legal Environments and Organizational Governance: The Expansion of Due Process in the American Workplace," *American J. of Sociology* 95:1401 (1990).

15. On this point, see Bradley R. E. Wright et al., "Does the Perceived Risk of Punishment Deter Criminally Prone Individuals? Rational Choice, Self-Control, and Crime," *J. Research in Crime and Delinquency* 41:180, 183 (2004).

16. Milgram, *Obedience to Authority.*

17. Christopher Browning, *Ordinary Men: Reserve Police Battalion 101 and the Final Solution in Poland* (1992), pp. 184–185.

18. Herbert C. Kelman and V. Lee Hamilton, *Crimes of Obedience: Toward a Social Psychology of Authority and Responsibility* (1989).

19. Ibid., p. 53.

20. Lawrence M. Friedman, *The Human Rights Culture: A Study in History and Context* (2011).

21. 1 Cranch (5 U.S.) 137 (1803). The right was controversial, in the beginning. Less controversial, and more commonly exercised in the nineteenth century, was the right to review acts of state legislatures.

22. Neil A. Lewis, "In Closing, Sotomayor Offers Concessions, Clearing Way for Vote," *New York Times,* July 17, 2009, p. A11.

23. James L. Gibson and Gregory A. Caldeira, "Has Legal Realism Damaged the Legitimacy of the United States Supreme Court?" *Law & Society Review* 45:195 (2011).

24. Fundamentalist religions are the exception. Legitimacy for members does not rest on democratic processes but on faithfulness to religious precepts.

25. Inga Markovits, *Justice in Lüritz: Experiencing Social Law in East Germany* (2010), p. 224. Lüritz does not really exist. Markovits conceals the identity of this town, with a population of about 55,000, to protect the identity of people she interviewed. The names of these and other people are also changed.

26. Maria Łoś, *Communist Ideology, Law, and Crime* (1988), p. 303.

27. Xin He, "Why Do They Not Comply with the Law? Illegality and Semi-Legality among Rural–Urban Migrant Entrepreneurs in Beijing," *Law & Society Review* 39:527 (2005).

28. Ibid., p. 548.

29. Ibid., p. 553.

30. The study is Raymond Fisman and Edward Miguel, "Corruption, Norms, and Legal Enforcement: Evidence from Diplomatic Parking Tickets," *J. Political Economy* 115:1020 (2007).

31. Tyler, *Why People Obey the Law*, p. 273. The importance of procedural justice is associated with the work of John W. Thibaut and Laurens Walker, especially *Procedural Justice* (1975). See also John Thibaut et al., "Procedural Justice as Fairness," *Stanford Law Rev.* 26:1271 (1974).

32. See Kees van den Bos, Henk A. M. Wilke, and E. Allan Lind, "Evaluating Outcomes by Means of the Fair Process Effect: Evidence for Different Processes in Fairness and Satisfaction Judgments," *J. Personality and Social Psychology* 74:1493 (1998).

33. See, for example, Tom Tyler, "Psychological Models of the Justice Motive: Antecedents of Distributive and Procedural Justice," *J. Personality and Social Psychology* 67:850 (1994); and van den Bos, Wilke, and Lind, "Evaluating Outcomes by Means of the Fair Process Effect: Evidence for Different Processes in Fairness and Satisfaction Judgments."

34. The study is Hartmut Koch and Gisela Zenz, "Erfahrungen und Einstellungen von Klägern in Mietsprozessen," in Manfred Rehbinder and Helmut

Schelsky, eds., *Zur Effektivität des Rechts*, Vol. 3, *Jahrbuch für Rechtssoziologie und Rechtstheorie* (1972), pp. 509, 527–528.

35. Harry Ball, "Social Structure and Rent-Control Violations," *Am. J. Sociology* 65:589 (1960).

36. Shiri Regev-Messalem, "Trapped in Resistance: Collective Struggle through Welfare Fraud in Israel," *Law & Society Review* 48: 741, 751 (2014). In a study of persistent drunk drivers in Australia, the findings did not prove either that "lack of respect for the law promotes reoffending" or that "such an attitude is the result of habitually reoffending." James Freeman, Poppy Liossis, and Nikki David, "Deterrence, Defiance and Deviance: An Investigation into a Group of Recidivist Drink Drivers' Self-Reported Offending Behaviours," *Australian & New Zealand J. of Criminology* 39:1 (2006).

37. Paul Cromwell and Quint Thurman, "'The Devil Made Me Do It:' Use of Neutralizations by Shoplifters," *Deviant Behavior* 24:535 (2003).

38. Rachel Shteir, *The Steal: A Cultural History of Shoplifting* (2011), p. 146.

39. David M. Engel and Jaruwan S. Engel, *Tort, Custom, and Karma: Globalization and Legal Consciousness in Thailand* (2010).

40. Ronet Bachman, Raymond Paternoster, and Sally Ward, "The Rationality of Sexual Offending: Testing a Deterrence/Rational Choice Conception of Sexual Assault," *Law & Society Review* 26:343, 367 (1992).

41. Richard H. Thaler and Cass R. Sunstein, *Nudge: Improving Decisions about Health, Wealth, and Happiness* (2008), pp. 66–67.

42. Lawrence M. Friedman, "Legal Culture and Social Development," *Law & Society Review* 4:29 (1969).

43. On this point, see Roger Cotterrell, "The Concept of Legal Culture," in David Nelken, ed., *Comparing Legal Cultures* (1997) and, in the same volume, my reply. Also see Lawrence Friedman, "The Place of Legal Culture in the Sociology of Law," in Michael Freeman, ed., *Law and Sociology* (2006), p. 185, and David Nelken, "Legal Culture and Social Change," in Dimitri Vanoverbeke et al., eds., *The Changing Role of Law in Japan: Empirical Studies in Culture, Society and Policy Making* (2014), p. 15.

44. Laura Beth Nielsen, *License to Harass* (2004), p. 7.

45. Patricia Ewick and Susan S. Silbey, *The Common Place of Law: Stories from Everyday Life* (1998).

46. Leisy J. Abrego, "Legal Consciousness of Undocumented Latinos: Fear and Stigma as Barriers to Claims-Making for First- and 1.5-Generation Immigrants," *Law & Society Review* 45:337 (2011). But younger members of this group, who came to the United States as children and are fully socialized, feel "stigma" more than "fear." Stigma, Abrego points out, is certainly a "barrier to claims-making," but the "threshold to overcome it is relatively lower" than the sense of fear, p. 363.

47. See, for example, Sally Engle Merry, *Getting Justice and Getting Even: Legal Consciousness among Working-Class Americans* (1990).

48. On this point, see, for example, John O. Haley, "The Myth of the Reluctant Litigant," *J. Japanese Studies* 4:359 (1978).

49. Eric A. Feldman, "Blood Justice: Courts, Conflicts, and Compensation in Japan, France, and the United States," *Law & Society Review* 34:661, 695 (2000).

50. Engel and Engel, *Tort, Custom, and Karma: Globalization and Legal Consciousness in Thailand*.

51. Merry, *Getting Justice and Getting Even: Legal Consciousness among Working-Class Americans*, p. 179.

52. Ibid.

53. See Robert C. Ellickson, *Order without Law: How Neighbors Settle Disputes* (1991).

54. The quote is from Raymond Paternoster and Sally Simpson, "Sanction Threats and Appeals to Morality: Testing a Rational Choice Model of Corporate Crime," *Law & Society Review* 30:549, 554 (1996). This conclusion seems quite sensible, although the way the authors tried to prove it was through presenting "scenarios" to business school students and a "group of corporate executives attending a business school executive education program."

55. Dorothy Thornton, Robert A. Kagan, and Neil Gunningham, "When Social Norms and Pressures Are Not Enough: Environmental Performance in the Trucking Industry," *Law & Society Review* 43:405, 407 (2009).

56. Ibid., p. 426.

57. Including my own, Lawrence M. Friedman, *The Legal System: A Social Science Perspective* (1975), pp. 67–166.

58. Julien Etienne, "Compliance Theory: A Goal Framing Approach," *Law and Policy* 33:305 (2011). See also Siegwart Lindenberg and Linda Steg, "Normative, Gain and Hedonic Goal Frames Guiding Environmental Behavior," *J. Social Issues* 63:117 (2007).

59. Etienne, "Compliance Theory," p. 310.

60. Ibid., p. 317.

61. Kelly Gallagher Mackay, "Teachers' Duty to Report Child Abuse and Neglect and the Paradox of Noncompliance: Relational Theory and 'Compliance' in the Human Services," *Law & Policy* 36:256, 257, 278 (2014).

62. The phrase is from Mark C. Suchman, "Compliance Theory: Rational, Normative and Cognitive Perspectives in the Social Scientific Study of Law," 1997, *Wisconsin Law Review* 475, 482.

63. See Lawrence M. Friedman, "Norms and Values in the Study of Law," in Aristides N. Hatzis and Nicholas Mercuro, eds., *Law and Economics: Philosophical Issues and Fundamental Questions* (2015), pp. 32, 34–35.

64. Suchman, "Compliance Theory," p. 487.
65. Ibid., p. 490.

9. Factors in Harmony; Factors in Battle

1. On this campaign, and "denormalization," see Eric A. Feldman and Ronald Bayer, "The Triumph and Tragedy of Tobacco Control: A Tale of Nine Nations," *Ann. Rev. Law Soc. Sci.* 7:79 (2011). The "triumph" was mostly in the developed countries; the "tragedy" is that there has been much less success in such countries as China and South Africa.

2. See Robert A. Kagan and Jerome H. Skolnick, "Banning Smoking: Compliance without Enforcement," in Robert L. Rabin and Stephen D. Sugarman, eds., *Smoking Policy: Law, Politics, and Culture* (1993), pp. 69, 79.

3. Scott Burris and Evan Anderson, "Legal Regulation of Health-Related Behavior: A Half Century of Public Health Law Research," *Ann. Rev. Law. Soc. Sci.* 9:95, 105 (2013).

4. Raymond Paternoster and Sally Simpson, "Sanction Threats and Appeals to Morality: Testing a Rational Choice Model of Corporate Crime," *Law & Society Review* 30:549, 554 (1996).

5. Ibid., p. 577. This study, like many others, did not study "corporate crime" directly; rather, the subjects—business school students and corporate executives attending a business school program in executive education—were given a bunch of "scenarios" and asked how they reacted to them.

6. Harold G. Grasmick and Robert J. Burski Jr., "Conscience, Significant Others, and Rational Choice: Extending the Deterrence Model," *Law & Society Review* 24:837 (1990).

7. Charles R. Tittle and Alan R. Rowe, "Moral Appeal, Sanction Threat, and Deviance: An Experimental Test," *Social Problems* 20:488 (1973).

8. Harold G. Grasmick and Donald E. Green, "Legal Punishment, Social Disapproval, and Internalization as Inhibitors of Illegal Behavior," *J. Criminal Law and Criminology* 71:325 (1980).

9. Ibid., Table 1, p. 331.

10. Charles R. Tittle, "Sanction Fear and the Maintenance of Social Order," *Social Forces* 55:579 (1977).

11. Ibid., p. 589.

12. Raymond Fisman and Edward Miguel, "Corruption, Norms, and Legal Enforcement: Evidence from Diplomatic Parking Tickets," *Journal of Political Economy* 115: 1020 (2007).

13. See David Freeman Engstrom, "Whither Whistleblowing? Bounty Regimes, Regulatory Context, and the Challenge of Optimal Design," *Theoretical Inquiries in Law* 15:605 (2014).

14. Yuval Feldman and Orly Lobel, "The Incentives Matrix: The Comparative Effectiveness of Rewards, Liabilities, Duties, and Protections for Reporting Illegality," *Texas Law Review* 88:1151 (2010).

15. Ibid.

16. Ibid., p. 1197.

17. Uri Gneezy and Aldo Rustichini, "A Fine Is a Price," *Journal of Legal Studies* 29:1 (2001); see also Uri Gneezy and John A. List, *The Why Axis: Hidden Motives and the Undiscovered Economics of Everyday Life* (2013), pp. 19–21.

18. When the fine was removed, behavior did not revert to the old status— perhaps because the "fine" had permanently altered how parents looked on the duty of the people who worked at the center; perhaps they considered their duty included caring for the kids until the parents came, even if the parents were late.

19. Michael Sandel, "Market Reasoning as Moral Reasoning: Why Economists Should Re-Engage with Political Philosophy," *J. Economic Perspectives* 27:121, 133 (2013). See also the discussion in Thomas S. Ulen, "Law and Economics, the Moral Limits of the Market, and Threshold Deontology," in Aristides N. Hatzis and Nicholas Mercuro, eds., *Law and Economics: Philosophical Issues and Fundamental Questions* (2015), pp. 203, 209. Much of the debate about the impact of "commodification" goes back to the classic study by Richard Titmuss, *The Gift Relationship: From Human Blood to Social Policy* (1971).

20. Uri Gneezy, Stephan Meier, and Pedro Rey-Biel, "When and Why Incentives (Don't) Work to Modify Behavior," *Journal of Economic Perspectives* 25:191, 201 (2011).

21. Ibid. They add, however, that "offering $20 worth of (unconditional) flowers might indeed make the desired partner happier."

22. See Bruno S. Frey, *Not Just for the Money* (1997), p. 26. Frey's book deals in general with the crowding-out issue.

23. Ibid., pp. 10–11.

24. Herbert L. Packer, *The Limits of the Criminal Sanction* (1968), p. 287.

25. There is a large body of work on the tangled history of Prohibition. See, for example, Daniel Okrent, *Last Call: The Rise and Fall of Prohibition* (2010).

26. Janice Nadler, "Flouting the Law," *Texas L. Rev.* 83:1399 (2005).

27. Katrina Murphy, "Procedural Justice and Tax Compliance," *Australian J. of Social Issues* 38:379, 395 (2003).

28. Fisman and Miguel, "Corruption, Norms, and Legal Enforcement."

29. See Franklin E. Zimring, *The City That Became Safe: New York's Lessons for Urban Crime and Its Control* (2012).

30. Richard D. Schwartz and Sonya Orleans, "On Legal Sanctions," *Univ. of Chicago L. Rev.* 34:274 (1967).

31. Kathleen M. McGraw and John T. Scholz, "Appeals to Civic Virtue versus Attention to Self-Interest: Effects on Tax Compliance," *Law & Society Review* 25:471 (1991).

32. Ibid., p. 485. There was, apparently, an impact on attitudes. The people who watched the normative tape, for example, came to believe that the system was fair; the people who watched the other tape, on the other hand, were "more likely to seek out information and discuss taxes during the tax season," p. 492. But actual taxpaying behavior did not change.

33. Barak Ariel, "Deterrence and Moral Persuasion Effects on Corporate Tax Compliance: Findings from a Randomized Controlled Trial," *Criminology* 50:27 (2012).

34. Ibid., p. 56.

35. Eva Hoffmann et al., "Enhancing Tax Compliance through Coercive and Legitimate Power of Tax Authorities by Concurrently Diminishing or Facilitating Trust in Tax Authorities," *Law & Policy* 36:290 (2014).

36. Jerzy Kwasniewski, "Motivation of Declared Conformity to a Legal Norm," *Pol. Soc. Bull.* No. 1, 74, 76 (1969).

37. The study is Noah J. Goldstein, Vladas Griskevicius, and Robert B. Cialdini, "Invoking Social Norms: A Social Psychology Perspective on Improving Hotels' Linen-Reuse Programs," *Cornell Hotel & Restaurant Administration Quarterly* 48:145 (2007).

38. Richard H. Thaler and Cass R. Sunstein, *Nudge: Improving Decisions about Health, Wealth, and Happiness* (2008).

39. Lawrence W. Sherman, "Defiance, Deterrence, and Irrelevance: A Theory of the Criminal Sanction," *J. of Research in Crime and Delinquency* 30:445 (1993).

40. Ibid., p. 448.

41. Ibid., p. 451. Sherman refers to Elijah Anderson, *A Place on the Corner*, 2d ed. (1978). Anderson studied the men who hung out at a bar and liquor store on Chicago's South Side. One group—Anderson calls them hoodlums—"view a possible encounter with the police as a chance for personal affirmation," p. 72.

42. Sherman, "Defiance, Deterrence, and Irrelevance," p. 459.

43. Seth Mydans, "900 Reported Hurt," *New York Times*, May 1, 1992, p. A7.

44. Les Ledbetter, "San Francisco Tense as Violence Follows Murder Trial," *New York Times*, May 23, 1979, p. A1.

45. Kristina Murphy, "Procedural Justice and Tax Compliance," *Australian J. of Social Issues* 38:379, 390 (2003).

46. James Freeman, Poppy Liossis, and Nikki David studied drunk drivers—real recidivists—in Australia, in an attempt, among other things, to test defiance theory. The results were basically negative on this point. "Deterrence, Defiance and Deviance: An Investigation into a Group of Recidivist Drink Drivers' Self-Reported Offending Behaviours," *Australian & New Zealand J. of Criminology* 39:1 (2006).

47. 98 U.S. 145 (1878).

48. 406 U.S. 205 (1972).

49. Feldman and Lobel, "The Incentives Matrix."

50. Ruth X. Liu, "The Moderating Effects of Internal and Perceived External Sanction Threats on the Relationship between Deviant Peer Associations and Criminal Offending," *Western Criminology Review* 4:192 (2003).

51. Harold G. Grasmick and Emiko Kobayashi, "Workplace Deviance in Japan: Applying an Extended Model of Deterrence," *Deviant Behavior: An Interdisciplinary Journal* 23:21 (2002).

52. Michael R. Gottfredson and Travis Hirschi, *A General Theory of Crime* (1990).

53. Jack Katz, *Seductions of Crime: Moral and Sensual Attractions in Doing Evil* (1988), p. 71.

54. Ibid., p. 231.

55. Ibid., pp. 116–118.

56. Paul D. Cromwell, James N. Olson, and D'Aunn Wester Avary, *Breaking and Entering: An Ethnographic Analysis of Burglary* (1991).

57. Richard T. Wright and Scott H. Decker, *Armed Robbers in Action: Stickups and Street Culture* (2003), p. 46.

58. Ibid., p. 119.

59. Ibid., p. 125.

60. Bruce A. Jacobs and Richard Wright, "Stick-up, Street Culture, and Offender Motivation," *Criminology* 37:149, 165 (1999).

61. Moshe Bensimon, Alon Baruch, and Natti Ronel, "The Experience of Gambling in an Illegal Casino: The Gambling Spin Process," *European J. of Criminology* 10:3 (2013).

62. Richard Wright, Fiona Brookman, and Trevor Bennett, "The Foreground Dynamics of Street Robbery in Britain," *British J. of Criminology* 46:1, 12 (2006).

63. Ibid., p. 13.

64. Heith Copes, "Streetlife and the Rewards of Auto Theft," *Deviant Behavior* 24:309 (2003).

65. Heith Copes and Lynne Vieraitis, "Identity Theft: Assessing Offenders' Motivations and Strategies," in Paul Cromwell and Michael L. Birzer, *In Their Own Words: Criminals on Crime*, 6th ed. (2014), p. 124.

66. Michael Wenzel, "The Social Side of Sanctions: Personal and Social Norms as Moderators of Deterrence," *Law and Human Behavior* 28:547 (2004).

67. John T. Scholz and Neil Pinney, "Duty, Fear, and Tax Compliance: The Heuristic Basis of Citizenship Behavior," *Am. J. Political Science* 39:490 (1995).

68. David S. Engel and Jaruwan S. Engel, *Tort, Custom, and Karma* (2010).

69. 410 U.S. 113 (1973).

70. Shauhin Talesh, "Legal Intermediaries: How Insurance Companies Construct the Meaning of Compliance with Antidiscrimination Laws," *Law & Policy* 35:209, 234 (2015).

71. *Roe v. Wade*, 410 U.S. 113 (1973).

72. Feldman and Bayer, "The Triumph and Tragedy of Tobacco Control."

73. See H. Laurence Ross, *Deterring the Drinking Driver: Legal Policy and Social Control* (1982), p. 111. See also Alexander C. Wagenaar et al., "General Deterrence Effects of U.S. Statutory DUI Fine and Jail Penalties: Long-Term Follow-up in 32 States," *Accident Analysis and Prevention* 39:982 (2007).

74. The essay is Joseph R. Gusfield, "Moral Passage: The Symbolic Process in Public Designations of Deviance," *Social Problems* 15:175 (1967).

75. See Loretta J. Stalans, Kent W. Smith, and Karyl A. Kinsey, "When Do We Think about Detection? Structural Opportunity and Taxpaying Behavior," *Law & Social Inquiry* 14:481 (1989).

76. Lawrence E. Cohen and Marcus Felson, "Social Change and Crime Rate Trends: A Routine Activity Approach," *Am. Sociological Rev.* 44:588 (1979).

77. Cromwell, Olson, and Avary, *Breaking and Entering*, p. 44.

78. Burglars in Santiago, Chile, as well as in the United Kingdom (and, for that matter, in the United States), strongly prefer an unoccupied property. Juan Carlos Oyanedel, "Cultura Criminal y Conocimiento Experto en Ladrones de Casas de Santiago de Chile," in Salvador Millaleo et al., *Sociología del Derecho en Chile, Libro Homenaje a Edmundo Fuenzalida* (2014), pp. 271, 290.

79. Timothy Coupe and Laurence Blake, "Daylight and Darkness Targeting Strategies and the Risks of Being Seen at Residential Burglaries," *Criminology* 44:431 (2006).

80. See Travis C. Pratt, Kristy Holtfreter, and Michael D. Reisig, "Routine Online Activity and Internet Fraud Targeting: Extending the Generality of Routine Activity Theory," *J. Research in Crime and Delinquency* 47:267 (2010).

81. Frances M. Weaver and John S. Carroll, "Crime Perceptions in a Natural Setting by Expert and Novice Shoplifters," *Social Psych. Quarterly* 48:349, 357 (1985).

82. Cromwell, Olson, and Avary, *Breaking and Entering*, pp. 29-32. Some burglars are skilled at dealing with burglar alarms, or fast enough to get out before the police arrive; nonetheless, the alarms have an impact. The same applies to dogs. Big dogs are a physical threat, and small dogs are very noisy.

83. Ian Ayres and Steven D. Levitt, "Measuring Positive Externalities from Unobservable Victim Precaution: An Empirical Analysis of Lojack," *Quarterly J. of Economics* 113:43 (1998). Since car thieves do not know if a Lojack is in a particular car, the device benefits a lot more people than the ones who actually use Lojack; hence, the authors conclude that the car owner who installs the device gets only about 10 percent of the total social benefit, "implying that Lojack will be undersupplied by the free market," p. 75.

84. Keith Guzik, "Taking Hold of the Wheel: Automobility, Social Order, and the Law in Mexico's Public Registry of Vehicles (REPUVE)," *Law & Society Review* 47:523, 524 (2013).

85. Federal Food, Drug, and Cosmetic Act, 52 Stat. 1040 (June 25, 1938).

10. A Concluding Word

1. Erhard Blankenburg, "Je mehr sich Gesetze von dem, was auch ohne sie ge-schieht, entfernen, desto mehr erweisen sie ihre Unwirksamkeit," "Über die Unwirksamkeit von Gesetzen," *Archiv für Rechts-und Sozialphilosophie* 58:31, 56 (1977).

ACKNOWLEDGMENTS

I want to thank Vivek Tata for his valuable help with notes and sources. I also wish to thank George Fisher, John Donohue, Robert Kagan, and two anonymous reviewers for their helpful comments.

INDEX